An empirical investigation of the componentiality of L2 reading in English for academic purpose

Studies in Language Testing... 12
Series editor: Michael Milanovic

Also in this series:

An investigation into the comparability of two tests of English as a Foreign Language: The Cambridge – TOEFL comparability study
Lyle F. Bachman, F. Davidson, K. Ryan, I - C Choi

Test taker characteristics and performance: A structural modelling approach
Antony John Kunnan

Performance testing, cognition and assessment: Selected papers from the 15th Language Testing Research Colloquium, Cambridge and Arnhem
Michael Milanovic, Nick Saville

The development of IELTS: A study of the effect of background knowledge on reading comprehension
Caroline Margaret Clapham

Verbal protocol analysis in language testing research: A handbook
Alison Green

A multilingual glossary of language testing terms
prepared by ALTE members

Dictionary of language testing
Alan Davies, Annie Brown, Cathie Elder, Kathryn Hill, Tom Lumley, Tim McNamara

Learner strategy use and performance on language tests
James Enos Purpura

Fairness and validation in language assessment: Selected papers from the 19th Language Testing Research Colloquium, Orlando, Florida
Antony John Kunnan

Issues in computer-adaptive testing of reading proficiency
Micheline Chalhoub-Deville

Experimenting with uncertainty: Essays in honour of Alan Davies
A. Brown, C. Elder, N. Iwashita, E. Grove, K. Hill, T. Lumley, K. O'Loughlin, T. McNamara

An empirical investigation of the componentiality of L2 reading in English for academic purposes

Cyril J. Weir, Yang Huizhong, Jin Yan

Published by the Press Syndicate of the University of Cambridge
The Pitt Building, Trumpington Street, Cambridge CB2 1RP, UK

CAMBRIDGE UNIVERSITY PRESS
The Edinburgh Building, Cambridge CB2 2RU, UK
40 West 20th Street, New York, NY 10011 – 4211, USA
10 Stamford Road, Oakleigh, Melbourne 3166, Australia
Ruiz de Alarcón 13, 28014 Madrid, Spain

© University of Cambridge Local Examinations Syndicate, 2000

First published 2000

Printed in Great Britain at the University Press, Cambridge, UK

British Library cataloguing in publication data

University of Cambridge, Local Examinations Syndicate
Issues in computer adaptive testing of reading proficiency

Authors: Cyril J. Weir, Yang Huizhong, Jin Yan

1. Education. Assessment 2. Education. Tests. Setting

ISBN   0 521 652995   hardback
           0 521 653819   paperback

Contents

Series Editor's note	vi
Preface	viii
Acknowledgements	x

Chapter One
Introduction — 1

Chapter Two
Establishing the parameters of EAP reading — 14

Chapter Three
Synthesising the *a priori* validation data — 52

Chapter Four
Operationalising the specification: test development — 57

Chapter Five
The quantitative studies. a posteriori validation of the
prototype AERT – version 1: quantitative studies — 73

Chapter Six
The *a posteriori* validation of the prototype AERT – version 1:
qualitative studies — 93

Chapter Seven
Conclusions and recommendations — 118

References	122
Appendices	128
Subject Index	298

Series Editor's note

This volume represents an interesting and important study in the assessment of reading for academic purposes. The approach adopted is very methodical and follows a clear development and validation pattern thus acting as a valuable case study for anyone developing language tests.

The project was based in China and financially supported both by the British Department for International Development (DFID) and the Chinese National College English Testing Committee. DFID has supported numerous English Language Teaching and Testing projects throughout the world and was particularly active in China during the 1980s and 1990s where it also helped in the development of the College English Test (CET) now widely used at the tertiary level in China. A forthcoming volume in this series will focus on the validation of the CET.

English Language Testing in China is characterised by projects like this one which demonstrate a genuine interest in developing effective and validated measures of English Language ability. Along side CET the public English Testing System (PETS) has been developed recently. This project, funded by the DFID and the State Education Commission (SEC) was carried out by the National Educational Examinations Authority (NEEA) and the EFL Division of the University of Cambridge Local Examination Syndicate (UCLES). Taking place between 1997 and 2000 the PETS project developed a five level system of English language tests that aimed to rationalize a much larger number of tests developed and implimented in a more haphazard manner over many years. The project was driven by the stated aim of the Chinese government to raise the standards of English throughout China. Testing is seen as an important tool in achieving this aim and for the first time the assessment of writing speaking and listening are integral parts of a testing system in China from the outset. Direct criterion-referenced asessment poses substantial logistic difficulties in China with its enormous population and it is to the credit of the authorities that they were prepared to undertake such an initiative.

Michael Milanovic
Cambridge
May 2000

Preface

This study reports on an empirical investigation of the componentiality of L2 Reading in English for academic purposes. The focus on careful reading in the theoretical literature has meant that we have somewhat ignored expeditious reading behaviours such as skimming, search reading and scanning in the teaching and testing of reading. We have theories of careful reading but very little on how readers process texts quickly and selectively, i.e., expeditiously, to extract important information in line with intended purpose(s).

Furthermore, because of a focus on the local level e.g. word recognition or syntactic parsing, only limited attention has been paid to careful reading at the global level ie comprehension of the main ideas in a text or of the discourse topic; the macropropositional as against the micropropositional level of text. In addition to careful reading at the local level, we felt it was important to explore a further four kinds of reading: Search reading, Skimming, Scanning, Careful Reading (at the global level).

The development of the Advanced English Reading Test (AERT) for University students in the People's Republic of China under the auspices of the National College English Test Committee was the vehicle for investigating the nature of and the relationships between these different types of reading at the macro level. The project was developed at CALS, University of Reading with colleagues from Shanghai Jiatong University in China. A number of CALS staff worked on the project with the Chinese members of the devlopment group and in particular Rita Green made a valuable contribution to the project activities reported below.

This volume reports on the methodological procedures that led to the development of this important test and discusses the results of the empirical investigations that were carried out to establish its validity both a *priori* and a posteriori. As such it offers a blueprint for those wishing to research in the area as well as generating data on these different reading styles of interest to both testers and teachers of reading in an additional language as well as researchers.

Acknowledgements

Many people were involved in the Advanced English Reading Test project (AERT) that was carried out by College English Test personnel in the Peoples Republic of China and academic staff in the Testing and Evaluation Unit (TEU) at CALS University of Reading between 1995–1998. Particular thanks are due to Luo Peng of Shanghai Jiaotong University PRC and to Rita Green, Hanan Khalifa, Amos Paran and Eddie Williams of CALS, UK for their numerous contributions to this project. Luo Peng helped greatly in generating the data that Chapter 4 is based on and in the proof reading.

We would like to acknowledge the financial support given by the Department for International Development (DFID) of the British Government and also by the National College English Testing Committee, PRC. Without their support, this project would not have been possible. We are also grateful to DFID for their permission to publish this material. Lastly, we must thank Barbara Wickham of the British Council who helped make this project the success it was.

1 Introduction

Background: the Chinese operational context

Reading in English at undergraduate level in China

Before 1985, the required speed of reading in English for Chinese university students was 17 words per minute. A survey by the Ministry of Higher Education (later the State Education Commission) showed that only one third of university graduates acquired this 'reading ability'.

In 1985, the National College English Teaching Syllabus (NCETS) was introduced by the State Education Commission. In this syllabus, the English course, which is compulsory for all university students across the country, is divided into six bands. All the students must meet the requirements of Band 4, which include a reading speed of 50 wpm for careful reading and 80 wpm for quick reading with 70% comprehension. The requirements of Band 6 are aimed at students who have successfully completed Band 4 study, the target reading speed being 70 wpm for careful reading and 120 wpm for quick reading with 70% comprehension. Band 4 and 6 together constitute the basic grounding stage of the College English Course. This course focuses primarily on the development of students' linguistic competence with only limited attention being paid to the development of language skills and strategies.

Despite this focus on linguistic competence, the publication of this syllabus has had a positive impact on English language learning at tertiary level in China. This can be seen in the data available on the College English Test (CET) based on the NCET syllabus which was inaugurated in 1987.

A recent 4 year research study has shown the CET to be a valid and reliable measure of general linguistic competence (Yang and Weir forthcoming). It has had a powerful backwash effect on the numbers learning English at the foundation stage in the university system with the candidature growing to over two million by 1997. Since the inception of the test ten years ago there has been an improvement in the language competence of university students as attested by institutional and national performance levels.

However, an important stated aim of English language teaching at the tertiary level in China is to improve access to scientific and technical literature

1 Introduction

through reading in English. Unfortunately linguistic competence is not the same as performance ability in language skills and strategies in reading. If providing students with the latter is the ultimate goal of English language teaching as specified in NCETS, then further steps need to be taken.

It was evident that many students and also their university authorities saw the foundation stage of English study as the end of English language learning and teaching. Furthermore, the end-users of the CET tended to misinterpret the value of CET and often expected too much from the certificate holders in terms of performance skills and strategies. Clearly the system was not providing university graduates with the requisite skills and abilities to access foreign academic and technical literature through the medium of English.

Rationale for the reading test project

It should be noted that to help achieve this criterial goal for English teaching in Chinese universities an EAP reading course is already stipulated in the syllabus for when the undergraduates finish foundation stage study after year 2. The problem is that the course is not given due attention and is neglected in many universities and institutions by university authorities, teachers and students.

The lack of an adequate and appropriate assessment tool is seen as a major reason for this neglect. A widespread tradition in China, as everywhere else, is 'what is tested is taught' and consequently 'what is not tested is not taught'. In this situation, an Advanced English Reading Test (AERT) could be the necessary catalyst for encouraging the achievement of the aim of the final stage of the college English course in China.

This project, therefore, set out to help achieve that end by developing an Advanced English Reading Test (AERT). The main benefits from this test would be:
- the availability of an appropriate tool for universities and teachers to monitor and evaluate students' performance in EAP reading
- the exertion of a much-needed positive backwash effect on English teaching in years 3 and 4 of college education in China in the sense of actually encouraging the teaching of reading skills and strategies where none may take place at present

Monitoring the impact of the reading project

Currently demographic statistics on the College English Test (CET – 4 and 6) are collected as a matter of routine and there is no reason why the same could not be done for the AERT. Scores by centre, region, institution, gender etc., are made available annually and can be compared to previous national and institutional averages.

Rigorous attempts are made to statistically equate the various forms of the CET test through IRT and an anchor test so comparisons can be made between cohorts from year to year. In this way it is possible to monitor whether there can be said to be improvement at a national or institutional level over a period of time. A similar system could be set in place for the AERT.

Empirical data can also be collected from institutions (staff and students) and end-users by self report (questionnaire survey and interview) in order to triangulate the descriptive statistics emanating from test administrations.

Such data will enable the authorities to monitor the impact of the AERT on the gain in reading ability in years 3 and 4 of Chinese universities. The most effective design would collect data relating to the state the students are at when they begin year 3 and where they get to by the end of year 4. Implementation data which established the amount and nature of mediated instruction in reading that went on within institutions might enable some useful pedagogical lessons to be drawn.

Failing such comprehensive evaluation, a comparison from year to year of exit behaviour would provide useful though less comprehensive data. At the very least it might show whether the test was having an impact in terms of gains in population reading scores across the various types of reading being tested over a period of time. The value added for the Chinese economy might then be investigated. This would involve end users calculating what progress in terms of performances at different levels on the test would contribute financially to their organisations. The enhanced value of improvement in the different types of reading measured by the test might then be estimated.

Background: developing tests to measure the construct of reading in English for academic purposes

The specification and operationalisation of the construct

In the past ESL examination specifications were either absent or extremely limited. Typically one met a spuriously circular argument relating examinations to the textbooks used to prepare the students for the examinations. The textbooks were viewed as a benchmark for establishing what levels such as intermediate and proficient meant. These text book writers would conversely refer to the examinations as their point of reference for both the content and level for their coursebooks.

In recent years a number of the major examination boards have taken a more principled and systematic approach to the development of tests. The University of Cambridge Local Examinations Syndicate (UCLES) is a good example of this (see handbooks produced for each examination by UCLES and **Users Guide** prepared for Council of Europe.). They have attempted to provide clear specifications for each of their major examinations and establish systematic development procedures to faithfully implement these.

1 Introduction

It is clear that a reading test/examination is only as good as the texts and tasks that are used to operationalise the construct it is intended to measure. Inadequacies or limitations in the texts and tasks employed will constrain the value of any comprehension test. Given the huge potential test population and national importance of the Advanced English Reading Test (AERT) in China it was imperative that we developed maximally valid operationalisations of what we believed to be the important elements of the construct of EAP reading in the form of texts and associated tasks. In order to develop a construct valid reading test we had to develop effective, efficient and replicable a *priori* and a *posteriori* procedures for test development. In this book we lay out a comprehensive set of procedures for the development of an advanced reading test in English as a Second Language.

Our initial studies indicated that reading research in this century has been constrained by a narrow view of reading (in the main focusing on careful reading at the local level) and by serious limitations in the tests used as research instruments (see Urquhart and Weir 1998). It was therefore imperative for us to develop a comprehensive specification with a sound theoretical and empirical base and implement this as faithfully as possible in the AERT. As well as helping us to develop a valid and reliable operational test, such research might also provide data which cast some light on the componentiality of the reading construct. Only through the development of a valid and reliable set of tests could we hope to resolve the issue of whether reading is a unitary activity or whether it is made up of separable components, for example: expeditious types of reading as in search reading, skimming, scanning for specifics, and careful reading at the global and local levels. Such a test might shed light on the relative contribution of the posited skills and strategies to the overall picture of a student's reading ability. It could also tell us about the relationship between the test components and inform us of the relative weaknesses and strengths of our students. Whether for formative or summative purposes such diagnostic evaluation might impact on whole educational systems as well as individual classrooms.

The data from the test development procedures described in this book are all grist to the construct validity mill. They can all shed light on what it is we are measuring and how well we are doing this. The more of these we can embrace in our research investigations into EAP reading the more valid and reliable the resulting data on academic reading ability.

Urquhart and Weir (1998: chapter 5.3) outline a principled set of procedures for investigating the componentiality of reading (see Figure 1.1 below). The a *priori* and a *posteriori* procedures outlined there were based on the development work behind the AERT in China and are discussed in detail in this volume. Such a methodology we feel is generic and should for the most part apply to all reading situations.

Figure 1.1
A methodology for investigating the EAP reading construct

A *priori* validation

Stage 1: Specification of the construct

The reading **strategies and skills** and the **conditions** under which these activities are performed might be established through:
- target situation analysis of target population's reading activities;
- theoretical literature review of reading processes;
- research literature review concerning the componentiality of reading;
- document analysis: EAP reading course-books/EAP reading tests.

Stage 2: Development of pilot tests to operationalise EAP reading specification

Systematic textmapping of appropriate texts:
- to establish the consensus information recoverable according to type of reading employed i.e. careful versus expeditious;

Produce pilot version of test(s):
- decide on most appropriate format in relation to operations;
- allow for attrition in texts and items by trialling extra;
- ensure intelligibility of rubrics;
- empirically establish timing;
- consider order of questions/process dimension;
- check layout;
- trial on small samples. Produce first draft of mark scheme;
- moderate tasks and mark scheme in committee.

A *posteriori* validation

Stage 3: Analysis of data on the test

Trial on reasonable sample
Item analysis
Establish item:
- facility values;
- discrimination indices;

Estimates of reliability
- marker reliability.

Estimates of internal validity
- internal consistency;
- correlations;
- principal component analyses;
- level of subtests: Means, t tests and cross-tabulation.

Estimates of external validity
Establish what items are testing through:
- qualitative expert judgement of items
- qualitative introspection/retrospection by test-takers
- feedback from test-takers (interview /questionnaire)

Revise
- administrator's instructions
- items
- timing
- rubrics
- mark schemes
- re-trial any new items

[Source: Reading in a Second Language, Urquhart A. H. and Weir C. J. (1998). Longman]

1 Introduction

Each of these stages is discussed in detail in the following chapters in this book as we describe the steps we took to try to achieve construct validity in our measuring instruments in terms of operationalising the skills/strategies underlying the various types of reading we wished to establish the empirical existence of.

In the next chapter, we will examine in close detail the a *priori* procedures which led to the specification of the AERT (see 3.1 for details of the construct). These constituted the first stage in the development of a systematic approach to developing our test of English for Academic Purposes reading ability. On the basis of the specification we then developed the AERT using a principled set of procedures described in 4.1 – 4.4.

A brief outline of these a *priori* procedures employed to define the construct of reading both theoretically and operationally is provided in the next section.

A prior validation

Establishing the parameters of the reading construct
To establish a specification of operations and performance conditions to be tested we pursued a number of avenues in the development of the Advanced English Reading Test (AERT) for undergraduates in China. We carried out:
- a review of research and theories of reading;
- analysis of EAP reading tasks in Course-books;
- analysis of EAP reading tasks in Public Tests;
- needs analysis.

The investigation of the theoretical construct of EAP reading and the development of a test for this required systematic research. The research began with a review of the literature on existing theories of the reading process (see 2.1 below). The study of various models of reading shed light on the construct of reading from various aspects though it was noticeable that these theories are mostly premised on only one of the identified types of reading, that is, careful reading. Nevertheless such research drew our attention to the importance of reader driven processing at the text level and the importance of goal setting, as well as more traditional text driven processing at the word/sentence level.

We also examined the empirical (largely test based) research literature concerning the divisibility of the reading construct into components and the salient performance conditions under which these types of reading are performed (see 2.1). This product focused empirical research relating to the componentiality of reading ability points to at least a bidivisible view of reading with vocabulary loading on a separate factor in addition to general reading comprehension in nearly all cases. The data suggest that a partially divisible view of reading is preferable to a unitary view.

The empirical study also involved a survey of Chinese undergraduates' EAP reading needs as viewed by subject teachers of advanced reading in English in China (see 2.2 below).

1 Introduction

For a view of what and how EAP reading is currently taught and tested, a survey was made of all the major EAP reading course books and EAP tests available (see 2.3 below) in terms of operations (skills/strategies) and performance conditions (length of texts, reading speed etc.).

The findings from these various strands of enquiry resulted in specifications of the types of reading to be included in the test as well as the conditions under which these reading activities should be performed (see 2.1 to 2.3 below).The types of EAP reading our research indicated we should include are listed below (see 3.1 for full details):

- careful reading for global comprehension of main ideas;
- careful local reading for understanding at the word level;
- expeditious reading (reading quickly, selectively and effectively) for global comprehension of main ideas;
- expeditious reading at the local level (scanning for specific details).

In addition our research suggested the following performance conditions had an important effect on performance on these tasks and must be carefully considered by the test developer:

- length of text must be appropriate for intended type of reading and time allocated be consonant with this;
- time allowed to complete to be empirically determined for each reading type tested;
- strict enforcement of such time controls at the passage/reading type level;
- nature of text must be accessible across three broad discipline areas;
- rhetorical organisation of texts appropriate for reading type;
- overtness of text organisation (markers of importance, textual signposting) for expeditious tasks;
- nature of vocabulary: appropriate degree of specialisation;
- topic familiarity: low to medium familiarity.

The test designed in line with the specified guidelines is expected to maximally operationalise the construct in question. Once appropriate operations and conditions are established these have to be implemented in a test.

Textmapping of main ideas in chosen texts

Having established the skills and strategies (see 2.1 – 2.3 and 3) we wanted to test located appropriate texts which lent themselves to the testing of these and which met the specified performance conditions (see 4.1), we moved on to constructing the test items.

The first step was to process the texts to establish the macro-propositions which might be extracted in line with the specified type of reading to be performed on that text (see 4.2). This utilisation-focused approach seeks to establish the main ideas of a passage through expeditious or careful 'textmapping' procedures.

1 Introduction

Urquhart and Weir (1998) describe how in each textmapping an attempt should be made to replicate a single type of reading on a single text, e.g. *reading a text slowly and carefully to establish the main ideas*. The product of the particular reading of a text can be compiled in the form of a spidergram or as a linear summary. This is first done individually and then the extent of consensus with colleagues who have followed the same procedure is established. The objective of the procedure is to examine whether what we have decided is important, in line with the specified type of reading activity, matches what colleagues consider important.

Urquhart and Weir (1998) see this as a crucial first step in trying to ensure the validity of our tests. The answers to the questions developed equate with the important information in the text that could be extracted by the particular type of reading being assessed. An ability to answer the items should indicate that the candidate has understood the passage in terms of successful performance of the specified operation(s).

Procedures such as textmapping should enable us to determine in a principled fashion the content we might wish students to recover from a text according to the type of reading employed. However, the format, which acts as the vehicle for testing reading activities may constrain the operations and conditions we attempt to include. So as well as carefully specifying the latter we need to consider carefully the method we are going to use so as to minimise the influence of method on measurement of the trait (see 2.3 and 4.3). The cardinal rule remains however: we must first decide what types of reading we want to test and develop systematic procedures for deciding the micropropositions and/or macropropositions that we would expect candidates to extract from texts in performing these types of reading. Only then do we consider test formats and decide which will most faithfully mirror the procedures and allow the appropriate propositions to be extracted.

The mapping procedure will provide the content to be extracted for each of the types of reading in the test. It will also show whether each passage is suitable for its intended reading purpose. Where it is possible to produce a consensus textmap, this then needs to be converted into appropriate test items in the format selected. Where consensus is not achieved or the textmapping produces too few items these texts must be rejected!

A *posteriori* validation

Once the first version of the test was ready a *posteriori* validation procedures were applied at the trialling stage to determine statistically whether the test was working in the way it was intended to and to closely examine the construct underlying the test. The a *posteriori* statistical procedures employed in the two trials of the AERT in China are discussed in detail in 5.1 – 5.2 below. They indicate that the components in the test do seem to be measuring differing parts of the reading construct and students do perform differentially on different types of reading.

1 Introduction

The stages of the quantitative and qualitative a *posteriori* validation of the AERT are briefly outlined next.

Trialling and quantitative analysis
It was important to trial the test on as broad a sample of the intended population in terms of ability as possible and then subject the results to statistical analysis to establish the test's value as a measuring instrument (see 5.1 – 5.2 below for detailed analysis).

The test data generated from the pilot and main trial were subjected to statistical analyses using the Statistical Package for the Social Science (SPSS). These included calculation of mean, discrimination and internal consistency as well as principal components analysis of the loading of test components, cross-tabulation of individual's performance on various components, ANOVA analyses to investigate differences in performance on components of the test in the whole sample and across disciplines.

It is important at the trialling stage to administer the research instrument to as normally distributed a sample as possible. This might mean purposefully sampling from top, medium and lower universities, institutions, schools and classes within these. Normally distributed data allows the researcher to apply the statistical analysis recommended below to establish how the items in the sub-tests are functioning. A skewed sample where the majority of students are too strong or too weak will not allow the researcher to do this.

To complement the result from the statistical analysis, qualitative data were collected through EAP reading experts' judgements on the skills and strategies tested in the AERT, students' introspection on the process of taking the AERT, and students' perceptions of the test conditions and the skills and strategies tested in the AERT (see 6.1 – 6.3 below).

Qualitative studies
The product of language tests tell us little of the processes that underlie reading and we need to employ different methodological procedures to investigate these. In particular introspective methods can help shed light on underlying thought processes. There are a number of problems associated with the method such as the time taken to administer and analyse, limited sampling and sensitivity to instructional variables. However, methods such as introspection and retrospection may offer insights into the perceived processes that take place during different types of reading and help us understand the nature of the differences in processing as well as the existence of such differences (Urquhart and Weir 1998). Such methods are considered in 6.1 – 6.3.

Internal statistical measures are necessary but not sufficient to establish the nature of the reading abilities under investigation. We needed to get a closer idea of what is actually happening during the test experience to accumulate evidence that the test is performing in an ecologically valid fashion i.e, in answering the items the students are processing text(s) as the test developer/

1 Introduction

researcher intended them to. For example, if test takers were using test-taking strategies to avoid skimming or search reading through faulty item construction the test statistics would not necessarily tell us this. We needed to generate data on the process as well as the product. In 6.– 6.3 below we examine a number of ways in which this was done including survey, introspection and retrospection. A brief description of these is provided next by way of introduction.

Structured feedback from test takers
The intentions of the test developer are always mediated by the response of the test takers. Their attitude to facets of the test are as important as the evidence arising from the statistical data as it can often explain why things have happened in a certain way.

Data from structured questionnaires are important because they give us a broad based view of how the sample is responding to the test. A lot of the features examined through these sample questionnaires (e.g., familiarity with text topic) might impact adversely on the measurement of the construct if we have not done a proper job at the development stage. They act as a check on our ability to faithfully implement the test specification. As well as this broad-spectrum data we also need more in-depth information on our test items. This is provided by qualitative research procedures such as introspection, retrospection and expert judgement. As well as data relating to students perceptions of the instruments, texts and tasks, we are also interested in their views on what they thought the items in the test were actually getting them to perform in terms of the skills and strategies in our posited construct. Qualitative data obtained from introspection, retrospection and questionnaire survey provided us with process information on what the test-takers thought the test was testing. This can usefully complement the quantitative data obtained through test administration.

Introspection
An introspection study into the students' process of reading texts and answering the questions was carried out to find out what skills and strategies students were using in completing each section of the test (see 6.3 for details). The students were trained to think aloud onto tapes in a language laboratory while taking a test. Students were allowed to use L1 if they wanted to in their verbal reports. The data were then transcribed and content analysed in terms of the test operations.

Retrospection
A separate retrospection study enabled the researchers to obtain a larger data set (than is possible through the time consuming spoken protocols) to establish student perceptions of the skills and strategies used in the process of taking the test. This can be carried out in the large-scale trialling of the test. It can

1 Introduction

be incorporated into the process of doing the test by providing a checklist for candidates to tick after they finish each section of the test (see 6.2 for details).

Experts' judgements
Apart from students' introspection and retrospection, language testing experts and reading experts should be asked to give us their professional opinion of the constructs being tested (see 6.1 for details).

Revision of the test instrument
As a result of the qualitative and quantitative investigations described above the researcher/test developer is well equipped to make any necessary amendments to the pilot version of the research instruments to make them more valid operationalisations of the intended construct.

On the basis of the procedures discussed above we had sufficient data to help us revise our test instruments to ensure they come closer to performing the job intended.

In conclusion we followed the following guidelines for the validation of the construct measured by the AERT:
- establish the type(s) of reading appropriate to the intended audience in terms of a framework of operations and performance conditions based on systematic analysis of the target situation of the intended test population, systematic review of the research based literature on the processes and componentiality of reading and document analysis of relevant tests and teaching materials.
- establish for appropriate texts according to the specification what would constitute an understanding of that text given closely defined purposes for reading it arrived at on the basis of target situation analysis.
- establish appropriate test development procedures to create test items that were most likely to elicit the desired reading behaviours in a testing mode.

Using the test to explore the construct reading
When the test instrument(s) have gone through the rigorous development phase described above (and in detail in chapters 2 – 6 below) then we can use them to investigate the nature of reading for the purposes and audience we have in mind. We can administer the revised version of test(s) to a representative sample of intended population and then subject the data to the same procedures outlined above in connection with the earlier trialling.

These investigations would help provide insight into the nature of the reading construct as defined by the specification and operationalisation in the test(s). They should tell us about
- The unidimensionality or divisibility of the reading construct under investigation;
- The relative contribution the different parts of the test were making to the measurement of an individual's reading ability;

1 Introduction

- The relative strengths of the sampled population in the different parts of the reading test;
- The nature of individual differences in performance on each of the components.

Stages in the study

The chronological progression of the project is laid down in the following flow-chart.

Figure 1.2

Chronological progression of the study

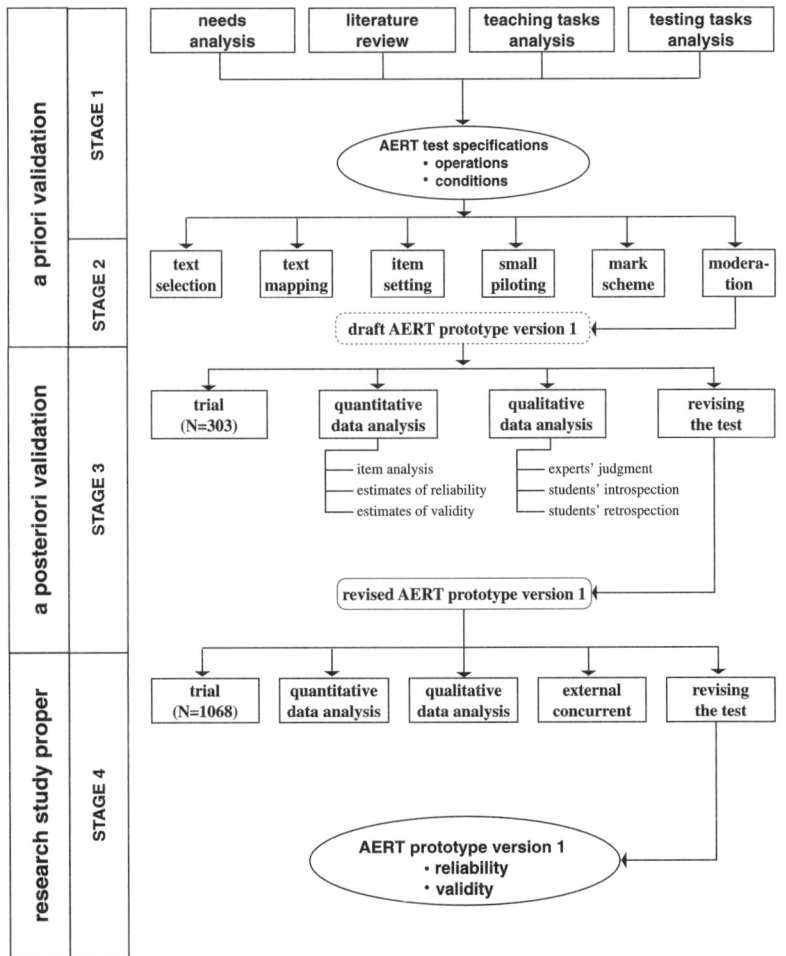

1 Introduction

In this introductory chapter we have looked at reading as a construct consisting of operations and performance conditions and surveyed the ways in which the AERT project sought to specify the construct of reading in English for academic purposes (EAP). We have mapped out a set of procedures for the specification and implementation of such a reading construct in the AERT. We offer this as a systematic methodology for others who might want to develop their own reading tests.

Additionally we have indicated how the AERT was conceived in its operational context and made a number of suggestions on how its impact on learning might be monitored in the long term.

In the following chapters we examine in detail each of the stages in the development of the AERT we have outlined above.

2 Establishing the parameters of EAP reading

Literature review: componentiality of reading and the ESP issue

The construct validity of an EAP reading test depends to a large extent on the view of reading on which it is based. Farr *et al* (1986: 135) argued for the necessity of study of the nature of reading as a necessary part of the test development process:

> *There is a need to synthesise that relevant research, to address the issues and problems raised by the recent wealth of information on reading, and to provide a context for direct application of solutions to the assessment of reading performance.*

To investigate the EAP reading construct, the literature on the process of reading and on the components of reading ability were reviewed as the first stage of the study. The main focuses of our inquiry were
  i. what happens during the reading process
  ii. can reading be broken down into underlying skill or strategy components for the purposes of teaching and testing

A further minor focus of our investigation was the ESP issue, in particular the effect of background knowledge on reading comprehension. This is a central theme in reading research but our interest is more restricted. We consider the extent to which reading comprehension, as shown by test performance, is affected by the reader's background knowledge. We were, however intent on minimising the effect of this in the AERT which we aimed to make accessible to all disciplines.

The distinction between EFL, ESL and L2 though meaningful and useful in many cases, is not of particular concern in this study. As traditionally distinguished, L2 and ESL refers to a language and in many cases English used as a secondary medium of communication in a language community for daily activities and school instruction. EFL, however, is not as frequently used in daily life but mainly taught and learnt for special purposes. Since the present study is set in the context of Chinese undergraduates learning English for Academic Purposes, EFL instead of L2 or ESL is used throughout the report. The distinction, however, is maintained when other researchers' studies are reported.

Componentiality of reading

Reading is for the most part an unobservable mental behaviour and as such it is generally regarded as inaccessible to researchers. What can be studied are either observable physical manifestation of the reading process such as eye movements and eye fixations or comprehension products such as verbal recalls and test results. Reading research is broadly classified into two categories: process-oriented and product-oriented.

Process-oriented studies aim to explain the reading process, i.e., they examine the psycholinguistic process of reading. Research methodologies such as eye-movement studies and computer on-line studies are employed to describe, according to temporal sequence, the reading process, that is, what exactly is happening while a task is performed. In the past two decades, three types of reading process models have surfaced: bottom-up models (e.g., Gough 1972; LaBerge and Samuels 1974), top-down models (e.g., Goodman 1967; Smith 1971) and interactive models (e.g., Just and Carpenter 1980; Rayner and Pollatsek 1989; Rumelhart 1977; Stanovich 1980).

Though this line of research is not the focus of the present study, the review of the literature throws light on our understanding of the process of reading especially at the lexical access and decoding level. What is important for this project is that a review of the process literature clearly demonstrates that existing theories of the reading process are mostly premised on careful reading. Expeditious reading i.e., quick purposeful efficient reading, is not adequately catered for in these careful reading process models.

Urquhart and Weir 1998 point out:

All the models of reading that have been looked at so far have been designed with careful reading in mind. Hoover and Tunmer (1993), for example, consider that their notion of the simple view 'assumes careful comprehension: comprehension that is intended to extract complete meanings from presented material as opposed to comprehension aimed at only extracting main ideas, skimming, or searching for particular details' (p.8). In fact many of the models of reading that have surfaced in the literature to date have been mainly concerned with careful reading; Rayner and Pollatsek (p.439) state that for most of their account of the reading process they are focussing on the skilled, adult reader reading material of the textbook variety. They point out that careful reading models have little to tell us about how skilled readers can cope with other types of reading such as skimming for gist (ibid: 477 – 478).

2 Establishing the parameters of EAP reading

There has for a long time been evidence from survey data that L2 readers found particular difficulty in reading quickly and efficiently in the target language (see also Carver 1992, Guthrie & Kirsch 1987, Weir 1983).

Slow careful reading also poses problems but the difference between L1 and L2 readers is most marked in expeditious reading. For reasons which are difficult to explain dedicated tests of the latter ability have not featured in examinations with the notable exception of the *Test for English Majors* in the People's Republic of China which has had a separate section on this since 1990. Data from this test support the view that candidates perform differentially in this section as against the careful reading section (see Zhou *et al* 1998).

> Urquhart and Weir 1998 *ask 'why have such differences not emerged in almost 50 years of research on this issue? The answer is depressingly obvious. Given that the research instruments used in the studies reported above almost universally failed to include items testing expeditious reading (skimming, search reading or scanning) then their claims to have demonstrated that reading is a unitary ability would seem to be questionable. If one does not take the time and trouble to carefully operationalise these strategies in tests then one should not be surprised that careful reading tests are just that, tests of careful reading with a possible division between global and local. Given the stranglehold this view of reading has had on research due to the different agenda of psychologists, it is perhaps not surprising that with a few exceptions (Pugh 1978) little attention has been paid to expeditious reading.'*

> *However, while such a restriction of focus to careful reading is perfectly legitimate for psychologists attempting to establish precise experimental data about the reading process, it is a luxury which we cannot allow ourselves, since the reading needs of students, and hence the teaching and testing of reading, requires a wider range of reading behaviours. We must thus, if possible, expand the model in order to accommodate this wider range.*

Careful reading models are limited in what they can tell us about what happens in expeditious reading. Rayner and Pollatsek (1989: 477 – 8) who provide one of the clearest accounts of the reading process had to admit that there is little hard information on what takes place in the process of expeditious reading. Paris *et al* (1991: 633) confirm this:

> *Testing is a mainstay of US education, and students endure a wide variety of criterion-referenced and norm-referenced tests every year. But educational tests of reading have not changed to conform with our notion of strategic reading. Instead, they are surprisingly uniform. The*

2 Establishing the parameters of EAP reading

common format of most reading tests requires the students to read brief paragraphs and answer multiple-choice questions about them. Although decoding, vocabulary, syntax and other features of language are often tested, comprehension scores are usually derived from reading several short paragraphs. Most of these paragraphs are disembodied prose – they do not have titles, pictures or structures like the selections used in basal readers or text encountered in content areas.

The overriding attention paid to careful reading in the theoretical literature has meant that in Britain at least (see 3.1 below) we have somewhat ignored expeditious reading behaviours such as skimming, search reading and scanning in both L1 and L2 teaching of reading. We have theories of careful reading but very little on how readers process texts quickly and selectively, i.e., *expeditiously*, to extract important information in line with intended purpose(s). Given the value of these types of reading to the work forces of states in the northern hemisphere let alone those of emerging nations, it is high time more attention was paid to them in the professional and 'academic' literature.

To accommodate expeditious reading strategies, such as skimming, search reading or scanning we need a more comprehensive processing model than is currently available (see Urquhart and Weir 1998 Chapter 2). Such a model will need to incorporate a variety of strategies for quick efficient selective processing of text which together with background knowledge and formal knowledge help establish which content is to be read more carefully.

The review of the literature showed that apart from sequential careful reading process models, various componential models have been conceptualised and in a few cases empirically validated. These componential models can be categorised by the number of components identified. The two-component models include Fries' (1962) recognition of graphic representation and comprehension of language, Venezky and Calfee's (1970) overall reading ability and the w-o ratio, Perfetti's (1977) formula:

Reading Comprehension = Language Comprehension + Decoding + X,

Gough and Tunmer's (1986) alternative formula to Perfetti's additive one

R=D x C,

and Hoover and Tunmer's (1993) simple view of reading comprising lower level decoding and higher level linguistic comprehension. What seems to have been identified in these models are the local level decoding of lexical meanings and global level comprehension of text with the caveat that the emphasis is in many cases laid on linguistic comprehension in these models.

17

2 Establishing the parameters of EAP reading

Urquhart and Weir (1998) point out that

> ...because of the focus on the local level e.g. word recognition or syntactic parsing the psychological literature has paid only limited attention to careful reading at the global level i.e. comprehension of the main ideas in a text or of the discourse topic; the macropropositional as against the micropropositional level of text.

The well-known three-component models are Coady's (1979) conceptual ability, language proficiency and background knowledge and Bernhardt's (1991) language, literacy and knowledge. These models have gained a great deal of currency in reading research in recent years most likely because of their better explanatory power.

In Coady's model, the process of reading is perceived as an interaction of the reader's conceptual abilities, process strategies and background knowledge. According to Coady's explanation, process strategies include the use of grapheme–phonem correspondence rules, grapheme–morphophoneme correspondence rules, syllable–morpheme rules, syntax, inferring lexical meanings and contextual meanings. The beginners progress from reliance on concrete processing strategies such as the application of grapheme–phoneme correspondence rules to more abstract ones like making use of contextual clues. Mature readers, however, are flexible and may resort to a variety of strategies should a problem arise.

Concrete processing strategies, combined with the use of background knowledge, can to a large extent explain expeditious reading strategies. In these cases the reader reads quickly and selectively to construct a discourse topic through determining the main ideas or to purposefully seek out predetermined information.

Elements of expeditious reading strategies such as goal-setting and comprehension monitoring are clearly indicated in the 'literacy' component of Bernhardt's (1991a) model. The model, which has been empirically validated, described the development of readers' processing abilities over time. Bernhardt suggests three variables to consider in a definition of reading: language, literacy, and world knowledge. For Bernhardt, 'linguistic variables entail the *seen* elements in a text, including word structure, word meaning, syntax, and morphology. Literacy variables include intrapersonal variables such as purpose for reading, intention, and preferred level of understanding, as well as goal-setting and comprehension monitoring. Knowledge entails the background information that a reader already possesses and may or may not use in order to fill in gaps in the explicit linguistic elements in a text.' (1991b: 32 – 33)

When readers have developed an awareness of and flexibility for employing various process strategies for different purposes of reading, and where there is a more need for the reader to read quickly and efficiently, reading becomes a much reader-driven process. It seems that with the development of the reader's literacy, reading becomes a purposeful strategic process involving the use of various cognitive and metacognitive strategies. Similar to Coady's process strategies, literacy combined with the use of appropriate background knowledge helps determine how to approach a text most efficiently, helps establish what should be read carefully, and how to monitor the process of reading in order to achieve the purposes of reading. So it does appear that there may well be a sub-component or a componential strategy of expeditious reading which is distinguishable if not separable from careful reading. Empirical studies might usefully search for the evidence for the existence of such a componential strategy.

What has also been revealed from the review is that componential models have some advantages over the process models in explaining the development of reading ability. This explains why componential models have gained much attention from EFL reading researchers. L1 reading studies are carried out for the most part by psychologists with their own rather narrow processing agenda and little concern for practical applications in teaching or testing. EFL reading studies have a much stronger applied linguistic bias. Setting as their ultimate goal to improve literacy or reading ability, applied linguists are more interested in the componential nature of reading, in identifying and isolating components or componential skills and strategies of the reading ability.

The distinction made here between 'skills' and 'strategies' is deliberate. The former refers to the largely subconscious nature of the linguistic processes involved in reading and the latter to purposeful and conscious aspects of the reading process. Skills are text driven whereas strategies are reader driven.

In their efforts to identify and validate componential skills and strategies, applied linguists employ largely product-oriented rather than process-oriented methodologies. Various comprehension tests have been developed based on researchers' understanding of the construct of reading, and various statistical analysis of test data carried out such as factor analysis and ANOVA. With its focus on EFL readers' EAP reading ability, the present study relies to a large extent on a product-oriented componential approach.

There are two major advantages for EFL reading researchers in resorting to a product-oriented componential approach. Firstly, the separation between L1 and EFL reading research can be avoided and best use can be made of the achievements from L1 reading research. Although there has not been a definitive or consensus view on how meaning is arrived at, EFL researchers have benefited a lot from the overwhelmingly L1 reading research.

Secondly, the clarity of the picture projected by a componential analysis helps EFL teachers and testers design exercises and test tasks with a clear objective in mind. Thus, components involved in reading can be dealt with

2 Establishing the parameters of EAP reading

step by step and in various ways. In the testing of reading, for example, it is a widespread practice to construct individual items or sections of items to measure individual reading skills or strategies. As pointed out by Weir and Porter (1996: 3) 'it is ... often claimed by practitioners that sets of reading skill components provide useful frameworks on which to base course design, teaching, and test and materials development. . .' Grabe (1991: 382), as cited by Weir and Porter (ibid.: 2), remarks on the usefulness of a componential approach that:

A reading components' perspective is an appropriate research direction to the extent that such an approach leads to important insights into the reading process. In this respect, it . . . is indeed a useful approach.

In this research, three views have emerged and have been to various degrees evidenced. These are summarised by Rost (1993: 80) as the holistic general-factor theories, the multiple-factor models and middle roaders' two factors of reading comprehension. Weir and Porter (1996) in their review of the studies in the field refer to them as the 'unitary', the 'multi-divisible' and the 'bi-divisible' views on the nature of reading.

Advocates of the unitary view often substantiate their claim using data from test results and typically employing factor analysis. Urquhart and Weir (1998) introduce this method as applied in the study of the construct of reading:

Factor analysis is a statistical procedure for extracting the extent to which putatively different variables – in our case the so-called 'skills and strategies' in reading, reading types – in fact function in a similar manner. If a number of putatively different skills and strategies function in a very similar manner it is said that they are not different at all, only a single construct in different guises. If all conceivably different skills and strategies load on a single factor, we have to consider the strong possibility that there are in fact no skills and strategies at all, only a single undifferentiated ability: reading.

To understand the single undifferentiated reading ability, often referred to as general reading competence, Rost (1993) put forward an intuitive explanation that for adult readers and presumably skilful readers, the subskills of reading comprehension which were originally distinct have become intermingled to such an extent (as a result of repeated common practice) that they can no longer be singled out and measured separately.

Empirical studies supporting the single factor hypothesis are cited in Rost

(1993). These include Spearritt (1972), Drahozal and Hanna (1979), and Carver (1992). Weir and Porter (1994) further cited Lunzer *et al.* (1979) and Rosenshine (1980) in which evidence for a fully unitary view of reading is presented.

In Rost's (1993) study, for example, younger children learning to read their L1 were experimented on to find out if a differential assessment of reading comprehension is possible. A factor accounting for 77% of the total variance was extracted and interpreted to be a 'general reading competence'. The high intercorrelations between various subtests supposedly testing various subskills were taken to indicate failure in operationalising 'different' subskills in reading comprehension. It is therefore suggested that 'an interpretation of 'typical' reading comprehension profiles should be discouraged …' (Rost 1993: 88).

In addition to the quantitative statistical studies, there is qualitative evidence supporting the unitary view. Alderson (1990a), for example, challenges the distinction of hierarchies of higher and lower order reading skills. The experiments reported demonstrate disagreement among judges on what skill an item is testing in an EAP reading test. This led to Alderson's conclusion that the assumed 'higher order' and 'lower order' skills are not distinguishable.

Weir *et al.* (1990) and Weir and Porter (1996), however, cast doubt on the accuracy and reliability of Alderson's qualitative study. Weaknesses of the study include the lack of a common understanding of the terms employed for the 'higher level' and 'lower level' skill components and of the categories of description employed in the study. The experience of the judges is also questioned as one possible source contaminating the reliability of the experiment.

The unitary view of nature of reading is not shared by other researchers. In the review of qualitative studies against a unitary view of reading, Weir and Porter cited Anderson *et al.* (1991), Bachman *et al.* (1988), Brutten *et al.* (1991), Lumley (1993), Weakley (1993) and Weir *et al.* (1990). In all these studies, a sufficient degree of agreement is reached on what skills are being tested by individual items.

Qualitative studies employing the introspection technique have provided further evidence for the multi-divisible view. Examples are Grotjahn (1987), Nevo (1989) and Anderson *et al.* (1991). The analyses of the verbal report data in these studies indicate the use of different skills and strategies in answering different types of questions.

Weir and Porter also suggest reanalysing Alderson's (1990) self report data in terms of two broader categories of level b and c in Weir's (1993: 73) three level checklist of operations in reading. The two levels represent skills of reading for a global comprehension and for specifically linguistic knowledge at the word level. They argue that if this were done 'there would be a majority agreement among the judges on which of these levels the items would fall in nine out of the ten cases selected by Alderson' (Weir *et al.* 1990: 466).

There is also some doubt as to the strength of the unitary argument in quantitative studies based on factor analysis. In their explanation of the use of factor analysis for the study of reading components, Urquhart and Weir (1998) noted:

If some putative skills and strategies function in a statistically similar manner, and so load fairly heavily on one factor, while other putative skills and strategies function statistically in another manner, and so load on a second factor, this is evidence that reading is at least bi-divisible.

In both Davis (1968) and Spearritt (1972) more than two factors are isolated. Davis, for example, identified five skills of reading which are identifying word meanings, drawing inferences, identifying a writer's techniques and recognising the mood of a passage, and finding answers to questions asked explicitly or in paraphrase.

A bi-divisible view of reading has been evidenced in studies that extracted two factors. Examples include Berkoff (1979), Carver (1992), Farr (1968), Guthrie & Kirsch (1987) and see also further studies cited in Weir and Porter (1994). In these studies, what turned out to be the second factor apart from the general reading competence is vocabulary. Weir and Porter (1994: 5) noted that 'the phenomenon of vocabulary loading on a separate factor is not uncommon'. Quantitative evidence (e.g., Berg 1973, Davis 1944, Rosenshine 1980, Spearritt 1972 etc.) suggests that 'in general it may not be consistently possible to identify multiple, separate reading skill components, *there does seem to be a strong case for considering vocabulary as a component separate from reading comprehension in general*' (Weir and Porter, ibid: 5, authors' original italics).

While arguing for a unitary view of reading, Rost (1993) did admit that the experimental data, i.e., the correlations of the eight subtests in a sample of N = 220 second-grade elementary-school pupils used in his experiment, can be accounted for by either one general factor, 'general reading competence', or two factors, namely, 'inferential reading' and 'vocabulary', with only a very small amount of unexplained reliable variance left over. It is noted that '... it is probably not wrong to assume that the second factor, F2, is a vocabulary factor ... "vocabulary" appears to be an adequate interpretation of the second factor (ibid.: 86)'.

Therefore, although the argument as to whether reading is a componential process composed of various reading skills and strategies is far from being resolved, there is a case for the argument that reading is at the very least likely to be bi-divisible, i.e., the ability of reading consists of at least two theoretically isolable and distinguishable factors: vocabulary and general reading competence.

2 Establishing the parameters of EAP reading

The direction for further research in the field, according to Weir and Porter (1994: 14), is to resort to '. . .more exigent statistical techniques to test whether the presence of each component is statistically significant'.

For the practice of reading teaching and testing, the dangerous implications of a fully unitary view have been pointed out by Weir and Porter (ibid.). One of the dangers results from the utilisation of test formats with a specifically linguistic focus. The apparent failure to separate skill components has encouraged some reading test developers to resort to a random sampling of microlinguistic skills, i.e., skills at the lower level of reading. According to Weir and Porter (ibid. 9), this is mainly for 'reasons of expediency rather than from a principled view of uni-dimensionality'. Tests that contain this type of items include well established IELTS and TEEP in UK and TOEFL in US, all of international standing and good repute. Evidence is provided in Weir and Porter (1994) and Urquhart and Weir (1998) to show the danger of relying solely on discrete linguistic items testing lower level elements of reading. It seems that some candidates while coping well with global comprehension items may not achieve pass scores on those items focusing on the microlinguistic local level.

Implications for the development of the AERT

The review of the background literature led to the following guidelines for the development of an EAP reading test:

- **skills and strategies:**
  Reading is at the very least a bi-divisible process. For the benefits of teaching and testing, a unitary view of reading should be discarded. The process of reading involves the use of different skills and strategies, the former indicating the careful and usually subconscious process of applying linguistic skills to extract main ideas and important details whereas the latter indicate the quick and usually conscious process of employing strategies for achieving the purposes of reading efficiently and quickly.

- **careful reading and expeditious reading:**
  There is a distinction to be made between careful reading and expeditious reading, the former being a slower overall process involving the use of probably different subconscious reading skills (such as accessing mental lexicon, syntactic parser and thematic organiser) and the latter a quicker process involving the use of reading strategies (as well as using careful reading skills as and when appropriate). In the latter expeditious mode the reader will not usually attempt to understand every word in a passage but focuses on overall meaning.

- **reading at the global and local level:**
  Both careful and expeditious reading can be at the global and local level. Global comprehension refers to the understanding of propositions beyond

the level of microstructure, that is, any macropropositions in the macrostructure, including main ideas and important details. Local comprehension refers to the understanding of propositions at the level of microstructure, i.e., the meaning of lexical items, pronominal reference, etc.

- **the process of careful reading:**
  In careful reading, the process can be sequentially bottom-up, from letters to words and from words to sentences and finally to texts. It can also be top-down, a process of confirming and correcting predictions by sampling the visual input. Most likely, the process is interactive involving both bottom-up and top-down reading by interactively using all sources of information and background knowledge.
- **skills in careful reading:**
  Careful reading at the global level is more likely to be an interactive process with some top-down use of strategies to facilitate the inferencing of propositional meanings and the extraction of main ideas at the macropropositional level. Careful reading at the local level is more likely to be bottom-up involving the use of skills at the micropropositional level such as inferring the meaning of lexical items and understanding syntactical structure of sentences.
- **the process of expeditious reading:**
  In expeditious reading, the reader's formal knowledge of the structure of the text and background knowledge can play an important role. Unlike careful reading, in expeditious reading, the linearity of the text is not necessarily followed. The reader is sampling the text, which can be words, topic sentences or important paragraphs, to extract information on a predetermined topic in search reading or to develop a macrostructure of the whole text as in skimming. The process can be top-down when the reader is deciding how to sample the text and which part(s) of the text to be sampled. It can also be bottom-up when the reader's attention is on the sampled part(s) of the text.
- **strategies in expeditious reading:**
  Expeditious reading at the global level involves the use of strategies such as skimming and search reading (and careful reading skills in accessing selected parts). Expeditious reading at the local level involves the use of the strategy of scanning.
- **purposes of reading:**
  For different purposes of reading, the reader resorts to different skills and strategies and thus different processes are involved. The test should encompass these different skills and strategies as far as possible. Urquhart and Weir offer the following descriptions of skills and strategies which are consonant with the specification developed for the AERT. For the moment we put forward the following rough working definitions:

2 Establishing the parameters of EAP reading

- **Skimming:** reading for gist. The reader asks: What is this text as a whole about?, while avoiding anything which looks like detail.
  Reading schemes like SQ3R recommend starting the reading to learn process with skimming, so that the reader has a framework to accommodate the whole text. The defining characteristics are (a) the reading is selective, with sections of the text either omitted or given very little attention; (b) an attempt is made to build up a macrostructure (the gist) on the basis of as few details from the text as possible.
- **Search reading:** locating information on predetermined topics. The reader wants information to answer set questions or to provide data for example in completing assignments. It differs from skimming in that the search for information is guided by predetermined topics so the reader does not necessarily have to establish a macropropositional structure for the whole of the text.
- **Scanning:** reading selectively, to achieve very specific reading goals, e.g., finding the number in a directory, finding the capital of Bavaria. The main feature of scanning is that any part of the text which does not contain the pre-selected symbol(s) is dismissed. It may involve looking for specific words/phrases, figures/percentages, names, dates of particular events or specific items in an index.
- **Careful reading:** This is the kind of reading favoured by many educationalists and psychologists to the exclusion of all other types. It is associated with reading to learn, hence with the reading of textbooks. The defining features are (a) that the reader attempts to handle the majority of information in the text, that is, the process is not selective; (b) that the reader adopts a submissive role and accepts the writer's organisation, including what the writer appears to consider the important parts; and (c) that the reader attempts to build up a macrostructure on the basis of the majority of the information in the text.

The effect of background knowledge

The effect of background knowledge on reading comprehension has always been a central theme in EFL reading research. Bernhardt was among the first to explicitly consider knowledge as a separate factor in L2 reading. Commenting on Alderson's question 'Foreign language reading: A language problem or a reading problem?', Bernhardt (1991b: 31) noted '... it became clear that a third proposition was being added to the question: a language problem, a reading problem, or a knowledge problem?' In her multifactorial model of L2 reading, Bernhardt has included knowledge variables as a third component.

In L2 reading, according to Bernhardt, both language features and textual features of a text are seen elements whereas knowledge elements entailed in the text are unseen. In her chapter on knowledge-driven processes in L2

2 Establishing the parameters of EAP reading

reading, Bernhardt (1991a: 93) defined knowledge as 'information held by the writer and assumed to be known to the reader' or 'information held uniquely by an individual reader'.

Bernhardt's division of knowledge structure (ibid.: 95–97) contains local-level knowledge (idiosyncratic knowledge held by individuals); domain-specific knowledge (acquired mainly from schooling); and cultural-specific knowledge (ritualistic knowledge and cultural-historic knowledge, transmitted from generation to generation). This division is based mainly on the sources where the knowledge is most likely acquired. It is a slightly different version of schema theoretician's division of content, cultural and formal knowledge.

The interaction between language proficiency and background knowledge is difficult to investigate. Research findings are in many ways inconclusive. Some suggest that background knowledge has a significant effect only on low language proficiency students and no effect will be shown on linguistically proficient readers whereas others suggest that the background knowledge effect exists regardless of readers' language proficiency. However, there is some evidence of linguistic thresholds being necessary for background knowledge to function, that is, background knowledge would only have an effect on readers who have passed a certain level of linguistic threshold. Whatever the findings, it seems that language proficiency levels play at least as important a role as background knowledge in the comprehension of reading texts.

Ridgway (1996, 1997) offered a framework which he contends to be able to account for some of the contradictory results found in a number of research studies into the effect of background knowledge on FL comprehension. In this theoretical framework, an upper threshold and a lower threshold are conceptualised. When the upper threshold is exceeded, the text is considered as 'easy' for the reader, who then resorts to mainly a bottom-up approach. Background knowledge is not necessary for readers at this level as all 'gaps' in comprehension are filled. When the lower threshold is not reached, the text is regarded as 'difficult' for the reader, who would try to adopt a top-down approach, but the lack of linguistic and background knowledge prevents comprehension and then a 'short-circuit' occurs. Only the intermediate level students are most likely to successfully use compensatory strategies. For readers of this level, background knowledge effect would be detectable.

Ridgway (1996: 72) further quoted Oxford and Cohen's report (1992) on Green's (1991) study as a support for his framework:

> *Green reports that his advanced language learners often have significantly lower strategy use than intermediate language learners, and that intermediates use strategies significantly more than do*

beginners. Thus strategy use in Green's study might appear to be curvilinear, with intermediates using language learning strategies far more than advanced and beginning language learners. One might speculate that advanced learners might have automatised their learning behaviours, so they might not use or need language learning strategies as much as do intermediates; and beginners might not yet have developed a large, conscious, and frequently tapped repertoire of strategies.

Apart from readers' linguistic proficiency, their content knowledge, i.e., their familiarity with the topic and the subject matter of the text, is also an important factor that determines the effect of background knowledge on the comprehension of reading, especially EAP reading.

While investigating whether an ESP approach to testing the reading proficiency of academic students is appropriate and feasible, that is, whether tertiary level EFL students should be given reading proficiency tests in their own academic subject areas, Clapham (1994) investigated the effect of background knowledge, in particular of subject or domain specific content knowledge, on reading comprehension. One of the important findings from her study is that the relative importance of language proficiency and background knowledge in reading comprehension is largely dependent on the specificity of the reading passages.

Her investigation into whether language ability affected the students' use of background knowledge supported the hypothesis that there is a threshold level below which learners have difficulty making use of this knowledge.

However, neither linguistic proficiency nor text topic familiarity nor text subject specificity are easily assessed and in most cases they are not specified by the researchers. Texts used in many studies, for example, lack comparability because they are either invented or rewritten by the researchers and the level of difficulty and subject matter specificity are most likely not noted. Therefore, findings from EFL reading studies should be interpreted cautiously.

The review of the studies of background knowledge effect suggests that:
- Background knowledge affects reading comprehension in different ways for readers with different linguistic proficiency;
- For readers whose linguistic proficiency is above a threshold level, only highly specific text has a background knowledge effect;
- For linguistically poor readers, activating relevant background knowledge can at least partially help them make up their inadequate linguistic proficiency;
- The reader's schematic knowledge, especially content and formal knowledge, influence how and which skills or strategies are to be used. So topic familiarity and formal schemata can have a marked effect on a reader's performance. The readers should at least have some familiarity with the topic of each text and the rhetorical structure of the text.

2 Establishing the parameters of EAP reading

The AERT project aimed to develop a test that could be taken by all students from whatever discipline. Highly subject specific texts would be avoided and the rhetorical structure of the texts selected would be familiar and appropriate for the skills and strategies being tested.

To examine whether we could eliminate the disciplinary effect on students from different subject areas and at different levels of language proficiency, the test used in the study would be deliberately designed to comprise three parallel subtests for the three broadly divided disciplinary areas. Students from the three areas at different levels of linguistic proficiency would be administered the test. We thereby wished to examine whether texts which avoided the extremes on a familiarity continuum could be used across disciplines for assessing reading ability.

A needs analysis of Chinese undergraduates' EAP reading

Purposes of the survey

As well as surveying the literature concerning the componentiality of EAP reading we wished to generate further data on which to base the AERT specification by investigating the actual needs of students in the Chinese EAP context. In order to arrive at a general picture of Chinese undergraduates' EAP reading needs as perceived by the teachers involved in EAP reading courses in universities, a questionnaire survey was carried out and data were collected from 55 teachers in the three broad discipline areas.

Design of the questionnaire

The design of the questionnaire (see Appendix 2.2), especially the section on EAP reading skills and strategies, was to a large extent based on the 'Ordered list of reading comprehension enabling skills in an EAP context' in Weir (1983). Munby's (1978) taxonomy of reading skills was also consulted for the inclusion of various skills.

For details on the nature, topics, length of academic reading texts, the requirements of vocabulary and average speed of academic reading, we also consulted the Teaching Syllabus for Specialized Reading Stage (for undergraduates of science and technology: draft version) and the Study Skills for Specialized Reading Stage (draft version). We also referred to the College English Teaching Syllabus and College English Testing Syllabus for the requirements on reading at the foundation stage of undergraduate study.

The inclusion of the open-ended 'other alternatives' part of the questionnaire in each section provided ample opportunities for teachers to supplement their responses with further comments. Jargon like 'conditions'

2 Establishing the parameters of EAP reading

and 'lexical range' were avoided in the hope of encouraging responses through the use of more explicit wording. In the survey a Chinese version of the questionnaire was used.

Responses to the questionnaire

Respondents

The Chinese version of the questionnaire was circulated in May 1995 with a letter explaining the purpose of the questionnaire to 6 universities covering comprehensive universities like FuDan University and Beijing University, universities of science and technology like Qinghua University, Zhejiang University and the University of Science and Engineering of South China and also liberal arts universities like the Law Institute of East China.

Due to poor responses, a follow-up letter was sent to specific personnel in the foreign language department of each university who were asked to take charge of the matter. Of the six universities, all but Qinghua University eventually responded.

However, the data collected from this survey are unbalanced with 24 respondents from science and technology departments but only 1 from biology and 7 from arts and humanities. The analysis based on this data will no doubt be severely biased towards academic reading in the field of science and technology. Further data from teachers in the humanities/management and life sciences/biology and medicine had to be collected before a more balanced view of Chinese 3rd and 4th year undergraduates' EAP reading needs could be arrived at.

In October 1996 during Dr Weir's consultancy visit to China for the AERT project, a further sample of 19 academic English reading teachers from five universities in Shanghai was consulted. These included 4 from science and technology, 4 biology and medicine, and 11 humanities and management teachers. During the same period, another 4 questionnaires were collected by the AERT project members in the UK from MA TEFL students in the Centre for Applied Language Studies, University of Reading, who are all EAP reading teachers in Chinese universities. These efforts resulted in a more balanced data set which covers all the three broad discipline areas. The data still, however, only represent a limited sample of the potentially huge number of such teachers in Chinese universities but they are a difficult group to trace.

Out of a total of 55 respondents, 45 are subject matter teachers, 10 are teachers from the English department. This confirms the finding of a research carried out in FuDan University in 1994 on the teaching of EAP reading in the universities or colleges in Shanghai (no reports available) that most of the academic English reading courses are given by subject matter teachers. Anecdotal evidence suggests that the emphasis of the EAP reading class conducted by those teachers is likely to be placed on matters concerning subject knowledge instead of English language or reading skills and strategies.

2 Establishing the parameters of EAP reading

Discipline areas covered by the sample

Subject courses taught by the respondents are grouped broadly into three discipline areas: science/technology, biology/medical science/life science and humanities/business/management (see table 2.1).

Table 2.1

Distribution of subject areas covered in the survey

Discipline areas	Number of questionnaires	Examples
science/technology	29	physics, computer science, microelectronics, electric motor and control, chemistry, applied mathematics, electrical engineering, mechanical engineering, chemical engineering
biology/medicine/life science	6	biology, biological and medical engineering
humanities/business/management	20	business commerce, international relations, political science, law, philosophy

From the table, it is clear that we now have a quite balanced sample of teachers in the discipline areas of science/technology and humanities/business/management. The inadequacy of the sample from biology/medicine/life science is within our expectation because the number of students in these areas is far smaller than that of the other two.

Results of the survey

In the course of frequency counting and data analyses, we received the impression that most respondents took the questionnaire survey seriously. This is evidenced to some extent by the fact that many of them filled in the blanks in the open-ended part of the questionnaire. The following is a brief discussion of the data in the sequence of the questions asked in the questionnaire.

01 Nature of academic texts

This question asked about the importance of different text types as viewed by subject teachers. From the frequency count, a general estimation of the importance of those text types is provided in the last column of the table (see Table 2.2).

The data suggest that both abstracts and chapters from books are rated by subject teachers as most important text types for their students, followed by journal articles and research reports. Alternative text types supplied by respondents in the open-ended part of the question include: thesis or dissertation, contract, biography, preface, and law suit case.

Table 2.2

Degree of importance of text types*

Text types	Degree of importance				Average degree of importance **
	H	M	L	N	
journal articles	19	22	9	4	M
newspaper articles	10	16	16	9	L
abstracts	21	16	8	5	H
research reports	17	21	9	4	M
chapters from books	29	16	5	4	H
manuals	6	15	18	11	L
business documents	5	16	13	17	L

* The total is sometimes less than 55 because some teachers consider the category irrelevant.
** H: high importance; M: medium importance; L: low importance; N: no importance

02 Topics of reading materials

In response to the second question about topics of reading materials, most of the respondents suggested topics from their own discipline areas as the most important.

Since it is difficult to elicit detailed opinions on topics in a questionnaire due to the numerous possibilities, an alternative way to find the suitability of topics of texts to be used in the AERT was to ask a number of teachers to rate the topic familiarity of a number of texts which appeared to the team to be suitable for inclusion. This was done by Dr Weir during his October 1996 consultancy visit on a sample of 19 EAP reading teachers from five universities in Shanghai. In addition, further information was collected by asking those teachers to list the topics they consider important for their students. A detailed list is provided in Table 2.3.

2 Establishing the parameters of EAP reading

Table 2.3
Topics listed by EAP reading teachers

Discipline Areas	Example of Topics	
Science and technology	environment protection computer science development space travelling development of automobiles development of aircraft	pollution semiconductor devices artificial intelligence meteorology
Life science, biology and medicine	simple medical knowledge health care embryo duplication	extraterrestrial talent (ET) research on human's brain
Humanities, business and social studies	justice and crimes legal system civil law and contract trade regulations & business pop songs historical events	education population science and mankind equality bet. men & women finance and banking cultural difference

03 Requirements of vocabulary for academic reading

This question inquires about the teachers' view on the vocabulary range that is needed for academic reading by their students. To assist respondents measuring the requirements of vocabulary, we provided two figures: the requirements of vocabulary for College English Band 4 and Band 6. The frequency of each option is listed below (see Table 2.3):2.4

Table 2.4

Requirements of vocabulary for EAP reading*

	Requirements of vocabulary (words)				Average requirement
	4000 – 5000	5000 – 6000	6000 – 7000	7000 – 8000	
Frequency	5	20	22	2	approx. 6500

* The total is less than 55 because some teachers didn't answer the question.

The estimated average requirement of vocabulary viewed by these teachers is about 6500 words, which is a requirement slightly higher than CET 6.

04 Average length of each type of text

This question is about the average length of the types of texts used in EAP reading courses. Table 2.5 lists the result from the questionnaire of the frequency for each option.

Table 2.5

Length of each type of EAP reading text*

Type of text	Average length of each type of text (words)				Average length of each type of text
	less than 1000	1000 – 2000	2000 – 3000	more than 3000	
Journal articles	10	16	11	2	<1000 – 3000
Newspaper articles	11	18	10	3	<1000 – 3000
Abstracts	33	7	2	1	<1000
Research reports	3	15	15	10	1000 – 3000
Chapters from books	8	15	17	8	1000 – 3000
Manuals	18	10	7	2	<1000 – 2000
Business documents	14	11	7	1	<1000 – 2000

From the table, we can see that the length of abstracts is the shortest and the length of chapters from books and research reports is the longest. The data suggest the possibility of using journal articles and abstracts for careful reading and chapters of books or research reports for quick reading in AERT.

05 Average speed of academic reading

Reading speed varies for different types of materials and for different purposes of reading, neither of which were specified in the questionnaire, and therefore the result of the average speed of reading should be interpreted with caution. What can be said from the results of the survey (see Table 2.6) is that the average speed of EAP reading can vary from 70 wpm to 150 wpm. The lower end might be taken to suggest the minimum speed of careful reading whereas the higher end the maximum speed of quick reading.

Table 2.6

Speed of EAP reading*

	Speed of EAP reading (wpm)				Average speed of reading
	60 – 90	90 – 120	120 – 150	above 150	
Frequency	13	20	11	3	60 – 150 wpm

* The total is less than 55 because some teachers didn't answer the question.

2 Establishing the parameters of EAP reading

06–18 Skills and strategies in EAP reading

This section inquires about the importance of various skills and strategies as viewed by the teachers of EAP reading. The frequency of each option is listed in the following table (see Table 2.7). An estimation of the average degree of importance is provided in the last column of the table.

Table 2.7

Degree of importance of EAP reading skills and strategies*

Frequency Skills/strategies	Degree of importance				Average degree of importance**
	H	M	L	N	
06 surveying for gist	29	13	5	4	H
07 scanning for specifics	14	18	12	4	M
08 understanding explicitly stated ideas	29	15	3	5	H
09 understanding inferred meanings	12	18	16	3	M
10 distinguishing main idea from supporting details	9	21	15	4	M
11 obtaining information through non-verbal form	15	15	14	4	M
12 summarising by extracting salient points	19	18	11	5	M
13 critical evaluation of author's view	16	12	11	10	M
14 reference skills (using bibliography, index, etc.)	11	19	16	2	M
15 deducing meaning of unfamiliar lexical items	5	26	10	8	M
16 using grammatical structures	11	18	17	5	M
17 using discourse markers	4	16	16	11	L
18 using grammatical cohesion devices	7	20	14	7	M

* The total is sometimes less than 55 because some teachers consider the skill/strategy irrelevant.
** H: high importance; M: medium importance; L: low importance; N: no importance

2 Establishing the parameters of EAP reading

What is clear from the survey is that teachers regard reading quickly for gist and reading carefully for explicitly stated main ideas as the two most important skills/strategies in EAP reading.

The results from this needs analysis concerning performance conditions are summarised in Table 2.8.

Table 2.8

EAP reading needs analysis: conditions

EAP reading needs		Teacher's view
Nature of the text	journal articles	M
	newspaper articles	L
	abstracts	H
	research reports	M
	chapters from books	H
	manuals	L
	business documents	L
Length of the text	journal articles	<1000 – 3000
	newspaper articles	<1000 – 3000
	abstracts	<1000
	research reports	1000 – 3000
	chapters from books	1000 – 3000
	manuals	<1000 – 2000
	business documents	<1000 – 2000
Requirement of vocabulary	root forms, functional & subtechnical approx. 6500	
Requirement of reading speed	careful reading: 60 – 90 wpm expeditious reading: 100 – 150 wpm	

Implications of the needs analysis for AERT

From this needs analysis, we obtained a general picture of EAP reading needs as viewed by subject teachers of advanced reading in English in China. The tentative implications of the needs analysis for AERT are as follows:
- There should be a variety of text types in AERT, including journal articles, abstracts, and chapters from books. Abstracts and chapters from books are the two text types for EAP reading most highly valued by subject teachers, followed by journal articles.

2 Establishing the parameters of EAP reading

- The average length of texts varies from one type of text to another with abstracts being the shortest (less than 1000) and chapters from books the longest (ranging from 1000 to 3000).
- The speed of EAP reading ranges from 60 to 150 wpm depending on the purpose of reading and the type of material to be read. It is likely that the speed of careful reading should be between 60–90 wpm and the maximum limit of expeditious reading should be no more than 150 wpm. This is in line with the national guidelines laid down for advanced reading in the curriculum.
- The requirement of vocabulary viewed by subject teachers is around 6500 words, which suggests a requirement slightly above that of CET 6 level. In Chinese universities, students are supposed to pass CET 4 after the first two years of study and then enter the academic reading stage. CET 6 is an optional test for undergraduates and compulsory for graduate students. So far as the requirement of vocabulary is concerned, the AERT should be about 1000 words more than CET 6. These words are likely to be the 1000–1200 most frequently used technical or semi-technical vocabulary, which students are required to learn during the academic reading course.
- The two most important skills and strategies viewed by subject teachers are 'surveying to obtain the gist' (SKM) and 'understanding explicitly stated ideas' (EXMI). The former is the type of expeditious reading strategy frequently referred to as 'skimming' and the latter is the type of careful reading for global understanding which is termed as 'careful reading for explicitly stated main ideas' in our overview of EAP reading skills and strategies. Search reading was not included in the original survey at the start of the project as this was a refinement that grew out of the research conducted in the UK. The basic difference between search reading and skimming is that in the former the information sought is predetermined whereas in the latter one has to develop an overview of (a macrostructure for) the text without prior guidance.
- Inferring propositional meaning (IPROP) and pragmatic inferencing (IPRAG) were considered of less importance than understanding explicitly stated main ideas.
- Decoding at the microlinguistic level (ILEX inferring lexical meaning and SYN understanding syntactic structure) is only considered of medium importance by subject teachers.

Analysis of texts and tasks in published EAP teaching materials and tests

Purposes of the analysis

The analysis of EAP reading teaching and testing tasks had two main aims: firstly to try to identify
- what skills and strategies were covered in EAP reading tests and textbooks
- the conditions under which these skills and strategies were performed in teaching and testing.

Identification of the textbooks and tests

Fourteen EAP reading textbooks, the majority published in the 1980s, were identified (see Appendix 2.3.1.1 for a list of the textbooks analysed). For the purpose of making a comparison, 6 textbooks of reading in English for General Purposes (EGP) (see Appendix 2.3.1.2) and 6 EGP reading literature books (see Appendix 2.3.1.2) were also analysed.

Ten major EAP tests with a separate reading component dating from the 1960s were identified (see Appendix 2.3.2 for details of the tests analysed). These comprised: the University Entrance Test in English for Speakers of Other Languages (UETESOL 2 versions), the International English Language Testing Service (IELTS), the Test of English as a Foreign Language (TOEFL), the Test of English for Educational Purposes (TEEP), the English Language Testing Service – General Academic Module (ELTS – GA/1), Social Science Module (ELTS – SS), and Technology Module (ELTS – T), the English Proficiency Testing Battery (EPTB) and the English Language Battery (ELBA).

Analysis of skills and strategies

Both teaching and testing tasks were analysed first of all in terms of the operations involved, i.e., the skills and strategies employed in EAP reading. Through the literature review and EAP reading needs analysis, potentially important EAP reading skills and strategies had been identified. These provided us with the descriptive categories for this analysis. We will provide a brief introduction to these skills and strategies below.

The skills and strategies fall into four broad categories: expeditious reading at the global level, expeditious reading at the local level, careful reading at the global level, and careful reading at the local level. Expeditious reading strategies at the global level include both *skimming* for the gist and *search reading* for information on predetermined topics. The expeditious reading strategy at the local level is *scanning* for a specific piece of information through pure matching of the target word or looking for a name, date or

2 Establishing the parameters of EAP reading

number etc. Careful reading skills at the global level can be employed for understanding explicitly stated main ideas, abbreviated *EXMI* (standing for Explicitly Stated Main Ideas), for inferring propositional meanings, abbreviated *IPROP* (standing for Inferring Propositional meanings), and for inferring pragmatic meanings, abbreviated *IPRAG* (standing for Inferring Pragmatic meanings); and finally careful reading skills at the local level are employed for inferring lexical meanings, abbreviated *ILEX* (standing for Inferring Lexical meanings) and for understanding syntax, abbreviated *SYN* (standing for Syntax).

In the process of identifying the skills and strategies involved in an individual teaching task or tested by an individual item, the reading research group at CALS, University of Reading experienced three main problems.

Firstly, it was felt that some of the tasks or items did not teach or test one skill/strategy alone, and in fact in some cases two or three skills/strategies were being addressed in one task or one item. In other words, the researchers found that there was sometimes an overlap between the skills/strategies used in completing a teaching task or in establishing an answer for a testing item.

Secondly, when the analyses were compared, a small number of differences in opinion surfaced among researchers. One of the factors contributing to the occasional disagreements was a lack of precise understanding of these terms. The researchers found it necessary to make sure that their understanding of certain terms used in the definitions was the same. For example, in identifying tasks and items that address the skill of careful reading for explicitly stated main ideas (EXMI), researchers felt it necessary to return to the discussion of what constituted a main idea and whether supporting details constituted main ideas. The type of tasks and items that the researchers had particular problems classifying were those addressing the two categories of expeditious reading strategies: 'search reading' and 'scanning'. In EAP reading literature there have been few clear distinctions drawn between the two. It was found necessary to revisit such tasks and items more than once in order to differentiate between those which should be classified as addressing search reading, and those which were addressing scanning. Ultimately, it was decided that where tasks and items directed the candidates to a word or symbol which matched exactly with one in the passage, these would be regarded as tasks teaching scanning and items testing scanning. It was also found helpful to further define the definition of search reading with regard to the wording 'predetermined topic' as meaning the use of not exactly the same words, but words belonging to the same or similar semantic field.

Thirdly, tasks and items of reading expeditiously and reading carefully were often based on the same texts. Therefore it was difficult to know which skills or strategies were being used to complete a task and to arrive at an answer as the reader was exposed to the same text more than once. For example, in the test tasks analysis, based on the passage entitled *Tennis*

Racquets (UETESOL June 1996 – Text A), the candidate has to answer a variety of items requiring the use of scanning, search reading, skimming, and reading for explicitly and implicitly stated main ideas!

Being aware of these problems, the researchers further clarified the skills and strategies and frequently re-visited their analyses before comparing their findings and making final judgements.

The distinctions elaborated in Urquhart and Weir (1998) were found to be helpful. Their summary is provided below.

Reading carefully for explicitly stated main ideas

Careful and thorough reading of text for explicitly stated main ideas and important information is an important purpose for reading. We often need to decode the whole of a text to understand it all or to establish its macrostructure. In this mode the reader has to read a text at a careful rate from beginning to end in a linear and sequential fashion with regressions as necessary. It will mainly be a bottom-up sequential process with some limited top-down processing.

This might involve:
- Separating explicitly stated main ideas from supporting detail by recognising topic sentences or by recognising lexical indicators of importance;
- Generating a representation of the text as a whole;
- Understanding the development of an argument and/or logical organisation.

Reading carefully for implicitly stated main ideas

In some texts the ideas may not be explicitly stated and students can be alerted to the nature of propositional inferences. These are made when the reader uses explicit statements in the text to form an inference without recourse to knowledge from outside the text (Chikalanga 1990). This might involve making:
- propositional informational inferences which are either referential, typically answering questions beginning with what and which, or spatio-temporal typically answering questions beginning with where and when;
- propositional explanatory inferences which are concerned with motivation, cause, consequence and enablement and will often answer questions beginning with why and how.

All the information required to make such propositional inferences is recoverable from the text. Readers' activities might include:
- discovering writer's intention;
- understanding writer's attitude to the topic;
- identifying the addressee;
- distinguishing fact from fiction.

2 Establishing the parameters of EAP reading

Inferring pragmatic meaning related to a text

Pragmatic inferencing takes place when readers rely mainly on their own schemata and/or opinions to interpret a text (Chikalanga 1990). This might involve making:
- pragmatic informational inferences which are either referential, typically; answering questions beginning with what and which, or spatio-temporal typically answering questions beginning with where and when;
- pragmatic explanatory inferences which are concerned with motivation, cause, consequence and enablement and will often answer questions beginning with why and how;
- pragmatic evaluative inferences where the reader makes an evaluation on the basis of the content of a text:
  - Applying the main idea(s) in the text into other contexts
  - Evaluating a point of view
  - Expressing own opinion on the subject

With reference to their own background knowledge and experience the readers would try to interpret, respond to, evaluate and possibly apply the writer's message(s) contained in the text.

Skimming

This involves processing a text selectively to get the main idea(s) and the discourse topic as efficiently as possible, which might involve both expeditious and careful reading and both bottom-up and top-down processing. The focus may be global or local and the rate of reading is likely to be rapid but with some careful reading. The text is processed quickly to locate important information which then may be read more carefully. Purposes for using this strategy might include:
- To establish a general sense of the text
- To quickly establish a macropropositional structure as an outline summary
- To decide the relevance of texts to established needs

Where appropriate to text type it might involve one or more of the following operationalisations:
- reading titles and sub-titles quickly
- reading the abstract carefully
- reading the introductory and concluding paragraph carefully
- reading the first and last sentence of each paragraph carefully
- glancing at words and phrases in particular for discourse cues

Search reading

This differs from skimming in that the purpose is to locate information on predetermined topic(s), for example in selective reading for writing purposes.

2 Establishing the parameters of EAP reading

It is often an essential strategy for completing written assignments.

The process like skimming is rapid and selective and is likely to involve careful reading once the relevant information has been located. Like skimming bottom-up and top-down processing is therefore involved. Unlike skimming, sequencing is not always observed in the processing of the text although it is likely to be more linear than scanning. The periods of closer attention to the text tend to be more frequent and longer than in scanning. It normally goes well beyond the mere matching of words to be found in scanning activities.

It might include the following operationalisations where appropriate
- Keeping alert for words in the same or related semantic field (not certain as in scanning of the precise form of these words);
- Using formal knowledge of text structure for locating information;
- Using titles and subtitles;
- Reading abstracts where appropriate;
- Glancing at words and phrases.

Scanning

This involves looking quickly through a text to locate a specific symbol or group of symbols, e.g., a particular word, phrase, name, figure or date. The focus here is on local comprehension and most of the text will be ignored. The rate of reading is rapid and sequencing is not usually observed. It is surface level rather than deep processing of text and is mainly bottom-up processing. There is a rapid inspection of text with occasional closer inspection. Pugh (1978: 53) describes it as:

finding a match between what is sought and what is given in a text, very little information processed for long term retention or even for immediate understanding

The operationalisations involved might include looking for/matching
- specific words/phrases;
- figures/percentages;
- dates of particular events;
- specific items in an index/directory.

Analysis of skills and strategies in teaching tasks

In the teaching tasks analysis, tasks were divided into three types chronologically: pre-reading, while-reading and post-reading. The four major categories of skills and strategies were observed to be mainly used in the while-reading tasks. At the pre-reading stage, two types of tasks were exploited: previewing (abbreviated PV) and prediction (abbreviated PD). At the post-reading stage, one type of post-reading task, writing summary (abbreviated WS), was identified. The results of the analysis of the 14 major

2 Establishing the parameters of EAP reading

EAP reading textbooks, 6 EGP reading literature books and 6 EGP reading textbooks were summarised in tabular forms (see Appendices 2.3.3.1 – 3).

For the 14 EAP reading textbooks, it can be seen from Appendix 2.3.3.1 that the most popular type of pre-reading activity is prediction. The strategy appeared in 12 out of the 14 textbooks analysed. This strategy is used to anticipate the content of a text and to make hypotheses about the macropropositions it might contain. The argument for this strategy is largely rooted in the psycholinguistic model of the reading process, in particular Goodman's (1967) top-down model, which claims that reading is a continuous prediction-confirming process. Activating appropriate schemata at the pre-reading stage is, therefore, viewed as a strategy for improving reading efficiency and enhancing comprehension.

Previewing is less emphasised in these textbooks, appearing in 5 out of the 14 books analysed. The strategy, in real life reading, is employed to judge the content relevance of a book, an article, or a text and then to make a decision whether to read it and how to read it. To be more specific, it might involve some or all of the following activities: thinking about the title, checking the edition and date of publication, and reading the table of contents, appendices, and indices quickly, and reading the abstract, the preface, the foreword and the blurb carefully. The reason why this task is not featured as much as prediction is that it is largely irrelevant in a teaching context, where coursebooks have been pre-selected by teachers and texts pre-selected by the compilers. So in general coursebooks and texts in the books are expected to be of relevance, interest and appropriate difficulty level to the potential readers.

The while-reading teaching activities in these coursebooks show an equal focus on the training of the four identified major categories of EAP reading skills and strategies, with a slightly low frequency for inferring pragmatic meanings (IPRAG). Out of the total 14 textbooks, the occurrences of these skills and strategies are 9 for skimming (SKM), 10 for search reading (SCH), 11 for scanning (SCN), 10 for understanding explicitly stated main ideas (EXMI), 10 for inferring propositional meanings (IPROP), 7 for inferring pragmatic meanings (IPRAG), 11 for inferring lexical meanings (ILEX) and 9 for understanding syntax (SYN).

Post-reading activities require readers to summarise and evaluate the text. Tasks at this stage provide readers with a chance to reflect critically on the text and thus promote interaction between the reader and the text. From the analysis, 6 out of the 14 textbooks have included post-reading tasks in the form of writing summaries (WS). Obviously less attention is paid to reading at this stage. However because this activity normally involves evaluation based on background knowledge, like pragmatic inferencing it has no place in testing because of our desire to reduce as far as possible the influence of background knowledge on test performance.

2 Establishing the parameters of EAP reading

As a comparison, the occurrences of these skills and strategies in EGP reading literature books and textbooks have also been tabulated (Appendices 2.3.3.2 – 3). The picture of pre-reading tasks is similar to that of the EAP reading textbooks which shows a preference for prediction activities. The picture of while-reading tasks is slightly different from that of the EAP reading textbooks. The pragmatic inference skill featured outstandingly in EGP textbooks (occurred in each of the 6 EGP textbooks analysed). The search reading strategy had a lower occurrence in EGP textbooks and appeared only once in the EGP reading literature book (Grellet 1981). At the post-reading stage, similar to EAP reading textbooks, little emphasis is laid on writing summaries.

Analysis of skills and strategies in test tasks

In the test tasks analysis two researchers first identified which skill(s)/strategy(ies) each item was felt to be testing and results were recorded in tabular forms, with one test in one table (see Appendix 2.3.4). Totals were then calculated and the findings were summarised (see Appendix 2.3.5) to illustrate the overall breakdown of skills/strategies tested in each paper. The tests have been listed in reverse chronological order covering the period from the 1990s to the 1960s. Some test items appear under two headings and are indicated by asterisks. Based on this table, several observations may be made.

Firstly, by arranging the tests in a chronological order, it is quite clear that there has been a move away from testing items at the microlinguistic level during the 1990s, with only the TOEFL testing this skill/strategy (maximum of 3 items). The table also indicates clearly that until the late 1970s there was an emphasis on careful reading.

Secondly, with the exception of EPTB and ELBA, all tests had items which tested scanning and reading carefully for explicitly and implicitly stated main ideas, though the percentage of the items was not always the same even within one test – compare for example, the UETESOL February paper with the June one. Nearly all papers tested search reading. Interestingly, all ELTS papers showed a preponderance of items testing reading carefully for implicitly stated main ideas (between 27.5% and 55%). However, very few items appear to test candidates' pragmatic knowledge since such items would not be equally fair to all candidates.

Thirdly, there are only a limited number of items testing the skimming strategy, which appears in a maximum of 3 out of the 10 tests analysed and a maximum of 1 item per test (UETESOL June and February 1996 test papers and TOEFL 1991 test paper). Given that skimming items often test comprehension of the text's discourse topic, and as each passage usually has only one discourse topic, this is perhaps not so surprising. On the other hand, given that the number of texts each test has varied from two to six, with a total of 40 texts for the 10 tests, perhaps more of such items might have been expected. This might be due to insufficient attention to the strategy and the

2 Establishing the parameters of EAP reading

difficulty of writing such items on the length of passages found in most of these tests. (See 2.3.4.2 Analysis of conditions in test tasks below for further details.)

Apart from these objective observations, the researchers' experiences indicated several other findings. Firstly, different skills and strategies are likely to be used by readers of different proficiency levels. In the identification stage of research, different options did occur between the native speaker of English (NS) researcher and non-native speaker of English (NNS) researcher. This was noticeable, for instance, in a few questions where the NNS felt obliged to use inferencing skills in order to reach an answer whilst the NS had felt the information to be explicitly stated. There were also occasions when the NS could read the whole text carefully whilst the NNS had to search read or scan the text given the time constraints due to the difference in reading speeds between the NS and the NNS researchers. However, since it was felt that the test was more accurately aimed at the NNS, differences of opinion on the skills and strategies used took this factor into account in determining which skill/strategy was thought to be tested.

Secondly, a superior knowledge of English may not be sufficient when dealing with highly subject-specific texts. This was witnessed, for example, in the ELTS (Technology) paper where the researcher (NNS) with more science-biased background had no problem interpreting such things as graphs whilst the researcher (NS) with more arts-biased background took much longer and had on occasion to employ guessing strategies. Clearly, the superiority of the native speaker's English did not help in this particular test when faced with insufficient schemata.

Analysis of performance conditions

The second aim of the teaching and testing tasks analysis was to identify the conditions under which the identified skills and strategies were performed.

Analysis of performance conditions in teaching tasks

In analysing the performance conditions of the teaching tasks, six prominent and recent textbooks were selected from the textbooks analysed for the skills and strategies. These comprised: McGovern *et al.*'s Reading (1994), Glendenning and Holmstrom's Study Reading (1992), Lynch's Reading for Academic Success (1988), Tomlinson and Ellis's Reading – Advanced (1988), Salimbene's Interactive Reading (1986), and Arnaudet and Barrett's Approaches to Academic Reading and Writing (1984).

Based on the conditions for reading tests laid down in Weir's *Understanding & Developing Language Tests* (1993), each of the six books identified was analysed in terms of the following conditions: stated purposes for reading; nature of the texts; rhetorical organisation; propositional features, for example, lexical range, topic areas, and background knowledge;

illocutionary features; channel of presentation; size of input/length of text; speed of processing; amount of help given; method factor/response mode; questions/answers in L1/TL; and receptive/productive.

In the analysis we describe the texts in terms of their rhetorical organisation breaking this term down into *collection of descriptions, causation, problem/solution,* and *comparison* in Meyer & Freedle's terms (1984. See Appendix 2.3.6 for details of the different expository types.) The aim in doing this was to see whether there was any relationship between the type of rhetorical organisation of the text and the type of reading skills/strategies that might be needed to understand the passage. It was recognised that such information would, obviously, be of great help to textbook writers and test developers at the stage of text selection.

The main difficulty surfaced was that most texts comprised elements from more than one rhetorical type. Clearly, as Carrell (1984) points out:

Most prose consists of combinations of these rhetorical patterns; for example, a folktale may contain description, causation, and time-sequenced events (that is, collection) within an overall problem/ solution organisation where the protagonist confronts and resolves a problem.

(ibid.: 444)

All the texts in the six textbooks and in the ten test papers were read individually by the researchers and it was found that Meyer and Freedle's 'model' applied quite well to these texts.

Secondly, due to the fact that most of the texts analysed teach skills of both reading expeditiously and reading carefully, it was felt important to add to the conditions information regarding the amount of control over both the skills/strategies employed and the time actually to be spent on each passage/task. Furthermore, in order to obtain a more accurate idea of the speed of processing required by candidates, the actual length of each of the passages was added to the conditions table.

A detailed account of the conditions of each textbook appears in Appendices 2.3.7.1–6. The information on which these conditions are based comes from two sources: firstly the textbook, for example, such information as the length of each passage; and secondly, the researchers' own interpretations, for example, rhetorical organisation as discussed above.

The analysis of the conditions underlying each of the six EAP reading textbooks analysed revealed similarities and differences between the textbooks. The table in Appendix 2.3.8 gives an overall summary of some of these conditions, on the basis of which the following tentative conclusions have been drawn.

2 Establishing the parameters of EAP reading

Firstly, the purpose of reading is stated clearly in all these textbooks. In general terms, the purpose is for the development of various reading skills and strategies so that candidates can have access to the necessary information for their academic study in a most efficient manner.

Secondly, texts are usually taken from academic books, journals, periodicals, textbooks and reference books. Topics vary greatly but are of general interest rather than of interest only to candidates majoring in a particular academic field. No special requirement on background knowledge is therefore needed.

Thirdly, channels of presentation are mainly textual with some graphics (table, charts, diagrams). Index, abstracts, content pages, bibliographies and encyclopaedic entries appear only in one of the textbooks.

Fourthly, the lengths and the rhetorical organisations of the passages used in these textbooks vary greatly. There is a good coverage of text lengths and rhetorical organisations within one textbook. This explains the wide range of skills and strategies covered by these textbooks (with the only exception of Arnaudet and Barrett's Approaches to Academic Reading and Writing, which is a combination of reading and writing textbook).

Fifthly, there appears to be little or no control over the skills/strategies candidates use on EAP reading teaching tasks. In most cases, teaching tasks which involve the use of both expeditious reading strategies and careful reading skills at both global and local levels are based on one passage. Candidates are therefore exposed to the same passage more than once in completing the tasks. As a result, it is virtually impossible to control the individual amount of time candidates should spend on each passage for each task, which is the most important factor in determining the use of skills and strategies.

Analysis of performance conditions in test tasks

Each of the ten EAP tests identified was analysed in terms of the conditions specified above for the teaching tasks, but two more conditions specific to testing were added: number and ordering of tasks and explicitness of weighting.

A detailed account of the conditions of each test appears in Appendices 2.3.9.1 – 10. The information on which these conditions are based comes from three sources: firstly the test paper, for example, such information as the length of each passage; secondly, any relevant supporting documentation such as test syllabi which sometimes provided information concerning such things as topic areas; and thirdly, the researchers' own interpretations, for example, rhetorical organisation as discussed above. It should be noted that the conditions describe the actual test version analysed, and that these may obviously vary a little in other years – for instance, in terms of the presence or absence of texts with diagrams, or in terms of the rhetorical organisation of the passages included.

2 Establishing the parameters of EAP reading

The analysis of the conditions underlying each of the ten EAP reading tests analysed revealed many differences between the papers. Appendix 2.3.10 gives an overall summary of some of these conditions, on the basis of which the following observations may be made.

Firstly, there appears to be little or no control over the skills/strategies candidates use on current EAP reading tests as questions testing both reading quickly and reading carefully are based on one passage.

Secondly, there appears to be little or no control over the individual amount of time candidates should spend on each passage. In IELTS, TEEP and EPTB times are suggested per passage/section but there is no enforcement of these times. Others simply state the time allowed for the reading test and leave the division of that time to the candidates' discretion.

Thirdly, the length of time given over to the reading tests varies from 15 minutes (EPTB) to 60 minutes (IELTS). The UETESOL does not offer any breakdown for its written paper. Candidates are given 2.5 hours within which to complete three components on writing, editing and reading.

Fourthly, the number of items varies from 27 to 40, the exception being EPTB which comprises a C-test of 50 items and a cloze elide test of 180. The number of texts also varies from 2 to 6, with lengths of between 50 words (C-test) and 1330 (ELTS-SS).

Fifthly, Appendix 2.3.11.1 displays the rhetorical organisation of each passage (according to Meyer & Freedle's 1984 classification), the length of each passage, and the skills/strategies tested by each passage. Appendix 2.3.11.2 is a breakdown of skills/strategies by rhetorical organisation of text. On the basis of these two tables it may be deduced that scanning items appear more often to be based on *collection of descriptions* passages (13 out of the 22 *collection of descriptions* passages had scanning items); that items testing reading carefully for explicitly stated ideas are evenly spread between *causation* (7), *comparison* (6) and a *collection of descriptions* (6); and that items testing the inferring of propositional meaning appeared predominantly in *collection of descriptions* (10) although they also appear in six *comparison* and six *causation* passages. Out of a total of forty passages, there were more *collection of descriptions* passages (17) than other types: *causation* (9), *comparison* (9) and *problem/solution* (5).

Test formats were also classified (see Appendix 2.3.12 for a glossary of test formats and a description of what each test format requires of the candidates). A total number of eleven types were identified, although only a maximum of seven appeared in any one test (IELTS) and in some tests only one test format was used, for example, multiple-choice questions in the TOEFL test. The eleven types comprised: gap-filling items, information transfer-type items, matching items, multiple-choice questions, sequencing items, short answer questions, table completion items, text completion items, true/false/no answer given items, and items in the forms of C-tests and cloze elide tests.

2 Establishing the parameters of EAP reading

In order to see more clearly which test used which test format and to what extent, a breakdown of test formats for each test is summarised in Appendix 2.3.13.1.

The MCQ format has been popular from the 1960s until the present with all TOEFL items utilising this format. The 1970s interest in C-tests and cloze tests is represented by examples of these formats in the EPTB, whilst the 1980s and 1990s saw the appearance of a greater variety of test formats in the EAP reading tests. Firstly, the 1980s witnesses the use of short-answer questions, sequencing items, and a text completion exercise in the TEEP. Then in the 1990s, other formats in the form of true/false/no answer given, matching, gap-filling, table completion, and information transfer appeared.

Appendix 2.3.13.2 illustrates the breakdown of test formats against skills/strategies tested in these tests. An analysis of the number of test formats used in each of the tests as displayed in Appendix 2.3.13.1, however, does not seem to indicate a particular pattern in terms of an optimal number of test formats which should be exploited by EAP tests. The ones analysed varied from 1 (ELTS, TOEFL & ELBA) to 7 (IELTS). This scenario does raise the question of whether there is an optimal number of test formats for one test, and whether certain test formats lend themselves to testing particular skills/strategies.

An analysis of the data in Appendix 2.3.13.2 indicates, for example, that the multiple-choice format has been utilised for the testing of every skill/strategy identified. It has been particularly heavily-used for testing reading carefully for implicit stated main ideas (more than 70 items out of a total of 176), but also quite often for testing scanning and reading carefully for explicitly stated main ideas (33 and 37 respectively).

With respect to the other test formats used, true/false/no information given seems to lend itself more to the testing of explicitly and implicitly stated main ideas (11 and 12 respectively out of a total of 26), whilst the table completion format appears to be preferred for the testing of scanning (19 items) and to a lesser extent for testing search reading (10 items). Gap-filling seems to be used more for the testing of explicitly stated main ideas (12 out of 15 items).

At the microlinguistic level, inferring lexical meaning and the testing of syntactic structures are mainly tested by means of text completion, C-test and cloze elide procedures (17, 50 and 180 respectively) with a small number of multiple-choice questions also being used (10–13 items).

The information in Appendix 2.3.13.2 might also contribute to our knowledge of which test formats might best lend themselves to being exploited for each and/or both of reading at the global and local levels. Based on the breakdown of which skills/strategies test global reading (search reading, skimming, reading for explicitly and implicitly stated main ideas) and which local (scanning, inferring lexical meaning and the testing of syntactic structures), Appendix 2.3.13.3 presents the information from Appendix 2.3.13.2 in a different format.

2 Establishing the parameters of EAP reading

From the analysis, it would appear that most test formats are used for testing at both the global and local levels. Of the 11 test formats present in the 10 tests 8 were used for testing reading both at the global and local level, 1 at the global level only (MATCH) and 2 at the local level only (TEXTC and CTEST), though admittedly, true/false/not given appears to be testing mainly global reading skills containing as it does only one scanning item.

Most test formats are used for testing both expeditious and careful reading (see Appendix 2.3.13.4). Of the 11 test formats present in the 10 tests 8 were used for testing both expeditious reading and careful reading. There are, however, a few formats which lend themselves better to testing either expeditious or careful reading. Table completion, information transfer are exploited only for expeditious reading whereas cloze elide, text completion, and C-test only for careful reading.

Implications for the development of AERT

The findings from this EAP reading teaching and testing tasks analysis throw light on the development of the test specifications for the AERT. The points arising out of the teaching tasks analysis provide some guidance for the development of the test operations:
- Skimming, search reading, scanning, reading carefully for main ideas (explicit and inferred) and understanding lexis are taught through a variety of exercise types in the 14 textbooks published from 1970 to 1994 we were able to analyse.
- There is however a greater prevalence of prediction activities and a number of exercises on previewing (rather like a pre-reading search activity) as compared to the test task analysis. This may reflect the fact that it is easier to teach these than to test them.
- There is also a greater incidence of exercises focusing on syntax in the teaching materials as against testing. As this has now been dropped completely in the CET 6 examination in China it was felt by the Project Team that this was added reason why it would not be appropriate to include this in AERT.

The analysis of testing tasks for EAP reading also points to a similar range of skills and strategies as to those discovered in the teaching tasks analysis. In addition, the test conditions analysis provides important implications for the design of the AERT. We summarise these points below:
- In expeditious reading of relatively long passages, scanning and search reading are the two most frequently tested strategies in these analysed papers. In careful reading of relatively short passages, most items test the understanding of explicitly stated main ideas and propositional inferences.
- The skill tested at the microlinguistic level of reading is inferring the meanings of unfamiliar lexical items using contextual clues.

2 Establishing the parameters of EAP reading

- Providing students with a brief description of the purpose of reading at the beginning of each passage might be useful for making the reading an authentic task and helping students adopt an appropriate skill or strategy in reading the passage.
- Texts should be of general academic nature but they should be written for a non-specialist audience.
- Topics of texts should be familiar to all students so as to avoid possible bias caused by topic familiarity. Several passages of different topics might be used to counter-balance the topic familiarity effect.
- Passages of various length should be used to allow the testing of different skills and strategies. Different passages should be used for the testing of expeditious and careful reading to make students aware of the flexibility of using different approaches to different texts and different tasks.
- Some texts might contain graphics, e.g., tables and charts, which is a general feature of expository academic texts.
- The most frequently adopted rhetorical organisation of texts is collection of description. This is also the type of text especially suitable for setting scanning items and quite suitable for testing inferring propositional meanings (IPROP). Texts with rhetorical organisations of causation, comparison and collection of description lend themselves equally to testing other skills and strategies. The less frequently used text type is problem/solution.
- The most flexible test formats for EAP reading tests include MCQ, T/F/NG, gap-filling (GF) and SAQ. Table completion (TABLE), information transfer (ITRN) are exploited mostly for expeditious reading whereas cloze elide (CLOZEL), text completion (TEXTC) and C-test (CTEST) for careful reading. Matching (MATCH) and true/false/not given (T/F/NG) are used more for reading at the global level than at the local level. Text completion (TEXTC), C-test (CTEST) and cloze elide (CLOZEL) are used more for local level reading than for global level reading.
- Questions can be put before or after the text depending on the nature of the questions. For long passages which are supposed to be read quickly using strategies of scanning, search reading and skimming, questions are preferably read in advance so that reading of the text will be more purposeful and realistic. Summarising questions might be put at the end of the passage.
- The weighting of items is usually marked explicitly on the test paper. Most tests give equal weighting to all the items, which makes it convenient for testers to compare students' performance on different parts of the test.

3 Synthesising the *a priori* validation data

The AERT test specifications

On the basis of:
- the survey of the literature;
- the analysis of EAP reading needs of Chinese undergraduates;
- the analysis of reading coursebooks;
- the analysis of tests of EAP reading,

we have developed a specification of the operations and conditions we feel should be tested in the AERT.

First, we list a taxonomy of the skills/strategies for academic reading. This is the operations section of the test specification. Table 3.1 includes strategies for expeditious reading at both the global and local level, and skills for careful reading at both the global and local level.

The research also indicates that a number of performance conditions would need to be built into the test and we list these at Table 3.2.

The development of these specifications was an iterative process and took place over a period of six months with frequent meetings of the reading research group at CALS, University of Reading.

The specifications constitute Stage 1 of the *a priori* validation of the AERT (see page 12) above. The next step was to operationalise these specifications by faithful implementation in the first version of the test (Stage 2).

Table 3.1
A taxonomy of skills and strategies in reading for academic purposes

Types of reading strategies and skills	Skimming	Expeditious reading strategies — Search reading	Scanning
Purpose	Processing a text selectively to get the main idea(s) and the discourse topic as efficiently as possible - which might involve both expeditious and careful reading. - To establish a general sense of the text; - To quickly establish a macro-propositional structure as outline summary without decoding all the text; - To read more efficiently; - To decide the relevance of texts to established needs.	Locating information on predetermined topic(s) (e.g., in the form of questions set on main idea(s) in a text). This normally goes beyond mere matching of words (as in scanning). The process is selective but is likely to involve careful reading once relevant information has been located.	Looking quickly through a text – not necessarily following the linearity of the text – to locate a specific symbol or group of symbols: e.g., a particular word, phrase, name, figure or date.
Operationalisations	Where appropriate to text-type: - Reading title and sub-titles quickly; - Reading abstract carefully; - Reading introductory and concluding paragraphs carefully; - Reading first and last sentences of each paragraph carefully; - Glancing at words or phrases.	- Keeping alert for words in the same or related semantic field (not certain of precise form of these words); - Using formal knowledge for locating information; - Using titles and subtitles; - Reading abstract where appropriate; - Glancing at words or phrases	Looking for (matching): - specific words/ phrases; - figures percentages; - dates of particular events; - specific items in index; - names.
Focus	Both global and local	Both global and local	Local
Text coverage	Selective reading to establish important propositions of a text	Selecting information relevant to pre-determined topic(s)	Ignoring most of the text
Rate of reading	Rapid with some careful reading	Rapid with careful reading when information is located	Rapid with some careful reading
Direction of processing	Sequencing observed	Sequencing not always observed	Sequencing not observed
Realtionship with the underlying process(es)	Interactive process involving both top-down and bottom-up processing	Interactive process - There is more observance of the linearity and sequencing as compared with scanning; - Involves some top-down processing, i.e., using formal knowledge. The periods of close attention to the text tend to be more frequent and longer than in scanning; - Also bottom-up involved because of close attention to the selected part(s) of the text. The periods of close attention to the text may be less frequent than skimming because of the predetermined searching.	Surface level rather than deep processing of a text. Mainly a bottom-up process: - exhibiting a mixture of rapid inspection of the text with an occasional closer inspection; - finding a match between what is sought and what is given in a text, very little information [being] processed for long-term retention or even for immediate understanding (Pugh 1978: 53) But for some items the top-down process may be involved (i.e, using formal knowledge to look for specific information in a fixed-pattern text, or to draw upon previous understanding established through skimming.

3 Synthesising the a priori validation data

Table 3.1 (cont.)

Types of reading Strategies and skills	Careful reading skills			
	Understanding a text	Understanding lexis		Understanding syntax
Purpose	Processing a text carefully and thoroughly in order to comprehend main idea(s) and supporting information; To decode all in order to comprehend all; To carefully establish a macro structure for the text.	Lexical inferences are of three kinds: the resolution of lexical ambiguity; the prediction of the meaning of unknown words; the identification of pronominal reference. (Chikalanga 1991)		When faced with a text whose meaning they can not untangle, [readers] may be able to identify the constituents of its sentences, e.g. the subject, the verb and to analyse these if they are complex. (Nuttall 1996:78)
Operationalisations	- Separating explicitly stated main idea(s) from supporting details through: a. recognising topic sentence(s) b. recognising lexical indicator(s) - Generating a representation of a text as a whole - Understanding the development of an argument and/or logical organisation - Distinguishing generalisations and examples	- Making propositional inferences Propositional inference is made when the reader uses explicit statements in the text to come to a conclusion that is not explicitly stated, without recourse to knowledge from outside the text. (Chikalanga 1991) Where appropriate to the text-type: - Making propositional informational inferences which are either referential typically answering questions beginning with what and which, or spatio-temporal (typically answering questions beginning with where and when). - Making propositional explanatory inferences which are concerned with motivation, cause and consequences, and enablement, and will often answer questions beginning with why and how. All the information needed to make propositional inferences is recoverable from the text. These may involve: * discovering writer's intention; * understanding writer's attitude to the topic; * identifying the addressee; * distinguishing fact from opinion.	- Resolving lexical ambiguity: the reader makes a choice between two or more meanings of a lexical item. - Predicting the meaning of unknown words: the reader infersthe meaning of unknown words from the context in a text. - Identifying pronominal reference: the reader identifies the pronominal anaphoric and cataphoric links within a text.	- Removing all the optional elements of complex sentences systematically until only the essentials remain and the bare structure of the sentence is clear. - Paraphrasing optional elements of complex sentences one byone, and fitting them into the whole structure to make sense of them.
Focus	Both global and local	Both global and local	Mainly local, occasionally global	Local
Text coverage	Reading from beginning to end	Will vary but will be selective	Normally use of immediate context and on occasion wider context	Local
Rate of reading	Reading the whole text carefully	Reading the selected parts carefully	Reading the selected part(s)carefully	Reading the selected part carefully
Direction of processing	Linear and sequential, with regressions if needed	Not necessarily sequential	Sequencing not observed	Sequential with some regression
Relationship with the underlying process(es)	Mainly text-based bottom-up sequential process with limited top-down process	Text based. Initially use bottom-up process to identify information from the text and then top-down process kicks in as needed to activate knowledge schemata to help make inferences based on the text.	Mainly bottom-up process. Occasionally with the help of top-down process.	Bottom-up process.

[Source: Reading in a Second Language, Urquhart A. H. and Weir C. J. (1998). Longman]

Table 3.2

Conditions for Advanced English Reading Test (AERT)

Conditions	Descriptions
Purpose(s) of reading	To test students' ability to comprehend academic texts and to extract important information from those texts.
Nature of texts	Texts written for a non-specialist audience with informative and interesting ideas.
Source of texts	Chapters from textbooks, journal articles, abstracts.
Rhetorical organisation	Mainly expository texts with rhetorical organisations of comparison, collection of description, problem/solution, and causation.
Propositional features	
Lexical range	Normally no technical jargon. Approximately 7000 words (root forms; functional and subtechnical lexis). Academic semi-technical words defined in the syllabus for section 5.
Topic areas	Familiar to students: humanities & management /science & technology /biology & medicine
Background knowledge	Within students' background knowledge but not totally given; students should not be able to answer test questions from background knowledge without recourse to the text.
Illocutionary features	To inform, to explain, to describe, to advise
Channel of presentation	Normally textual. Some texts might contain graphics.
Size of input/length of text	3 short passages (approx. 600 – 900) for careful reading (global) 15 items 3 short passages (approx. 250 – 500) for careful reading (local) 15 items 3 long passages (approx. 1000 – 1800) for expeditious reading (global) 15 items 3 long passages (approx. 1000) for expeditious reading (local) 15 items
Speed of processing	144 minutes for a total of 12 passages About 60 – 90 wpm for careful reading; 100 –150 wpm for expeditious reading
Control over skills/strategies	Three passages for each skill/strategy, one from arts and humanities, one from science and technology, one from life and medical science. For careful reading, passages are short and may sometimes have relatively implicit text structures. For expeditious reading, passages are long and may sometimes have relatively explicit text structures.
Control over time spent	Time is strictly controlled both for each section and for each passage within the section. Careful reading (global): 60 minutes 20 for each passage; Expeditious reading (skimming): 15 minutes 5 for each passage; Expeditious reading (search reading): 21 minutes 7 for each passage; Expeditious reading (scanning): 18 minutes 6 for each passage; Careful reading (local): 30 minutes 10 for each passage.
Amount of help	General instructions (in Chinese) to candidates are provided 15 minutes before the test. Instructions for each section are clearly written on a separate page in the question booklet and students are reminded to read instructions before texts. An *Example* is provided for the truth/false/justification items since candidates may not be familiar with the format.
Number and ordering of tasks	Order for the five sections: careful reading (global), skimming, search reading, scanning, careful reading (local)
Method factor/ response mode	Formats include: SAQ, true /false, table /flow chart /sentence /text completion.
Question/answer in L1/TL	Mainly in English but could be in Chinese if necessary.
Receptive/productive	Mainly receptive, some limited writing involved in SAQ but only brief answers will be required (no more than 10 words).
Explicitness of weighting	All items equally weighted.

[Source: Reading in a Second Language, Urquhart A. H. and Weir C. J. (1998). Longman]

4 Operationalising the specification: test development

Text selection – operationalising conditions

In selecting appropriate texts for the AERT test, we were concerned with the test conditions under which reading activities should be carried out. Special attention was paid to topic familiarity, subject specificity, language difficulty, rhetorical organisation, length of the abridged text, text structure, and the skill/strategy to be tested by the text.

Obviously the rating of some of these facets is problematic for the individual researcher so an attempt was made to arrive at text selection on a principled basis. The major task involved was to determine the suitability of texts for testing the skills and strategies covered by the operations of the AERT test specification. Research was carried out at the a *priori* stage to ensure the maximal operationalisation of the test conditions, and at the a *posteriori* stage to confirm the selection using candidate retrospection. The procedure that has been followed in the project is illustrated in the following flow-chart.

4 Operationalising the specification: test development

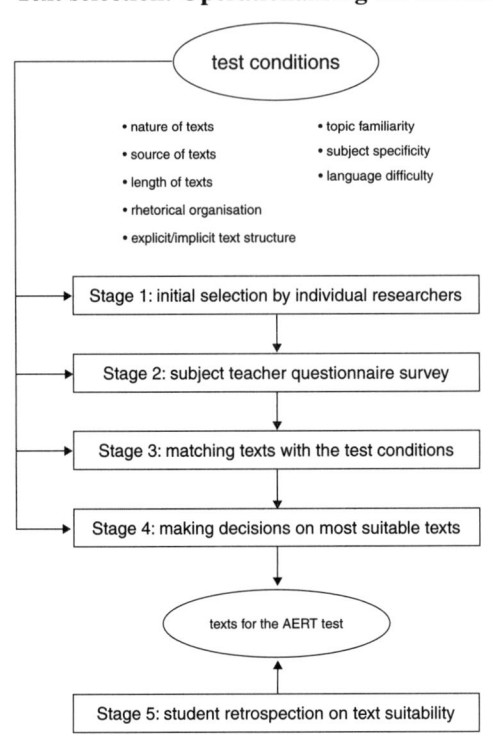

Figure 4.1

Text selection: Operationalising the conditions

```
                    ( test conditions )
                    
        • nature of texts        • topic familiarity
        • source of texts        • subject specificity
        • length of texts        • language difficulty
        • rhetorical organisation
        • explicit/implicit text structure

    → Stage 1: initial selection by individual researchers
                          ↓
    → Stage 2: subject teacher questionnaire survey
                          ↓
    → Stage 3: matching texts with the test conditions
                          ↓
    → Stage 4: making decisions on most suitable texts
                          ↓
               ( texts for the AERT test )
                          ↑
        Stage 5: student retrospection on text suitability
```

Initial selection by individual researchers

At the first stage of selection by individual researchers, consideration was given to parameters that could be determined either through individual researchers' subjective judgements such as the nature and the rhetorical organisation of texts or through researchers' objective observation such as sources of texts and length of texts. Details of these considerations are described below:

Nature of texts

AERT is not intended to be a highly subject-specific modular test. Instead, it is meant to be an academic reading test catering for candidates who are undergoing undergraduate foundation stage studies in three broad academic fields, i.e.,
- arts and humanities, business and social studies (abbreviated AH);
- physical science, engineering and technology (abbreviated ST);

4 Operationalising the specification: test development

- biology, medical and life sciences (abbreviated ML).

So texts written for a non-specialist audience were considered and priority was given to those with informative and interesting ideas.

Sources of texts

The needs analyses carried out both in Britain (Weir 1983) and in China suggest that academic journal articles, chapters from subject matter textbooks in English and abstracts are the three most frequently employed sources of texts for EAP reading courses. In our selection, academic journals, and textbooks provided texts for the expeditious reading sections (both global and local level) and the careful reading section (global level). For careful reading at the local level, i.e., the test of contextualised lexical meanings, texts were initially selected from the SJTU corpus which exhibited a high incidence of academic vocabulary.

Length of texts

Clear evidence emerges from the needs analysis that a variety of text types are met by the majority of students. Almost all are exposed to extensive as well as intensive reading. Most have to read at least chapters from books which can be up to 3000 words in length. Furthermore, the length of texts varies according to the purposes of reading. For expeditious reading tasks, longer texts together with the requirement of time limits ensure the use of the strategies. For careful reading tasks, shorter texts with sufficient time provided ensure that texts will be indeed read carefully. In selection, both longer texts (1000 words) and shorter texts (about 500 words) have been included.

Rhetorical organisation of texts

From the analysis of EAP reading teaching textbooks and test papers, it is clear that texts with different rhetorical organisations, e.g., comparison, collection of descriptions, causation, and problem/solution (Carrell 1984) lend themselves better to testing different reading skills and strategies, that is, for testing a particular skill/strategy, there might be an optimal rhetorical organisation.

Urquhart and Weir (1998) emphasise that the skills and strategies it is wished to test will influence selection: problem/solution, causative or comparison texts from journals or textbooks may well lend themselves better to testing reading carefully for main idea(s) comprehension than more descriptive texts with lots of detailed information. In careful reading the texts may not necessarily have clear main ideas for selection and main ideas might have to be constructed through propositional inferencing whereas in skimming and search reading they should be explicit.

4 Operationalising the specification: test development

Where candidates are expected to skim or search read lengthier texts these ideally would have a clear overt structure, and be clearly sequenced with a clear line of argument running through them. A journal article or chapter from a textbook with clear sections and headings and where paragraphs contain topic sentences in initial position which signal the information to be presented may prove suitable for testing these expeditious reading strategies. Problem and solution, causative and comparison texts may have the clearest, tightly organised structures (Carrell 1984, Meyer and Freedle 1984 and Meyer 1975). One might also look for texts which are overtly organised into sections. Texts without a clear structure may well be authentic but they do not lend themselves easily to use in testing expeditious reading just as in real life they are difficult to follow quickly, to summarise or to make notes on. Collection of description texts (Carrell 1984, Meyer and Freedle 1984) may be the best vehicle for testing scanning for specific detail. They have been found to be more frequently used for teaching and testing scanning in EAP reading courses.

Explicit/implicit text structure

The explicitness or implicitness of the text structure was also considered in selecting texts. This is a criterion related to but not exactly the same as the rhetorical organisation of texts. Texts of collection of descriptions, for example, may have an implicit structure which make them less suitable for search reading or skimming. On the other hand, texts of comparison may be explicitly organised with subtitles and clear topic sentences and hence lend themselves better to being read expeditiously.

Based on these considerations, 15 texts (5 from each major discipline area) were considered for inclusion in the AERT for testing careful reading at the global level and expeditious reading at both global and local level and 6 (2 from each major discipline area) were chosen from the SJTU corpus for the lexical section.

Subject teacher questionnaire survey for text suitability

At the second stage of text selection, a number of meetings were organised with groups of subject teachers within the faculties who were asked to rate 15 preselected texts on the basis of likely familiarity of the topic for their students; the subject specificity of the text and the level of language difficulty they thought it might present for the students they taught (See Appendix 4.1 for a copy of the questionnaire). In all 19 attended these meetings from 5 universities in Shanghai. Questionnaires were collected from all but one of these teachers making a total of 18 for the survey of the text suitability.

4 Operationalising the specification: test development

Familiarity with topic:

Research has indicated that in selecting texts for EAP reading examinations it is the degree of students' familiarity with the topic that has a major effect on their performance (Khalifa 1997). A crucial part of the AERT development was to ensure that students are reasonably familiar with the topics of each of the texts selected from the three broad discipline areas.

Ideally, the topic should be generally accessible, i.e., not too obscure and not too familiar, to all candidates. On the one hand, bias in the content background knowledge can be avoided if all candidates share the necessary background knowledge for reading the text. On the other hand, a certain degree of unfamiliarity is necessary to attract readers' attention, to arouse their interest and, what's more important, to prevent them from answering questions from background knowledge without recourse to the text. Therefore, texts with subject tutors' assessment on topic familiarity level of 'M' (medium) are preferable.

Subject specificity:

Research has suggested (Clapham 1996 and Khalifa 1997) that the degree of subject specificity of each text is a key consideration when developing an EAP reading test. The subject specificity of texts therefore needs to be established carefully in advance. Texts selected have been seen to be from one of the three subject groupings but at the same time they should be accessible to students across all three discipline groupings.

Evidence suggests that it is only when the texts are highly specific that the influence of background knowledge on test performance can be demonstrated (Clapham 1996). General academic texts taken from these discipline areas are unlikely to disadvantage students from one discipline against another. In addition, highly subject specific texts may divert the focus of test from reading skills and strategies to subject knowledge. Therefore, preference is for the texts of 'L' (low) subject specificity but sometimes we can be content with 'M' (medium) level subject specificity if the topic is quite familiar and the language is not too difficult.

In the piloting phase we decided to select 12 texts, 4 from each of the three broad discipline areas to test each of the four operations we have identified above in the test operations. All students would take all tests on all texts in the development phase. This would enable us to determine if there is any effect of subject knowledge on test performance.

Thus the research would address the two key issues in EAP testing, viz. the effect of background knowledge on performance in EAP reading tests and the issue of the unitary or componential nature of the reading construct.

4 Operationalising the specification: test development

Language difficulty:

It is not easy to determine the difficulty level of language in a text. Readability might be a rough index but the criterion has met serious challenge from many reading researchers. Urquhart and Weir comment:

> *The literature abounds with warnings against reliance on readability formulas for estimating text difficulty (Klare 1984: 682 et seq, Weaver and Kintsch 1991). According to Klare at best they are oversimplistic at worst seriously distorting.*

Subject teachers' judgements were seen as the best method for ensuring selection of texts of a medium level of language difficulty.

Frequencies for subject teachers responses to the questionnaire were counted and tabulated in Table 4.1. At this stage, 10 texts with favourable comments from these teachers were marked in the table (*) for their potential suitability, namely:
- high or medium topic familiarity;
- medium or low subject specificity;
- medium or low language difficulty.

Matching the selected texts with the test conditions

From the texts we made available for initial screening seven texts were selected as being suitable. We needed two further texts for the scanning section, one from the discipline area of medical and life science and the other from the humanities and business. These were selected by the research team based on the experience in initial selection. For the lexical section, the preselected six texts were discussed by the research team one by one to identify possible words that could be tested. Two were chosen and a third one was subsequently selected from a journal.

These twelve texts were matched against the test conditions by the research team (see Table 4.2).

Making decisions on the most suitable texts

AERT is intended to be a test applicable to all undergraduate students who have successfully completed the foundation stage study of English in Chinese universities. All candidates of the test should have a feeling that they are being catered for. Therefore, the topics of the texts should be of at least medium familiarity and the language should not be overly difficult. Most importantly the subject specificity should be kept to the medium level or below. Texts satisfying these conditions were considered if appropriate in terms of the further conditions of length, explicitness of macrostructure and rhetorical organisation. Final decisions were made on twelve texts listed in Table 4.3.

4 Operationalising the specification: test development

Table 4.1
Results of questionnaire survey on the texts (N=18)

Text	Topic familiarity H	M	L	N	Subject specificity H	M	L	N	Language difficulty H	M	L	N
*1 Technological change in industry in …	4	10	4	0	0	9	7	2	1	9	6	2
*2 Universities in transition in Asia	7	7	3	1	1	6	7	4	0	7	9	2
*3 Africa's adjustment	4	7	7	0	0	12	4	2	0	8	7	3
*4 Japanese women	9	7	2	0	1	3	10	4	0	8	6	4
*5 Asia: a billion consumers	7	6	5	0	0	7	8	3	2	8	6	2
*6 Sugaring the pill	0	6	8	4	7	6	5	1	3	14	1	0
*7 Cancer-stranglers go on trial	1	7	7	2	3	9	5	1	5	10	3	0
*8 Tomorrow's bitter harvest	1	11	5	2	3	4	10	1	1	12	5	0
9 The veiled goddess	1	2	11	3	8	8	1	1	8	10	0	0
*10 Tricks of nature	1	7	6	4	7	7	3	1	3	11	2	2
11 Is the solar system stable?	2	4	10	2	5	9	3	1	3	11	3	2
*12 Mindless machines	4	8	4	2	6	9	2	1	3	9	5	1
13 High-performance parachutes	1	4	8	5	9	3	4	2	4	8	5	1
14 Sacred cows in physics education	3	6	4	5	7	2	6	3	4	9	4	1
15 Things fall apart	3	4	6	5	10	5	1	2	5	10	2	1

61

4 Operationalising the specification: test development

Table 4.2
Matching the selected text to the test conditions

	1 Asia	2 Cancer	3 Mindless	4 Japanese	5 Sugaring	6 Harvest	7 Tricks	8 Themes	9 Ads.	10 Andropov	11 Quark	12 Elephant
Purpose(s) of reading	+	+	+	+	+	+	+	+	+	+	+	+
Nature of texts	+	+	+	+	+	+	+	+	+	+	+	+
Source of texts	Journal	Journal	Journal	Journal	Journal	Journal	Journal	Textbook	Internet	Corpus	Journal	Corpus
Rhetorical Organisation	Comparison	Problem/solution	Comparison	Comparison	Problem/solution	Causation	Collect. of description	Collect. of description	Collect. of description	Comparison	Problem/solution	Problem/solution
Lexical range	+	+	+	+	+	+	+	+	+	+	+	+
Topic areas	Arts/humanities	Medical/life science	Science/technology	Arts/humanities	Medical/life science	Science/life science	Science/technology	Medical/life science	Arts/humanities	Arts/humanities	Science/technology	Medical/life science
Background knowledge	+	+	+	+	+	+	+	+	+	+	+	+
Illocutionary Features	Inform	Explain	Inform	Inform describe	Explain	Explain	Describe	Describe	Describe	Inform	Explain describe	Explain describe
Channel of presentation	Textual	Textual	Textual	Textual	Textual	Textual	Textual	Textual	Textual	Textual	Textual	Textual
Size of input / length of text	695 words	658 words	855 words	1161 words	1036 words	987 words	1030 words	1077 words	973 words	501 words	375 words	286 words
Speed of processing	60 - 90 wpm	60 - 90 wpm	60 - 90 wpm	100 - 150 wpm	100 - 150 wpm	100 - 150 wpm	100 - 150 wpm	100 - 150 wpm	100 - 150 wpm	60 - 90 wpm	60 - 90 wpm	60 - 90 wpm
Control over skills/strategies	Careful reading	Careful reading	Careful reading	Skimming search reading	Skimming search reading	Skimming search reading	Scanning	Scanning	Scanning	Decoding lexical items	Decoding lexical items	Decoding lexical items
Control over time spent	20 minutes	20 minutes	20 minutes	5 minutes / 7 minutes	5 minutes / 7 minutes	5 minutes / 7 minutes	6 minutes	6 minutes	6 minutes	10 minutes	10 minutes	10 minutes

4 Operationalising the specification: test development

Table 4.3
Final results of text selection for the AERT

Text	Discipline	Parameters						skill/strategy to be tested
		Topic familiarity	Subject specificity	Language difficulty	Rhetorical organisation	Length of abridged text	Explicit or implicit structure	
5 Asia: a billion consumers	AH	H/M	M/L	M/L	comparison	700	implicit	EXMI/IPROP
7 Cancer-stranglers go on trial	ML	M/L	M	M	problem/solution	720	explicit	EXMI/IPROP
12 Mindless machines	ST	M	M	M	comparison	910	implicit	EXMI/IPROP
4 Japanese women	AH	H/M	L	M/L	comparison	1790	explicit	SKM/SCH
6 Sugaring the pill	ML	M/L	H/M	M	problem/solution	1040	explicit	SKM/SCH
8 Tomorrow's bitter harvest	ST	M	L	M	causation	990	explicit	SKM/SCH
10 Tricks of nature	ST	M/L	H/M	M	c. of description	1030	explicit	SCAN
16 Themes in the study of life	ML	*	*	*	c. of description	1070	explicit	SCAN
17 Advertising strategies	AH	*	*	*	c. of description	980	explicit	SCAN
Andropov	AH	from the SJTU corpus			comparison	501		ILEX
Quark	ST	journal article			problem/solution	375		ILEX
Elephant	ML	from the SJTU corpus			problem/solution	286		ILEX

* Not evaluated by teachers

63

4 Operationalising the specification: test development

Text diagramming – operationalising tasks

Having operationalised the test conditions through appropriate text selection, the next step was to operationalise test tasks as faithfully as possible in order to maximise the validity of test activities as compared to those in real life. Test formats, time limits and control over the employment of skills and strategies on one text were all important considerations. The key decision for item setters is what would the reader be expected to take away from the text having read it for a specified purpose under the additional performance conditions.

Purposes of consensus text diagramming

The usual practice of test construction leaves the decision on what to test to the individual test writer. This can be problematic and, for example, may lead to a situation such as described by Urquhart and Weir (1998):

All too often test constructors take considerable periods of time reading and rereading texts and they peel off deeper and deeper levels of meaning. They then give candidates 20 minutes or so to reach the same depth of understanding under exam conditions. This is obviously a nonsense.

Therefore, in order to establish, on a principled basis, the content that should be extracted from a text in line with the established purpose for reading it, a practical and 'utilisation-focused' (Urquhart and Weir 1998) procedure, frequently referred to as 'mindmapping' (Buzan 1974), text mapping or text diagramming, has been followed in the development of AERT. The main purposes of employing the method were:
- to explore the possibility of whether the selected texts allow for the testing of the intended operations (i.e., skimming, search reading, scanning, EXMI, IPROP and ILEX);
- to facilitate the process of identifying the content in a text that should be used to test these operations;
- to avoid the idiosyncratic views of the individual test writer;
- to arrive at a consensus view of the main ideas and important details of a text; and
- to provide a benchmark for the actual test time.

Method

The major principle of text mapping is that the procedure should replicate posited separate processing for the skills and strategies as far as possible. Therefore, for mapping texts that test different operations, separate sessions with different instructions are necessary. In each session, participants should

4 Operationalising the specification: test development

be provided with detailed written instructions informing them of the purposes of the mapping. Furthermore, the time for the mapping activity should not exceed the actual test time. For expeditious reading texts, for example, participants should be instructed to read under time pressure so that the items set on those points generated in the mapping are not only testing important main ideas or supporting details but also are achievable within the time limit by proficient candidates.

The mapping process starts with participants reading individually the text at a speed at which they feel confident to achieve the required purpose within the time limit. This is followed by a group discussion. Consensus views are arrived at by frequency count of those who share a point. Normally agreement of n-1 is necessary, i.e., if there are five people in the group at least four must have included the point for a consensus.

There are variations in the implementation of these procedures. Some researchers, for example, would prefer participants to highlight the most salient points in the process of reading. Others tend to rely on recall protocols. The main argument for the highlighting method is that less mental pressure is imposed on the reader, who is thus able to concentrate on text comprehension instead of memorising the content. But the extent to which these highlighted points have indeed been comprehended by the individual reader is questionable. In addition, it is often very difficult to set a limit for the number of points to be highlighted because different readers are likely to go into different levels of detail. Recall protocol users support their method arguing that only the points that have been genuinely comprehended and that have left a deep impression on the reader can be recalled. Meanwhile the number of points generated from a recall is automatically controlled because of the limited capacity of a reader's memory.

For the 12 texts of AERT, four sessions of text mapping were organised, each for a different type of operation. In each session, participants were first briefed of the AERT project and the purpose of mapping. The instructions for text mapping were then discussed in detail (see Appendices 4.2.1.– 4).

The timing for each session was calculated according to the required reading speed of the session and the length of the text. Texts used for testing expeditious reading at the global level (skimming and search reading), for example, are about 1000 words and the required reading speed is 100 to 150 wpm. Each text would take 7 to 10 minutes. So the time given for each text in this session of text mapping was 8.5 minutes, the average of 7 and 10 minutes. Similarly, the time limits in other sessions were 5 minutes for scanning as less has to be processed, 15 for careful reading at the global level and 8 for careful reading at the local level.

The recall protocol method was employed in mapping texts intended to test skimming and search reading, scanning and careful reading at the global level. For texts intended to test contextualised lexical meanings, however,

4 Operationalising the specification: test development

instead of providing a recall protocol, participants were required to highlight the lexical items considered to be academic and to bear important contextualised meanings in the text. The reason for this change was mainly due to the difficulty of the mappers in achieving a precise definition of semi-technical or academic vocabulary. In trialling the recall method for mapping texts in this section, it was found to be very difficult to reach consensus views on the lexical items. Very often participants recalled the same content area but different lexical items. By using highlighting, readers had a chance to compare words in terms of their academic degree and importance in the context.

Participants

A further important factor in text mapping is the participant. A combination of item writers, native speaker readers at about the same academic level as the potential test population and proficient readers from the potential test population forms an ideal group of participants. In reality, however, it is often difficult to achieve such a satisfactory combination.

The AERT mapping participants consisted of one native English speaker reader and teacher from CALS, the University of Reading, one ELT teacher from China and two Chinese PhD attachment students and researchers in CALS.

Results

In each session, all points raised by individual participants in the group discussion were noted on a master sheet of paper. The number of people who agreed on them were noted beside each point e.g., 3/4 (three out of four agreed). In setting items, priority was given to those points which had majority agreement, i.e., those consensus points which were agreed by at least n-1 participants. Appendix 4.2.5 lists the text mapping points that were generated from the discussions and were finally used for setting items.

Task construction

The appropriate texts having been chosen and the content areas for setting items in these texts having been mapped, careful attention was then given to deciding on task construction including the issues of a modular or a general test, test formats, time limits, control over the employment of skills and strategies in one text, rubrics and test paper layout.

Decision on a modular or general test

In the development of an EAP reading test it is always a central issue whether the test should be a subject specific modular test, i.e., different tests catering

4 Operationalising the specification: test development

for candidates with different backgrounds and directions in future professional development, or whether it should be a general academic reading test catering for students across disciplinary areas.

It is clear from the IELTS revision project that when there is more than one module available it is often quite difficult for candidates to decide which to choose; e.g., should it be based on their previous learning experiences or future? Which module should an engineering graduate going on to take a post graduate degree in management select?

The problem is compounded the more modules that are available. The immense difficulty of constructing multiple, parallel, valid and reliable subject modules cannot be underrated. There is little evidence from any of the major validation studies that have been carried out to support the development of multiple subject specific modules. Clapham (1996) only reports a limited background knowledge effect in a few cases where the texts selected were highly discipline specific. There was no apparent discipline effect when general academic texts were employed.

In text selection, we sought texts written for a non-specialist audience and with low or medium subject specificity as ranked by subject tutors. It was our hope that a significant effect of subject-specific background knowledge could be ironed out and the AERT test could be an academic reading test catering for candidates who are undergoing undergraduate foundation stage studies in three broad academic fields. However, before we obtained the data from the test, it was difficult to claim definitively that the subject-specificity of our texts was not discriminating between students across discipline areas. ANOVA analyses would show us whether a discipline effect was apparent in the test data.

Therefore, the AERT has been designed to comprise three subtests, which are parallel in terms of the test conditions such as language difficulty and topic familiarity of the texts, test formats, weighting and time limits. The only difference between the subtests is the broad discipline area from which each text is extracted. The idea was for candidates from each of the three discipline areas to sit the whole test i.e., all three subtests. If no significant effect between the performance of candidates from each discipline on each subtest could be found from the test data analysis, we might reduce the test size. If the effect was significant, the test would be split into three modular versions; three 'subject-specific' EAP reading tests.

Decision on test formats

From the analysis of EAP reading teaching and testing tasks, it was observed that in recent years, there is a strong movement away from MCQ in favour of alternative formats. Given the potential scale of the AERT test in China, however, practicality in marking the test is an essential concern.

4 Operationalising the specification: test development

For the section of careful reading at the global level, both the objective format of true/false judgement and the subjective format of SAQ were used. For the three expeditious reading sections, only subjective formats were used including SAQ, table/flow-chart/sentence completion and writing summarising sentences. The amount of writing was to be strictly controlled. The lexical section was employed banked cloze where answers were selected from a bank of possibilities.

On the one hand, efforts were made to control the subjectivity of the open formats. For SAQ, the number of acceptable answers to each question and the number of words needed for answering each question have been both controlled. For table/chart/sentence completion, it has been ensured that there is only one unequivocal answer to each question and this is likely to be a single word or phrase. On the other hand, a reasonably comprehensive marking scheme was drawn up after the two trials to make sure that acceptable variations in wording used in answers have been accommodated. For the skimming section which uses the most open format of summarising sentences, spelling and grammar were not punished. Credit was given to the summary sentence as long as its meaning is clear and it covers the point(s) listed in the marking scheme.

With these efforts, the AERT would hopefully achieve a balance of open and objective items, which marked a welcome shift away from the grip of MCQ tests in China at present.

Consideration of other test conditions

After the draft version prototype version 1 was completed, it was trialled on a small sample available to the research team. Alterations were made to the rubric, the timing, the order of sections, passages and questions and the layout. The rubrics were made simpler and clearer. In addition, before the test, general instructions in Chinese would be given to candidates informing them of the test structure, the time limits for each section and the control over time spent on each section. For the careful reading at the global level section, an example was given to help familiarise candidates with the format of true/false/not given with a supporting sentence from the passage.

The initial setting of the time limit for each section was based on the requirement of the reading speed specified in the test specification and on the experience from proficient readers' text mapping. This was confirmed from the small-scale trialling. However, after the first trialling on a sample of 303 students in March 1997, the time for the careful reading at the global level section was extended from 45 minutes to 60 minutes and the times for the search reading and the scanning sections were shortened from 25 and 20 minutes in the first trialling to 21 and 18 minutes. The purpose was to make each section more distinguishable, i.e., to maximally ensure the expected performance on each section by candidates.

4 Operationalising the specification: test development

The order of sections was revised based on the suggestion from the small-scale trialling that students might panic if the expeditious reading section (skimming) was put at the beginning. Careful reading was chosen as the first section instead of skimming in the draft version because careful reading is believed to be the type of reading Chinese learners are most familiar with. The skimming section has to come before the search reading section because the two sections share the same three passages and readers are expected to skim a passage before going on to search for more detailed information. The passages of the three discipline areas have been arranged to appear in different orders in different sections so as to minimise the effect of passage order in comparing the performance on the three subtests of the three discipline areas. The language difficulty, topic familiarity and subject specificity of these passages were also taken into consideration. The general principle was to put the easier, more familiar and less specific passages before the more difficult, less familiar and more specific ones. The order of questions within a passage followed the order of the content that appeared in the text.

The layout of the test was also revised several times in order to make it easier for testtakers to work efficiently and for invigilators to check conveniently. The text-booklet was in a different colour to avoid possible confusion of testtakers. The instructions for each section appear on a separate sheet of paper before each section and warnings were given in italicised and bold type to emphasise the importance of using an appropriate skill/strategy for achieving the best performance. A bar or several bars with the label 'section X' on top of the bar(s) appear on each page of the question booklet so that invigilators could easily tell whether test-takers were working on the right section or not.

The answer sheet for each section has been designed on separate pages so that they could be collected at the end of the time limit of each section. Candidates were informed of this requirement in the Chinese instructions given before the test. Candidates were also instructed not to move on to other sections even if they have finished one section in advance of the time limit. In the final large-scale trialling, the requirement of time for each passage within each section was also put down in the instructions. But due to the practical difficulty of using different colours for different passages within a section, the control over the timing for each passage was found to be very difficult to control.

The prototype version 1 was finalised after two triallings, the first in March 1997 on a sample of 303 and the second in October 1997 on a sample of 1068. The final version of the test is described in the following section.

A description of the AERT prototype version 1

The AERT prototype version 1 consists of five sections testing:
- careful reading at the global level (15 items);
- expeditious reading at the global level: skimming (3 items);

4 Operationalising the specification: test development

- expeditious reading at the global level: search reading (12 items);
- expeditious reading at the local level: scanning (15 items);
- careful reading at the local level (15 items).

Within each section, three passages are used (skimming and search reading sections use the same three passages), one from each of the three broad discipline areas. To facilitate statistical analysis, five items were set on each passage. Thus the AERT has a balanced number of passages (4) and items (20) for each of the three broad discipline areas (Table 4.4) and a balanced number of items (15) for each of the four skills and strategies to be tested (Table 4.5). The analysis of the data from a test with such a structure would allow us to investigate both the componentiality of the reading construct and the effects of background knowledge.

Table 4.4

Subtests for investigating the effects of background knowledge

Subtests	Passage in each section				Questions in each section			
	I	II/III	IV	V	I	II/III	IV	V
A/H	1	4	9	10	1–5	16/19–22	41–45	46–50
S/T	3	6	7	11	11–15	18/27–30	31–35	51–55
M/L	2	5	8	12	6–10	17/23–26	36–40	56–60

Table 4.5

Subtests for investigating the componentiality of the reading construct

Subtests	Passages	Questions
1 EXMI & IPROP	1–3	1–15
2 SKIM & SEARCH READING	4–6	15–30
3 SCANNING	7–9	31–45
4 ILEXT	10–12	46–60

The test materials comprise:

- a question booklet: instructions for five sections; questions 1 to 45 for sections I to IV; 3 passages and 15 items for section V;
- a source booklet: passages 1 to 9 for sections I to IV;

4 Operationalising the specification: test development

- answer sheets: for each section with one section on one page;
- marking scheme: keys and acceptable variations;
- invigilator manual: instructions to invigilators;
- candidate instruction: general instructions and test regulations in Chinese to candidates.

The test starts with Section I of careful reading at the global level, which is a more familiar type of reading to Chinese students. The section uses three passages of 600 to 900 words and the time limit is 60 minutes. Test formats are short answer questions and true/false judgements. In the former, a maximum of 8 words are allowed for each answer. In the latter, candidates are required firstly to decide whether a given statement is true or false or information not given and secondly to support their judgement by identifying a corroborative sentence from the passage.

The second and the third sections test the two important expeditious reading strategies: skimming and search reading respectively. Passages of 1000 words are used and the time limit is 15 minutes for skimming (3 items) and 21 minutes for search reading (12 items). For skimming, one summarising sentence is required for each passage. For search reading, the formats include flow-chart, table and sentence completion. Answers are required to be no longer than 8 words.

The fourth section tests a third important expeditious reading strategy: scanning for specific information. Three passages of around 1000 words were used and the time limit is 18 minutes. The same formats as for search reading are used, i.e., flow-chart, table and sentence completion. Answers are usually single word or phrase.

Section V tests the understanding of contextualised meanings of academic words in passages of about 500 words each. Five words were deleted from each passage and the student has to fill in the blanks with words chosen from a bank of 10 words. The time limit for the section is 30 minutes.

The whole test lasted 144 minutes for 12 passages and 60 questions.

Table 4.6 describes the test in terms of the arrangements of sections, passages, questions, formats, aims of each section and types of passages used for each section.

4 Operationalising the specification: test development

Table 4.6

A Description of the Advanced English Reading Test

Section	I	II	III	IV	V
Passages	1 – 3	4 – 6	4 – 6	7 – 9	10 – 12
Questions	1 – 15	16 – 18	19 – 30	31 – 45	46 – 60
Formats	SAQ, T/F/NG & supporting sentence	summarising sentences	flow-chart/ table/ sentence completion	flow-chart/ table/ sentence completion	banked cloze
Time limits	60 minutes	15 minutes	21 minutes	18 minutes	30 minutes
Aim of the section	careful reading for explicitly stated main ideas and propositional inferences	expeditious reading for the discourse topic of the text	expeditious reading for information on a pre-determined topic	expeditious reading for specific information	careful reading for contextualised meanings of academic vocabulary
Type of passages	c. 600-900 words causation, problem/ solution	c. 1000 words causation, comparison, problem/ solution	c. 1000 words causation, comparison, problem/ solution	c. 1000 words collection of descriptions	c. 500 words

This brings us to the end of Stage 2: test construction, and to the end of the *a priori* validation procedures in the development of the AERT. We now turn to the *a posteriori* validation of the test where quantitative and qualitative procedures were used to investigate how well we had tested what we intended to test in the AERT developed through the systematic *a priori* validation procedures described in the last three chapters of this study.

5 The a *posteriori* validation of the prototype AERT version 1: quantitative studies

Quantitative studies

In previous chapters we have examined how the AERT was developed. Experience gained in this project illustrates clearly the value of establishing systematic procedures for test development both at the design and implementation stages. The hubristic view that pragmatic test developers know what to test without any a *priori* theoretical or empirical investigation has meant that in the past numerous tests have been premised on a restricted careful reading model (see Part 2.1). As a result scant attention has been paid to testing expeditious reading strategies (skimming, search reading and scanning) with the notable exception of the Test for English Majors in China.

The admittedly limited a *priori* validation which underpins the AERT consisted of:
- a review of the theoretical literature;
- a target situation analysis of Chinese students' reading needs;
- an analysis of materials for teaching EAP reading;
- an analysis of EAP reading tests;
- a specification of operations and conditions for an EAP reading test.

On the basis of these data, rather than armchair speculation, we attempted to operationalise a prototype version of a reading test which faithfully implemented the specification. As described in Part 4 we developed a systematic set of procedures which included:
- selecting appropriate texts to match conditions (e.g., familiarity, specificity, language difficulty);
- textmapping the content areas;
- principled selection of test formats;
- careful consideration of timing, rubrics, layout, and the order of sections, texts and tasks.

We are not claiming that these procedures are perfect but they certainly represent an advance in reading test design which may be of interest to test developers elsewhere.

For the validation of the test at the a *posteriori* stage, the first step was to trial the AERT on a small but as representative a sample of the potential test population as possible and then subject the test data to statistical analysis.

5 The a posteriori validation of the prototype AERT version 1

First trial

Test administration

The first version AERT prototype test was trialled in March 1997. Students from six universities had been invited to compete in a competition. Certificates were to be awarded by the administrative office of the Shanghai Education Commission together with prizes ranging from a 1000 yuan first prize to encouraging prizes of 100 yuan (29 in total). This helped ensure those taking the test were well motivated and the results credible.

Sample

340 candidates from the Shanghai area took the pilot test in March 1997. We had requested students from a range of ability, top, middle and low, be put forward by their universities.

Marking and data entry

During this phase the markers kept careful notes of decisions taken and where candidates gave an alternative answer which looked acceptable these were carefully discussed and if acceptable added to the marking key. A double check on the marking was carried out as the scores were read into the computer from the candidates' scripts. The process helped determine:
- whether the items had been marked correctly (with very few exceptions this was the case);
- any other acceptable responses to the open ended questions not initially anticipated by the test designers.

Changes were incorporated into a revised marking scheme for use in the main trial in October 1997.

A large part of the April 1997 AERT Development Team meeting was taken up with refining the mark scheme for the five sections of the test using the 303 complete scripts from the first trial, marking the scripts, and then entering the data into SPSS. This was extremely time consuming because potential alternatives had to be discussed every time they cropped up. However, this was an essential stage because it meant that we then had a 'comprehensive' mark scheme for use in the second major trial planned for October 1997.

Descriptives of the test data

The test data were entered onto a computer and analysed using SPSS (see Appendix 5.1). Descriptive statistics were generated for the test at the item, passage, section and whole test level. The test as a whole seemed to be working well. The reliability of each section of the test was examined carefully

5 The a posteriori validation of the prototype AERT version 1

together with the discriminating power of each item. The overall alpha for the test was a respectable 88 and the individual sections were all above .68. All bar four items discriminated at more than .2 within their own section.

Factor analyses

A Principal Components Analysis (PCA) demonstrated that the careful global comprehension items, items 01 to 15, were all loading on a different factor than the linguistic comprehension items, the careful local reading items 46–60 (see Table 5.1 below). This offers some support for at least a bidivisible view of reading with a local linguistic comprehension factor and a global comprehension factor emerging in these particular data.

The attempt to see if there was an expeditious factor as against a careful factor was hampered by the lack of sufficient control over the time the candidates spent on any one passage in a section. In the careful reading it looks as though they spent most of the time on the first two passages turning the last passage into an expeditious rather than a careful reading test. The same is true in the search reading with most of the time being spent on the first two texts. This interpretation is supported by the number of those not offering an answer to an item increasing markedly on the last passage in these two sections (see Appendix 5.1.3).

Table 5.1

PCA factor loadings

	Factor 1	Factor 2		Factor 1	Factor 2
ITEM01	.35419	.07147	ITEM46	.43179	-.33806
ITEM02	.25198	.02516	ITEM47	.50645	-.31203
ITEM03	.39938	.04971	ITEM48	.30775	-.09041
ITEM04	.36344	.19864	ITEM49	.24747	-.07246
ITEM05	.35125	.41042	ITEM50	.33496	-.23607
ITEM06	.22666	.13507	ITEM51	.42613	-.13725
ITEM07	.38603	.19247	ITEM52	.32176	-.34385
ITEM08	.37549	.34387	ITEM53	.27668	-.41138
ITEM09	.20756	.48369	ITEM54	.24263	-.14900
ITEM10	.47791	.09945	ITEM55	.37222	-.31271
ITEM11	.41513	.03979	ITEM56	.47017	-.11028
ITEM12	.35698	.20657	ITEM57	.38027	-.03741
ITEM13	.42686	.12114	ITEM58	.38288	-.30800
ITEM14	.31132	.29858	ITEM59	.51289	-.01229
ITEM15	.42710	.42185	ITEM60	.41676	-.02467

5 The a posteriori validation of the prototype AERT version 1

When we subjected the data to varimax rotation on the part scores from each section a first factor indicating global and local separation of parts is suggested (see Table 5.2 below). The lower loadings on the third parts may be due to the lack of time spent on these by candidates (see above).

Table 5.2

Varimax rotated factor matrix

	Factor 1	Factor 2	Factor 3	Factor 4
TOTCARE1	.62663	.06843	.14628	.35600
TOTCARE2	.68429	.18215	-.02032	.29792
TOTCARE3	.24659	.77317	.07610	.05948
TOTSKCH1	.66732	.14945	.35875	-.24400
TOTSKCH2	.63147	.22176	.20415	.16141
TOTSKCH3	.19237	.70827	.10002	.14803
TOTSCAN1	.23178	.05967	.20672	.74158
TOTSCAN2	.13408	.36250	.11138	.60733
TOTSCAN3	-.00418	.59897	.45727	.23528
TOTLEXI1	.13906	.20804	.70249	.16867
TOTLEXI2	.18398	-.01130	.76645	.03382
TOTLEXI3	.15465	.31186	.53667	.32259

Cross-tabulations

Cross-tabulating individuals' scores on the various sections of the test gives us a clearer picture of what is happening at the level of the individual candidate (see Figure 5.1 below). If candidates were performing the same on different parts of the test one would expect similar numbers in each of the quadrants. There is some evidence that over 60% of candidates who would pass a reading test with a cut off score of sixty percent on the careful global reading items (totcare) would fail on the search reading/skimming items (totsksch). A larger percentage of candidates would pass on the careful global comprehension items (totcare) but fail on the careful local comprehension (totlexi).

Individuals do not perform in the same manner on all four parts of the test. There is some support for a partial divisibility view of reading.

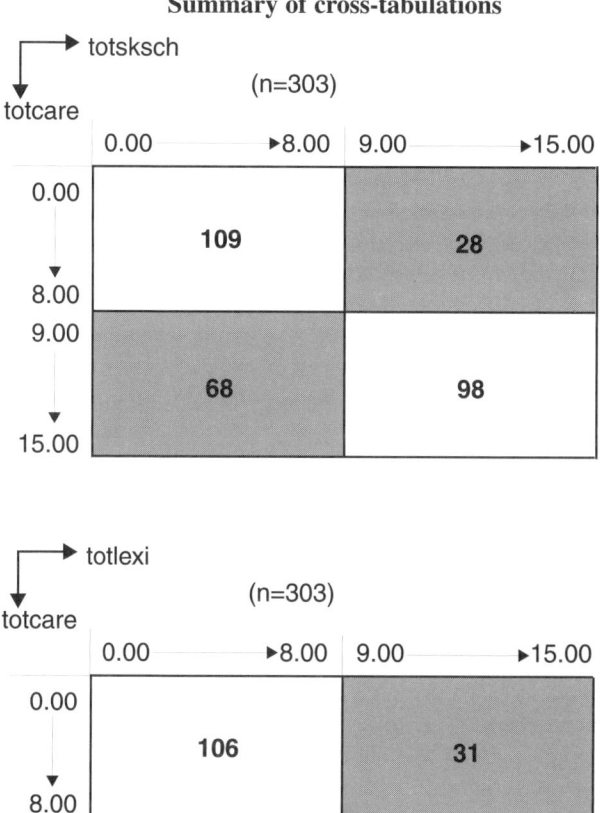

5 The a posteriori validation of the prototype AERT version 1

Figure 5.1

Summary of cross-tabulations

totsksch (n=303)

	0.00 — ▶8.00	9.00 — ▶15.00
totcare 0.00 — ▼ 8.00	109	28
9.00 — ▼ 15.00	68	98

totlexi (n=303)

	0.00 — ▶8.00	9.00 — ▶15.00
totcare 0.00 — ▼ 8.00	106	31
9.00 — ▼ 15.00	85	81

[Source: Reading in a Second Language, Urquhart A. H. and Weir C. J. (1998). Longman]

Questionnaire survey

In addition a feedback questionnaire had been filled out by every student (see Appendices 5.1.15 – 16). This provided us with information on:
- candidates' perceptions of the language level of each passage;
- their familiarity with the topic of each passage;
- the discipline area they feel the passage was from;
- the specificity of the passage;
- their familiarity with the format;

5 The a posteriori validation of the prototype AERT version 1

- their attitude to the formats;
- whether the timing was sufficient for each section of the test;
- which section they thought the easiest/most difficult/heaviest time pressure/least time pressure.

The results of the questionnaire data were similar to those we obtained for the main trial in October reported in full later in this chapter. The data for the April trial are included at Appendix 5.1.16.

The degree of familiarity with each passage, the language level and the subject specificity of the passages all fell within the desired ranges, and extremes had been successfully avoided.

Candidates were on the whole familiar with the formats employed with the exception of the table completion in Section 3, although many had some familiarity even with this. On the whole they claimed to have liked rather than disliked the formats.

Their main source of dissatisfaction was with the sufficiency of the time for the expeditious sections 2 – 4. On the whole the majority of candidates thought they had sufficient time for the careful reading sections 1 and 5. Section 5 careful reading local was seen as the easiest by 36% and the least time pressured by 69% of all candidates. Section 4 scanning was seen as the most time pressured followed by section 2 skimming and section 3 search reading.

Overall candidates reported that they liked the format, the content, the design and the rubrics of the AERT. They were less happy about the length and the time allowed. The amount of time given to the expeditious reading sections must be carefully controlled. These are the areas they are weakest in and where reform needs to be made. Without strict control and delimited time the test would not be measuring these abilities. One can see in the no response to items data that they are already spending too much time on the earlier items within a section at the expense of later items precisely because of limited ability to read quickly, selectively and efficiently.

Conclusions

About the EAP reading construct

The evidence from the factor analysis and from the cross tabulations encouraged us in our desire to maintain the quadripartite division of the test.

Revision of the prototype AERT

Changes to performance conditions for the test

A number of changes to test performance conditions are recommended as a result of the analysis. The time for each section is already strictly controlled. It was felt that in addition there should be strict time controls on the items in each passage within each section in the October trial. The data indicated that in the skimming section (2), scanning section (4) and to a certain extent in the

5 The a posteriori validation of the prototype AERT version 1

search reading section (3) performance dropped on the third passage indicating that candidates may in fact have spent more time carefully reading the items on the first two passages in the section. The data on the careful reading section (1) shows that performance fell on the third passage items in this section perhaps as a result of less time spent on items 11 – 15. The factor analyses support this interpretation. A further check of non responses to items in each section also suggest that this was the case (see Appendix 5.1.3).

As regards careful reading it is proposed that in addition to enforcing strict time controls at the passage as well as the section level, we should also increase the time allowance to 60 minutes for this section. In the Principal Components Analysis (see Appendix 5.1.11), the marked loadings of the items in the third passage (items 11 – 15) on the same factor as the skimming items in section 2 (items 16 – 18) suggest that this would be sensible. Our aim is to ensure that items in each section as far as possible are maximally valid operationalisations of the constructs we are trying to test. There is nothing to lose by ensuring students have sufficient time to carefully read the items in section 1.

In order to rigidly control the maximum time spent on each passage in the search reading section it is sensible for the 3 passages to be roughly equivalent in terms of length. This necessitated cutting passage 4 on Japanese Women down in size. We feel that the time allocated for this section should be reduced accordingly from 24 to 21 minutes; 7 minutes per passage. They have already had 9 minutes to skim these 3 passages in Section 2. At roughly 1000 words per passage the minimum speed for faster reading might be estimated at 100 wpm. Thus they would have 10 minutes for fast processing of each passage of a 1000 words.

The time spent on each passage in the scanning section (4) will also need to be tightly controlled. There is a noticeable fall in performance on the items in the third passage in this section (41 – 45). This again is probably a result of the students spending less time on the items on the third passage. Again the factor analysis and the non responses in this part suggest this to be the case.

As scanning is supposed to involve only selective reading of the text and as matching helps identify required information more quickly than is possible in search reading or skimming, we proposed cutting the time down for this section slightly from 20 to 18 minutes. This would allow us to ensure that 6 minutes only are available for the scanning items on each passage. This should further help make this subtest a maximally valid test of scanning activities.

It was felt that it might be useful for the test invigilator to orally reinforce the purpose for reading for each section of the test. The instructions already attempt to make this clear but perhaps oral reinforcement and instructions in Chinese would drive home even further the point that different types of reading are needed for each section i.e., NOT careful reading in every section.

5 The a posteriori validation of the prototype AERT version 1

Changes to actual items

Apart from the reduction in size of passage 4 and strict control on the time spent on each passage, very little change seems necessary to the test itself. Item 22 was revised to make it clearer; the amendment of one of the options ('components') in the banked cloze on passage 12 should improve item 58. Item 15 was also altered because of a potential overlap with item 12. Item 31 has a facility value of .87 which in part explains its low discrimination. Item 49 has a discrimination of .19 which is only marginally below our notional cut off point, as is item 2 at .18. We left items 2, 31 and 49 as they were, deciding they would be reviewed again at a later stage when more data become available.

The main trial

Test administration

The registration and organisation of the test was much helped by the support of the Provincial Higher Education Commission of Shandong. Six universities were selected for the test. The two comprehensive ones (Shandong University and Qingdao University) were expected to provide students from the disciplinary areas of arts and humanities; the two science and technology ones (Shandong Engineering University and Qingdao Oceanographic University) students from science and technology; and the two medical ones (Shandong Medical University and Qingdao Medical University) students from medical and life science. Both the university authorities and candidates were informed that the test was an assessment of the students' EAP reading ability and that the results would help establish baseline data for the probable large-scale administration of this test in the near future. That the test was taken seriously was confirmed by the small number of absentees (12 out of 1080), by the fact that no candidates quit before the end of the test and by the completion of the questionnaire by all the candidates.

All candidates took the test in the same order completing the items on passages 1 through 12 serially. It would have been too complicated to vary the order in which the passages were taken.

All invigilators took part in a 20-minute training session before each administration, in which they were talked through the whole process of the test. Emphasis was given to the importance of keeping strictly to the time limit set for each section. A detailed set of instructions including a time-table for the whole test was given to each invigilator. 10 minutes before the test, candidates were provided with Chinese instructions telling them how they might achieve their best performance in the test and the time limit of each section. During the test, a reminder was given to students 5 minutes before the end of each section. Answer sheets were collected section by section.

5 The a posteriori validation of the prototype AERT version 1

A major setback was that some students did not follow the instruction of allocating the same amount of time for each passage within one section, which was put clearly in the instructions for each section. This resulted in a larger number of blank answers for the third passage in each section than for the first two, especially in the expeditious reading sections. Serious attention must be paid to the control of the time limits for each passage in any further trialling of the test.

Sample

A total of 1080 candidates were initially selected. Thanks to the effort of organisers in each university, 1068 candidates sat the test, 533 CET 4 certificate holders and 535 CET 6 certificate holders. Divided by their disciplinary areas, 207 are from arts and humanities, 446 from science and technology, and 415 from medical and life science. They constitute a broad sample of fourth year undergraduates who have passed either CET 4 or CET 6 in the last twelve months (January 1997, June 1996) and who have completed the EAP reading course in the third year.

Marking and data entry

The marking of the 1068 scripts took three consecutive working days to complete. Four experienced teachers were invited from the Foreign Languages Department of Shanghai Normal University. The first two hours were spent on familiarising the markers with the test paper and the marking scheme. To ensure the reliability of the marking, one marker was put in charge of a single section (Sections 1 to 4) and frequent and close checking was done on the papers of the first university. To familiarise markers with the marking scheme, a good university was chosen to start with because variations in acceptable answers were more likely to appear in good candidates' papers. The marking scheme proved to be very helpful and markers came up with very few new acceptable variations.

When the marking was reviewed in the November Moderating Committee meeting a number of issues arose. Sections 4 and 5 of the test posed few problems for the markers as they were only checking the presence and absence of a particular word on the candidate's script. However, in Section 2 of the test, where the candidate has to skim the text to establish the discourse topic a number of problems were noted when the scripts were checked. Acceptable variations in wording which deviated from the mark scheme had been marked wrong and this served to depress the item total correlation for that item. To a lesser extent this was also noted in section 3 in the marking of some of the search reading items.

It should be pointed out that reviewing and revising the marks for just one question in Sections 2 and 3 took 4 hours for two people to complete. We looked closely at 6 items in these sections alone. It was an extremely time consuming operation. Thus it is crucial in the next administration of the AERT that one can rely on the first markers. In the future, markers for the sections testing skimming and search reading as well as being very familiar with the passages in the test and the marking scheme will need to be linguistically sophisticated. The marking scheme can never be fully exhaustive (as we found even after the earlier piloting on 300 students), so while markers should be closely guided by the acceptable answers provided in the marking scheme, they will also have to be adaptive to possible acceptable variations. To achieve this, the markers need to have a sufficiently advanced command of language to give credit to any additional acceptable variations.

It took the team seven days to check both the marking and the data entry. Though extremely time consuming it was an essential part of the process. It led in nearly every case to improved discrimination at the item level and to an enhanced reliability coefficient for each section. It also expanded the range of acceptable answers in the mark scheme. Such direct involvement was also valuable in that it alerted us to the tail off in responses towards the end of each section indicating that time was a considerable problem for a large number of candidates especially in the expeditious reading sections (Sections 2 and 3).

The experience suggests that markers for the test will need to be linguistically sophisticated and highly trained to avoid the need to remark. This is one of the drawbacks of direct skill/strategy based testing through short answer questions as against the ubiquitous multiple choice.

Descriptives of the test data

Descriptive statistics were generated for the test at the item, passage, section and whole test level (see Appendix 5.2.1). The indications are that the test as a whole seems to be working well with only 3 items exhibiting relatively weak statistical properties. The reliability of each section of the test was examined carefully together with the discriminating power of each item. The overall alpha for the test was a respectable .85 and the individual sections were all above .65. All bar 11 items discriminated at more than .2 within their own section and the alphas of each section (1 – 5) would not be improved by deleting any item.

At the component level the ANOVA analyses showed that careful reading is significantly easier for this sample of students than expeditious reading, and reading for global comprehension significantly easier than reading for local comprehension. Skimming and search reading were the most difficult of all reading tasks.

5 The a posteriori validation of the prototype AERT version 1

P.C.A. and varimax rotation

The principal component factor analysis provides some evidence that careful reading global items (section 1 items 1 – 15) are behaving in a different manner than careful local items (section 5 items 46 – 60). This accords with our earlier research in this area. In addition we employed varimax rotation on the sub-components of the test at the passage level. The results indicate that the global items (with the exception of TOTSKCH 3 seriously affected by time) are loading on this factor in a different manner to the local items (see Table 5.3 below). They also indicate a second factor on which the lexical parts load the most heavily. The fourth factor is possibly best explained as a scanning factor but again we see an effect occasioned by serious problems with timing in the third passage (see breakdown of non responses in Table 5.5 below). Factor 3 may be a reflection of that problem as three of the third passages where the highest incidence of non responses occur load heavily on that factor. To explore the componentiality issue further, serious attention needs to be paid to ensuring an equal amount of time is spent on each passage within each section in future research on AERT.

Table 5.3

Varimax rotation of October part scores

	Components			
	1	2	3	4
TOTCARE1	.633	.279	-1.24E-02	.183
TOTCARE2	.782	6.362E-02	2.408E-02	.112
TOTCARE3	.451	-4.47E-02	.421	.279
TOTSKCH1	.522	.196	.203	.160
TOTSKCH2	.579	.198	.311	4.261E-02
TOTSKCH3	.145	6.335E-02	.752	.135
TOTSCAN1	.267	.192	-2.02E-04	.730
TOTSCAN2	.110	.147	.253	.773
TOTSCAN3	7.666E-02	.194	.744	4.345E-02
TOTLEXI1	.194	.571	9.333E-02	.263
TOTLEXI2	.104	.793	1.265E-02	.111
TOTLEXI3	.195	.667	.223	3.553E-02

Cross-tabulations

The cross-tabulations of individual students' performances on the four parts of the test also show clearly that the majority of students are weak in expeditious reading as against careful reading and are better at careful global

5 The a posteriori validation of the prototype AERT version 1

comprehension than careful local comprehension (see Figure 5.2 below). Setting a notional pass mark at 60% clearly evidences the need for the profiling of reading ability.

Figure 5.2

Summary of cross tabulations October trial

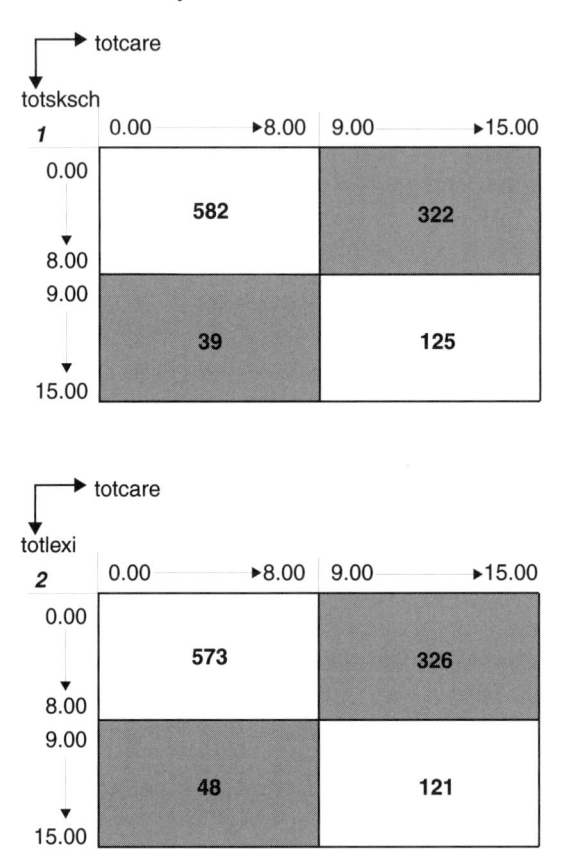

	totcare 0.00 — ►8.00	totcare 9.00 — ►15.00
totsksch 1 0.00 — ▼ 8.00	582	322
9.00 — ▼ 15.00	39	125

	totcare 0.00 — ►8.00	totcare 9.00 — ►15.00
totlexi 2 0.00 — ▼ 8.00	573	326
9.00 — ▼ 15.00	48	121

ANOVA analyses of differences between test sub-components

The means of the careful global (factor 1) versus expeditious global (factor 2) reading are also significantly different as can be seen in Table 5.4 below. There is clear water between the two with a much better performance on the former. This accords with questionnaire data where the evidence is for a lot more training having been received in the former and also a lot more use of the skill in real life as against little use of expeditious reading.

5 The a posteriori validation of the prototype AERT version 1

Table 5.4

ANOVA analyses of differences between subtest mean scores in October Trial

ANOVA

		Sum of Squares	df	Mean Square	F	Sig.
SUBSCORE	Between Groups	3571.643	2	1785.821	226.208	.000
	Within Groups	25270.600	3201	7.895		
	Total	28842.243	3203			

Post Hoc Tests
Multiple comparisons
Dependent variable: SUBSCORE
Bonferroni

(I) facnumb	(J) facnumb	Mean Difference (I–J)	Std. Error	Sig.	95%Confidence Interval Lower Bound	Upper Bound
1.00	2.00	2.2453*	.122	.000	1.9541	2.5366
	3.00	2.2341*	.122	.000	1.9428	2.5253
2.00	1.00	-2.2453*	.122	.000	-2.5366	-1.9541
	3.00	-1.12E-02	.122	1.000	-.3025	.2800
3.00	1.00	-2.2341*	.122	.000	-2.5253	-1.9428
	2.00	1.124E-02	.122	1.000	-.2800	.3025

In global reading (factor 1) as against careful local reading (factor 3) there is a significant difference and a clearly superior performance in the former. As in the previous comparison this may of course be because of ease of passage or questions or because of difference in abilities in these areas.

Analysis of questionnaire data

A revised feedback questionnaire was filled out by the 1068 students taking the test. This provided us with information on:
- candidates' perceptions of the language level of each passage;
- their familiarity with the topic of each passage;
- the discipline area they feel the passage was from;
- their perceptions of the specificity of the passage;
- their interest in the content of the passage;

5 The a posteriori validation of the prototype AERT version 1

- their familiarity with the format;
- their attitude to the suitability of formats for testing their reading ability;
- whether the timing was sufficient for each section of the test;
- which section they thought the easiest/most difficult/heaviest time pressure/least time pressure;
- their views on the whole test (time sufficiency, layout, instructions);
- the frequency of use of each skill/strategy in real life;
- the training they have received in each skill/strategy.

Descriptive statistics were calculated for all the questionnaire items and these are included at Appendix 5.2.33 – 34. In general the data suggest the following:

- Levels of difficulty, familiarity and specificity of the passages fall within the desired ranges. Only a small percentage of the respondents marked the extremes of difficulty and familiarity for any of the 12 passages. In most cases passages were regarded as easy or quite difficult and quite familiar or not so familiar.
- The candidates' views of the discipline area the text had been selected from on the whole matched those of the examiners with some differences in opinion evident over passages 6, 8 and 12.
- No passage was seen as very specific to any one subject discipline.
- The majority of the passages appeared to be of some interest to the candidates. Passages 5 – 8 and 10 – 11 however elicited a majority of not so interesting to not interesting at all responses. Clearly this may be an area where developers in the future will need to do more a *priori* screening. It may also result from test fatigue.
- With the exception of flow chart completion the majority of candidates were reasonably familiar with the formats and once practice tests are available and prior teaching is taking place, this should not be problematic.
- The majority of the candidates thought all formats of the test were suitable for testing their EAP reading ability though interestingly sentence completion and banked cloze were clearly regarded as less suitable than the other formats.
- Candidates thought that the time allowed for the careful reading sections (1 and 5) was sufficient but that for the expeditious reading was not. As regards the test as a whole only c 30% thought time was quite suitable
- They perceived the expeditious sections (2 – 4) as being more difficult than the careful reading sections 1 and 5.
- A majority were positive about the layout despite the necessary complexity of the test procedure. A clear majority were positive about the test rubrics. Overall then they were satisfied with the layout and the accessibility of the instructions but were less satisfied with the time

allowed (probably because of the pressure they felt in the expeditious sections).
- Candidates appear to read carefully for global comprehension and focus on words quite often in real life. Some skimming also takes place but they do not appear to search read or scan very often at all.
- Candidates appear to have had very little training in expeditious reading.

Effect of perceptions on test scores

So far we have examined candidates' background and responses to facets of test design to ascertain whether we have done a reasonable job in test development. Next we will examine whether some of these independent variables have affected the dependent variables of test scores. The effects of independent variables such as:
- language difficulty;
- topic familiarity;
- specificity;
- interest;
- format familiarity;
- format suitability;
- sufficiency of time allowed;
- perceived section difficulty;
- use of skills strategies in real life;
- prior training in the skills/strategy.

were calculated on test scores at the passage and (where appropriate) at the section and test level (Appendix 5.2.35).

The results show that in general:
- the less difficult they perceived the language of the passage the higher the scores;
- the more familiar students claimed to be with the topic of a passage the higher the scores;
- the more interesting they thought the text the higher the scores;
- the more sufficient they thought the time for a section the higher the scores;
- the more frequent the use of the activities tested in real life the higher the scores;
- the more training they had received in a particular skill/strategy the higher the scores;

These results can also be interpreted in reverse. For example the higher the score, the more interesting, more familiar, etc., they thought the texts.
- the students in the top third of the score range (41 – 60/60) were also satisfied with the sufficiency of time allowed, the layout and the clarity of the rubrics. The degree of satisfaction falls when we move to the

middle range (21 – 40/60) and is at its lowest in the bottom range of scores (<20/60). The fall in satisfaction with the sufficiency of time appears the most marked.

Conclusions

Revision of the prototype AERT

The sample for the second administration of the test was much weaker than those in the first trial who had entered for the reading competition. This was perhaps inevitable in that this time we had to accept the actual population in the six universities whereas in the first trial the best students had in a sense pre selected themselves for the competition. It had not been possible to hold a second competition in Shanghai for administrative reasons in the office of the Shanghai Higher Education Commission. The result was that the overall mean in the second trial was 24.9 and the s.d. 8.68 against a mean of 32.9 and an s.d. of 9.91 in the first trial.

This meant that in the second trial there were 11 items with a facility value of less than .2 whereas in the first trial there had only been one. The net result was that this probably served to depress some of the item total correlations with a knock on effect for the sub-component alphas.

Revisions at the item level

Item 6
This item had performed weakly in the first trial and this time the corrected item total was similarly unimpressive at .1454. The item is still making a contribution albeit small to the internal consistency of its section. This is the only item with a facility value above .8 (.83).

Item 22
This item had not worked over well in the first piloting but had been left in because it was considered an important piece of content. The corrected item total correlation of .1831 is probably just about acceptable as the alpha for the test would not be improved by deleting this item.

Item 35
This item did not work as well in this administration with a corrected item total correlation of .1886. This is probably acceptable as the alpha for the test would not be improved by deleting this item.

Item 52
This item did not work as well in this administration with a corrected item total correlation of .1526 because the distractors *similarity* and *demonstrations* proved very strong for this weaker sample.

5 The a posteriori validation of the prototype AERT version 1

Item 58

This item had performed well in the earlier trial (.38 as against .1466) but the mark scheme was changed as *components* had been considered an acceptable alternative to *variables*. Its replacement *varieties* has, however, proved to be too strong a distractor and thought might be given to changing this in future administrations. The item is still making a contribution albeit small to the internal consistency of its section.

Items 46, 48, 49, 50

These items also had item subtotal correlations below .2 (.1873, .1974, .1603 and .1825) but these (with the marginal case of 49) had performed satisfactorily in the first trial (.3866, .2637, .1918 and .2846). The items are all still making a contribution to the internal consistency of section 5 and the alpha of this sub-component would not be improved by removing any of them.

Revisions at section level

A number of changes to test performance conditions are recommended as a result of the analysis. The time for each section is already strictly controlled. However, as yet the team have still not been able to achieve strict time controls on the items in each passage within each section. The data indicated that in the skimming section (2), scanning section (4) and to a certain extent in the search reading section (3) performance dropped on the third passage indicating that candidates may in fact have spent more time carefully reading the items on the first two passages in the section (see Figure 5.7 below). The data on the careful reading section (1) show that performance fell on the third passage items in this section perhaps as a result of less time spent on items 11 – 15. The factor analyses support this interpretation. A further check of non responses to items in each section also suggest that this was the case (see Table 5.5).

Thus, in spite of putting clear instructions in both Chinese and English in the candidates test booklet, and despite invigilators advising them of the necessity of doing this to score well, the candidates are still not distributing their time equally between the questions set on the three passages in each of the sections of the test. This is particularly the case in the expeditious reading sections 2 – 5 (items 16 – 45) of the test. The number of missing values in the final passage questions in each of these three sections gives clear evidence that many candidates have not even attempted these items. This may be because of deficient abilities in expeditious reading but we cannot state this conclusively at the moment.

5 The a posteriori validation of the prototype AERT version 1

Table 5.5

Number of non responses for each item in the main trial in October 1997

Section 1		Section 2		Section 3		Section 4		Section 5	
Item No	No. of non-responses	Item No	No. of non-responses	Item No	No. of non-responses	Item No	No. of non-responses	Item No	No. of non-responses
1	15	16	4	19	24	31	20	46	7
2	29	17	64	20	35	32	52	47	7
3	11	18	148	21	61	33	61	48	6
4	8			22	70	34	99	49	9
5	5			23	116	35	430	50	10
6	6			24	181	36	115	51	6
7	48			25	301	37	283	52	7
8	10			26	222	38	255	53	10
9	6			27	288	39	452	54	13
10	14			28	419	40	420	55	13
11	103			29	615	41	503	56	7
12	130			30	609	42	769	57	9
13	74					43	846	58	9
14	79					44	872	59	20
15	66					45	883	60	24

As a result performance tails off on the items set on the last passage in the first three sections of the test (see table 5.5 above). Unfortunately this also restricts our ability to determine the subject specific effect of the passages on performance discussed in the next section. It is difficult to tell whether lower performance on the final passage in a section was due to the subject of the passage or simply reflected running out of time.

The possible solutions all appear extremely unwieldy. If we were to have 15 answer sheets each of which was collected after the allotted time for the questions on each passage this would be both hard to organise and costly and difficult in terms of the amount of paper handling involved. However if we are ever to be fully confident of the relationship between expeditious and careful reading then we will have to explore ways of ensuring that candidates spend an equal amount of time on each of the three passages in each section. This might mean printing each of the passages in a different colour and collecting each after the allotted time period.

Revisions at the test level

There is both qualitative and quantitative evidence to support the case that we have avoided the extremes of familiarity and topic specificity. For the most part the effect of background knowledge on performance would seem to have been filtered out.

5 The a posteriori validation of the prototype AERT version 1

Simple inspection of the means (Appendix 5.2.8 – 9) shows the arts students performing slightly better overall with not a great deal of difference between the Physical Sciences students and the Life Sciences. Performances on the Arts part of the test are fairly similar to those on the science parts but the Life Science parts appear easier for all groups. The Analysis of Variance (ANOVA) data support these initial observations and show where the significant differences lie.(Appendices 5.2. 23 – 5.2. 31.)

For the whole test sample there is no significant difference between performances of the whole test population on the Arts and on the Science parts of the AERT (Passage 1, 4, 9 and 10 as against passages 3, 6, 7, and 11). In terms of parallelness these two elements of the test are the closest. The alpha for these parts of the test (40 items) is .79 against a total test alpha of .85. There is, however, a significant (and meaningful) difference between the performance on the third part based on Life Science passages (2, 5, 8 and 12), as compared to the Arts and Science passage based sub-components.

The ANOVA analysis shows that the Arts students significantly outperform the Life Science students and Science students on the test overall, on the global and local, expeditious and careful components. Arts students are significantly better than the other two on the Arts parts, better than the Life Science students but not the Science on the Science parts and better than the Science but not the Life Science students on the Life Science parts. In nearly all cases these differences were less than 1 point in 20.

In the ANOVA analysis on the individual parts (12) of the test, i.e., at the passage level, there is a small but significant difference between the three groups in five cases out of 12. Two of these occur in the careful reading section, one in the skimming and search reading, scanning and lexis. In all cases it was the Arts student group that was significantly better than the other two.

Thus apart from a slightly superior performance on the part of the Arts students it is difficult to maintain a subject effect for the passages except in so far as the Life Sciences passages were easier for all. The cross-tabulation data also support this. With a notional cut off pass score of 60% individuals are not disadvantaged by either the Arts or the Science parts of the test. However considerably more would pass on the Life Science components overall than on the Arts or Science.

There is slight evidence that the Scientists reduced the deficit as compared to the Arts students on the Science parts overall and likewise for the Life Science students on the Life Science passages. If one wished to reduce the size of the test as part of the evidence one might remove the passage from each section which exhibits a significant difference between the groups. In section 1 there are two of these so the passage with the biggest difference might be considered.

5 The a posteriori validation of the prototype AERT version 1

In this part we have looked at the quantitative data generated by administering the AERT in two trials. In many ways these are our best data as the sample size is acceptable and statistical analysis tells us whether we can support various statements. These then are 'hard' data. Next we turn to qualitative self report data, which, because of the inevitable limitations on sampling, must be seen as illuminative rather than definitive. However, such soft data do shed light on the test taking process which test data can tell us little about. For this reason alone they are of interest.

6 The *a posteriori* validation of the prototype AERT version 1: qualitative studies

Introduction

At the *a posteriori* stage of test validation, test data analysis is the most revealing but this can be complemented and triangulated by qualitative data, which provides us with information on:
- what experts think the various parts of the test are testing,
- what skills and strategies students retrospectively think the various parts of the test are testing,
- what skills and strategies students introspectively think the various parts of the test are testing.

These three types of qualitative data were collected through an experts' questionnaire survey, a students' retrospection study and a students' introspection study.

Expert judgements

In order to obtain experts' professional opinion of the skills and strategies being tested in the AERT, a questionnaire (see Appendix 6.1) was designed, in which subject tutors were invited to select from a range of five types of skills and strategies the primary focus and the secondary focus (if there is one) being tested by each section of the AERT prototype version 1.

In the questionnaire, technical terms of skills and strategies (i.e., skimming, search reading, scanning, EXMI, IPROP, ILEX) were avoided and the five types of reading were described in simple academic terms. Thus it was hoped that misjudgements caused by the misunderstanding of the technical terms could be avoided. In addition, in each section, an open-ended choice was provided for the experts to specify the type of reading being tested in the section if it was considered that none of the given types of reading was being tested.

6 The a posteriori validation of the prototype AERT version 1

Data collection

The questionnaire together with the test paper was distributed to the teachers involved in the study of text characteristics described above. They were 19 teachers involved in teaching academic English reading to 3rd or 4th year students in 6 universities in Shanghai. 17 questionnaires were completed and returned to the project team. The return rate was 89%. Among the 17 respondents of the survey, 5 were English teachers and 12 subject matter teachers. Among the 12 subject matter teachers, 4 were from the departments of arts and humanities (e.g., politics, laws etc.), 4 science and technology (e.g., computers, microelectronics, electric machinery etc.) and 4 medical, biology and life science (e.g., biology, biology and medical engineering etc.). So the respondents constitute a balanced sample from the three broad discipline categories covered by the test.

Data analysis

Frequency was counted for the 17 questionnaires and the results were recorded in Table 6.1. It was noticed in the frequency count that the total of both the primary and secondary focus for each section could sometimes exceed 17. This was because no limit was set in the instructions for the number of skill(s)/strategy(ies) as the primary and secondary focuses in one section. Some respondents chose more than one primary or secondary focus for one section. In section 1, for example, all the 17 experts agree that the section is testing reading carefully for main ideas as its primary focus, but there are 5 (among these 17) who consider that the section has a second primary focus in addition to the careful reading for main ideas. In calculating the percentage, however, the total was kept as 17 simply because for one type of reading in a section the maximum could only be 17.

From Table 6.1, it is clear that the AERT test developers' expectations has been confirmed to a large extent by the experts' judgements. The percentage of respondents who agreed with the test developers' view of the primary focus of each section ranges from the lowest 88% (for the skimming and search reading sections) to the highest 100% (for the two careful reading sections).

6 The a posteriori validation of the prototype AERT version 1

Table 6.1

Experts' judgements of the skill(s)/strategy(ies) being tested in each section (N=17)

Skill/strategy	Section 1 p*	Section 1 s**	Section 2 p	Section 2 s	Section 3 p	Section 3 s	Section 4 p	Section 4 s	Section 5 p	Section 5 s
reading carefully for main ideas	17 100%	0	0	2	1	1	1	0	0	2
reading quickly to get the overall idea of a text	1	4	15 88%	2	1	2	0	4	0	6
reading quickly to search for information on main ideas	2	8	3	4	15 88%	1	2	1	0	3
reading qiuckly to find specific information: words/numbers/ symbols	2	1	2	1	3	5	16 94%	1	1	4
carefully working out meaning of words from context	0	3	0	2	1	3	1	4	17 100%	0
others (please specify)	0	0	0	0	0	0	0	0	0	0

*: primary focus of the skill/strategy being tested in the section
**: secondary focus (if there is one) of the skill/strategy being tested in the section

For each section, most of the respondents considered that a secondary skill/strategy was being tested. For a clear view of the skills/strategies as a secondary focus in each section, a separate table was drawn for the analysis (Table 6.2).

From the table, it can be seen that the skills/strategies with high frequencies of being considered as a secondary focus in the test are expeditious reading strategies. This is especially true for the two careful reading sections where 13 (78%) experts agreed an expeditious reading strategy was being tested as a secondary focus. The total frequency of expeditious reading strategies as a secondary focus is 47, whereas that of careful reading skills is only 17.

6 The a posteriori validation of the prototype AERT version 1

Table 6.2

Experts' judgements of a secondary focus of skill/strategy being tested in each section (N=17)

Secondary focus	Section 1 careful reading (global)	Section 2 skimming	Section 3 search reading	Section 4 scanning	Section 5 careful reading (local)	Total
Expeditious reading strategies	13	7	8	6	13	47
Careful reading skills	3	4	4	4	2	17
Total	16	11	12	10	15	64

This may reflect a wider use of expeditious reading strategies. In careful reading for main ideas (Section 1), for example, 4 experts agreed that skimming was a secondary focus being tested and 8 agreed that search reading was a secondary focus. This seems to suggest that a text could be skimmed for gist and/or search read for main ideas before it is read more carefully for precise comprehension. Similarly, in careful reading for understanding contextualised lexical meanings (Section 5), 6 experts agreed that skimming was the secondary focus being tested, suggesting that texts could be skimmed first for a general idea to facilitate the understanding of individual lexical items.

On the other hand, the high frequency of expeditious reading strategies being considered as secondary focuses in the test might well indicate that time was felt to be a factor influencing candidates' performance throughout the AERT test.

Conclusions

On the whole, experts' judgements confirm the test developers' expectations in terms of the skill/strategy being tested as a primary focus in each section. In addition, expeditious reading strategies of skimming and search reading were considered to be tested as secondary focuses in the two careful reading sections.

Student retrospection

In addition to the experts' questionnaire survey, a student retrospection study was carried out in order to obtain a larger data set to establish students' perceptions of the skills and strategies being used in the process of taking the test.

6 The a posteriori validation of the prototype AERT version 1

Data collection

The collection of the students' retrospection data was incorporated into the introspection study of the revised AERT prototype version 1 (to be reported in Section 6.3). CET-4 and CET-6 certificate holders from three universities in Shanghai were invited to participate in the introspection study and the questionnaire survey for the retrospection study. Students were given the questionnaire (the same as the one used for expert judgement: see Appendix 6.1) immediately after they finished the test. Instructions were given to students to select from a range of five types of reading the primary and the secondary focus (if there is one) of skill/strategy being used for each section of the test.

A total of 69 retrospection checklists were obtained from:
- 27 Shanghai Jiao Tong University students (as a science/technology sample);
- 24 Shanghai Medical University students (as a medical/biology/life science sample);
- 18 East China Normal University students (as an arts/humanities/business sample).

The respondents thus constitute a quite balanced sample of students from the three broad categories of subject matters concerned in the study.

Data analysis

Frequency was counted for each of the three universities (see Appendix 6.2) and the results were then summarised in Table 6.3 for the total of 69 student respondents.

In general, it seems that students' perceptions conformed to a lesser degree with the test developers' expectations than do the experts' judgement. This is perhaps to be expected because it is less likely for students to have a clear idea and a strong awareness of the skills/strategies being used in the test than experts.

From Table 6.3, it is clear that students were quite certain about the use of the skimming strategy in Section 2 and the scanning strategy in Section 4 as the primary focuses, with 70% and 65% agreement respectively.

The section with poorest agreement among students is search reading (Section 3). 31 (45%) students agreed that they were reading quickly to search for information on main ideas. The confusion here is clearly the distinction between search reading and scanning. 26 (as against 31) considered that in Section 3 they were reading quickly to find specific information: words/numbers/ symbols. Simple matching with words in the stems of the test items may indeed be the test taking strategy they adopted as certain of those introspecting were later to confirm. If they have never been taught to search read (see Appendix 5.2 34 for summaries of 1068 test takers feedback on this) then they are not likely to be able to do it in the manner intended.

Table 6.3

Students' perceptions of the skill(s)/strategy(ies) being tested in each section (N=69)

Skill/strategy	Section 1 p*	Section 1 s**	Section 2 p	Section 2 s	Section 3 p	Section 3 s	Section 4 p	Section 4 s	Section 5 p	Section 5 s
reading carefully for main ideas	**38 55%**	11	6	4	6	6	4	4	13	17
reading quickly to get the overall idea of a text	14	17	**48 70%**	15	7	18	8	18	11	8
reading quickly to search for information on main ideas	13	15	10	27	**31 45%**	17	17	19	6	8
reading quickly to find specific information: words/numbers/symbols	10	14	8	10	26	17	**45 65%**	19	4	14
carefully working out meaning of words from context	2	13	0	3	6	7	3	7	**37 54%**	14
others (please specify)	0	1	0	0	1	0	0	1	0	1

*: primary focus of the skill/strategy being tested in each section
**: secondary focus (if there is one) of the skill/strategy being tested in each section

The agreement of the primary focus of the careful reading for main ideas section (Section 1) is much lower (55%) than the experts' judgement (100%). More than half of the students went for expeditious reading strategies (14 for skimming, 13 for search reading and 10 for scanning), suggesting the time pressure felt by most of the students in the careful reading for main ideas section.

Section 5 is designed as a test of understanding lexical meanings from the context, which is expected to be testing careful reading at the local level. However, the agreement for the primary focus of the section is only 54%. What seems to be difficult to explain is that 24 students went for a global reading skill/strategy as the primary focus of the section (13 for careful reading for main ideas and 11 for reading quickly to get an overall idea of the text).

6 The a posteriori validation of the prototype AERT version 1

Given that the construct validity of the test has in large part been supported by the statistical data analysis and the experts' judgement, one possible explanation for the relatively low agreement of students' perceptions of the skills/strategies being used in Section 1 (careful reading at the global level), Section 3 (search reading) and Section 5 (careful reading at the local level) could be that the data were affected by those students whose general reading ability was too poor to have any idea of reading skills and strategies.

This prompted the idea of looking into the perceptions of those students who performed well in the test. Our anticipation was that proficient readers may have a stronger awareness of the skill/strategy than those less proficient readers and as a result of this awareness they might be more likely to perform in the manner expected by the test developers and consequently achieve a good performance.

A frequency count for the top 21 students was carried out and the results are recorded in Table 6.5. The perceived skills and strategies in these data are more consonant with the test developers' expectations. The highest agreements were again on the use of skimming and scanning strategies (86% and 71% respectively). The percentages of agreement for the two careful reading sections were both improved a little (57% and 62% respectively). The least agreed section was again Section 3 (search reading) due to the difficulty in distinguishing it from scanning. 9 (as against 10) went for the scanning strategy in the search reading section.

Earlier comments about the lack of knowledge concerning search reading apply here. This result also indicates that qualitative data of this sort must be treated with some circumspection when participants do not share a common metalanguage of skills and strategies and have little experience of some of them.

Table 6.4 and Table 6.6 were drawn for the analysis of the secondary focuses of the skills/strategies. The perceptions of students are similar to experts' judgements. The total frequency of expeditious reading strategies as a secondary focus is 62, whereas that of careful reading skills is only 21. Except for the careful reading at the local level section (Section 5), where the secondary focus was considered to be the skill of careful reading for main ideas, the frequencies of expeditious reading strategies as the secondary focuses in the four sections range from 12 (57%) to 15 (71%).

6 The a posteriori validation of the prototype AERT version 1

Table 6.4

Students' perceptions of a secondary focus of skill/strategy being tested in each section (N=69)

Secondary focus	Section 1 careful reading (global)	Section 2 skimming	Section 3 search reading	Section 4 scanning	Section 5 careful reading (local)	Total
Expeditious reading strategies	46	52	52	56	30	236
Careful reading skills	24	7	12	11	31	85
Total	70	59	64	67	61	321

Table 6.5

Proficient students' perceptions of the skill(s)/strategy(ies) being tested in each section (N=21)

Skill/strategy	Section 1 p*	Section 1 s**	Section 2 p	Section 2 s	Section 3 p	Section 3 s	Section 4 p	Section 4 s	Section 5 p	Section 5 s
reading carefully for main ideas	12 57%	3	1	2	0	1	1	1	5	6
reading quickly to get the overall idea of a text	3	4	18 86%	2	2	5	1	5	1	1
reading quickly to search for information on main ideas	4	6	2	8	10 48%	6	4	6	2	1
reading quickly to find specific information: words/ numbers/ symbols	2	5	0	2	9	4	15 71%	4	0	3
carefully working out meaning of words from context	0	2	0	0	0	1	0	0	13 62%	5
others (please specify)	0	0	0	0	0	0	0	0	0	0

*: primary focus of the skill/strategy being tested in each section
**: secondary focus (if there is one) of the skill/strategy being tested in each section

6 The a posteriori validation of the prototype AERT version 1

Table 6.6

Proficient students' perceptions of a secondary focus of skill/strategy being tested in each section (N=21)

Secondary focus	Section 1 careful reading (global)	Section 2 skimming	Section 3 search reading	Section 4 scanning	Section 5 careful reading (local)	Total
Expeditious reading strategies	15	12	15	15	5	62
Careful reading skills	5	2	2	1	11	21
Total	20	14	17	16	16	83

Conclusions

The students' retrospection study lends some support to the hypothesised construct validity of the AERT prototype. However, serious questions still remain concerning the students' awareness of the various skills/strategies in the process of reading for different purposes. In real life, training is obviously necessary particularly in the expeditious strategy of search reading. In terms of the methodological procedures employed in this study, some concern must be expressed over the need to train participants in a common metalanguage. Finally we must also repeat our reservations concerning the generalisability of such findings. Only 69 students out of a total of 1068 participated so we must be necessarily tentative in any conclusions we might wish to draw.

We next turn to the introspection study carried out as part of the development of the AERT to see what light it can shed on the skills and strategies being employed to answer test questions.

Student introspection

In order to investigate what skills and strategies students were using in reading the texts and completing the tasks of the AERT test and how the use of these skills and strategies might affect the performance of readers at different levels, an introspection study was carried out as part of the qualitative research for the AERT test validation. We realise that our sample is very limited. Still we feel it is worth reporting because of the light it sheds on the test taking process. It peels off yet another layer and shows us what is actually happening during the test for the limited sample we have managed to collect data from and analyse. The analysis of students' verbal report data provided us with some evidence to support the content validity of the test.

6 The a posteriori validation of the prototype AERT version 1

Data collection

Test material

The AERT prototype version 1 contains 12 texts totalling about 9600 words and 60 items and lasts 144 minutes. Allowing sufficient time for verbal reporting, it would take students about three hours to introspect on the whole test. The fatigue that could be brought about by this lengthy experiment would jeopardise the reliability of the introspection data. Therefore, it was decided that the test should be split into three subtests according to the disciplinary areas of texts, namely, arts, humanities and business (the A/H subtest), science and technology (the S/T subtest), and medical and life sciences (the M/L subtest). Each subtest consists of 4 texts and 20 questions testing four categories of skills/strategies: careful reading at the global level, skimming and search reading, scanning, and careful reading at the local level (see Table 6.7).

A further alternative would have been to divide the whole sample into four groups, each group taking a subtest testing one of the four categories of skills/strategies, but the choice we adopted was considered a better solution because it would allow us to compare one student's performance across the range of skills/strategies. In addition, since students from the three broad discipline areas were used in the experiment and students of one discipline area were divided into three groups for the three subtests (see 6.3.1.3 of the report), this would allow us to investigate the possible background knowledge effect.

In the introspection study, the revised version of AERT prototype version 1 was used. Modifications made to the April trial version of the prototype paper include wording of some items and the time limit of the global level careful reading section, the search reading section and the scanning section

Time limit for each section

Time limits were marginally prolonged to take into account the time needed for the verbal report. Decisions were made on the basis that we should not give students too much time as this might contaminate the nature of the skill/strategy on which that section focused. So the time limit was prolonged from 20 to 22 for the careful global section, 5 to 6 for the skimming section, 7 to 8 for the search reading section, 6 to 7 for the scanning section, and 10 to 12 minutes for the careful local section respectively, making a total of 55 minutes (see Table 6.7 below).

6 *The a posteriori validation of the prototype AERT version 1*

Table 6.7

Test materials and time limits for the introspection study

Section	Skill/Strategy tested	Time Limit (minute)	A/H subtest P*	A/H subtest Q**	S/T subtest P	S/T subtest Q	M/L subtest P	M/L subtest Q
I	careful reading (global)	20+2=22	1	01 – 05	3	11 – 15	2	06 – 10
II	skimming	5+1=6	4	16	6	18	5	17
III	search reading	7+1=8	4	19 – 22	6	27 – 30	5	23 – 26
IV	scanning	6+1=7	9	41 – 45	7	31 – 35	8	36 – 40
V	careful reading (local)	10+2=12	10	46 – 50	11	51 – 55	12	56 – 60
Total (each subtest):	five sections				55 minutes		4 passages and 20 questions	

*: passage number
**: question numbers

Sample

Since the potential AERT test population are the third or fourth year college students, the subjects used in the study were selected from CET-4 or CET-6 certificate holders, who have successfully completed the foundation college English study. As reported in the students' retrospection study, the whole sample consists of 27 Shanghai Jiao Tong University students (as a science and technology group), 18 East China Normal University students (as an arts, humanities and business group), and 24 Shanghai Medical University students (as a medical and life science group). Students in each university were divided into three groups, each introspecting on one subtest, hence 23 students for each subtest (see Table 6.8 below).

Table 6.8

Participants of the introspection study

	A/H students	S/T students	M/L students	Total
A/H subtest	6	9	8	23
S/T subtest	6	9	8	23
M/L subtest	6	9	8	23
Total	18	27	24	69

All 69 tapes were listened to but those which were found to be lacking in clarity or where introspectors did not follow the instructions were eliminated. Considering the time needed for transcribing each tape, we also decided to exclude the tapes of some students who were from the same discipline group doing the same subtest and who achieved the same scores. Finally it was decided that 27 tapes would be transcribed in detail for our analysis. These

6 The a posteriori validation of the prototype AERT version 1

comprise 9 for each subtest, 9 for each level and 9 for each discipline group (see Table 6.9). This offered us a chance to explore if there was any difference between performances of readers at different levels and if there was any effect of background knowledge on students of different disciplines and at different levels.

Table 6. 9

Candidates whose verbal reports were transcribed and their test scores

	Top group			Middle group			Bottom group			Total
A/H subtest	H12	J10	J15	H8	M15	J16	M8	M14	H9	9
(score)	17	16	14	12	12	11	8	6	5	
S/T subtest	H18	J20	H17	M2	J25	M5	M1	J24	H15	9
(score)	18	17	15	12	11	11	6	5	2	
M/L subtest	J9	M22	H6	M20	H2	J1	M16	J3	H4	9
(score)	17	17	15	12	12	10	7	6	4	
Total	9			9			9			27

H: representing candidates from the A/H group
J: representing candidates form the S/T group
M: representing candidates from the M/L group
The number after the letters is candidates' serial number

Data elicitation

Simultaneous verbal reporting was adopted in the study to tap into the students' reading process. The students were required to think aloud onto tapes in the language laboratory while taking the test. Students were allowed to use Chinese if necessary in their verbal reports. Separate cells in the lab prevented interference from neighbouring subjects.

A training session was provided before the experiment to emphasise that they should simply report on what they were doing. First, students were briefed on the purpose of the study. It was made very clear that this was not a test of their proficiency but an investigation into the reading process. This probably relieved some of the subjects enabling them to report as much as possible instead of concentrating only on getting correct answers. Then students were informed of the structure of the test and the time limit for each section. They were also reminded to read the instructions of each section carefully before doing the test. Most important of all we provided a detailed explanation of 'think-out-aloud' by means of a sample tape from the introspection study of the CET reading test which was listened to by all participants.

To eliminate the possible contamination of the introspection data by misunderstanding test instructions, all the instructions were translated into Chinese.

6 The a posteriori validation of the prototype AERT version 1

Since students were not used to this type of experiment, some of them slipped into silence when they concentrated on reading or task completion. So reminder slips with sentences 'Keep reporting please!' or 'Louder please!' were showed to these students individually by experimenters.

Tape transcription

The most difficult and time consuming part of an introspection study is the tape transcription, especially for an introspection of a 55 minute test. To get an idea of how tapes of this experiment could be transcribed, several tapes were listened to before an appropriate transcribing method was decided. From this experience, we designed two tables to facilitate data transcription (see Appendix 6.3.1). In these tables, notes were taken on:

- the text processing and the task completion performance, including: how the text was read, selectively, expeditiously or word-by-word carefully; what contributory reading monitoring skills or strategies were used in reading the text, e.g., translation, re-reading, reading topic sentences, making use of sub-titles, etc.; item responses, i.e., whether the item was correctly answered; and how a correct answer or a wrong answer was arrived at;
- typical examples of the expected performance of using a particular skill/strategy;
- examples of the unexpected performance of text processing and task completion;
- the general impression of the student's use of background knowledge, language competence and use of skills/strategies.

Out of the 27 tapes we transcribed, verbal reports of the twelve students were cited as typical examples of performance. These constituted a sample of four from each level (top, middle and bottom), four from each subject discipline (A/H, S/T and M/L) and four taking each subtest (A/H, S/T and M/L) (see Table 6.10 below). Since the four students from the high group achieved the highest scores (one 18 and three 17 out of the total 20), the four from the middle group achieved typical middle scores (two 11 and two 12) and the four from the bottom group achieved typical low scores (one 5 and three 6), it was hoped that these twelve reports would provide us with most typical examples of performance in line with the test designers' purpose of reading and performance not in line with the test designers' purpose of reading (see also Appendix 6.3.2 for the records of these twelve candidates).

6 The a posteriori validation of the prototype AERT version 1

Table 6.10

Twelve candidates whose verbal reports were cited in describing the AERT test taking performance

	Top group		Middle group		Bottom group		Total
A/H subtest (score)	H12 17			J16 11	M14 6	H9 5	4
S/T subtest (score)	H18 18	J20 17	M2 12	J25 11	M1 6		4
M/L subtest (score)		M22 17	H2 12		J3 6		4
Total	4		4		4		12

We realise that the sample, though carefully selected, is very limited so it is not possible to extrapolate too much from the resulting data. In quantitative studies, samples are in most cases randomly selected, and thus quantitative data lend themselves better to stringent statistical analysis and we are able to generalise to some degree about the result. However, it is very difficult for a qualitative study to achieve this randomness of sampling. Therefore, we are less able to extrapolate from a qualitative data analysis, in other words, this type of analysis is informative and often illuminative but not definitive.

Data analysis

Description of students' performance

From the 27 tapes that were transcribed, typical performances which were in line with the test designers' purpose of reading in each section of the test and the performances which were not in line with the test designers' purpose of reading were summarised and one or several examples from the twelve candidates are provided below to illustrate the performance being described.

Section 1: Careful reading for EXMI and IPROP

Typical performance in line with the purpose of reading carefully for EXMI and IPROP
In this section, all candidates whose reports were transcribed seemed to be reading carefully, that is, word by word sequential processing of the text. Some read questions before they started to read the text and thus the text was read with questions in mind. While reading the text, possible areas for answering the questions were marked or noted. There were also some students who started with a quick overview of the text and then went on to read questions. Having achieved some idea of both the text and the questions, the text was read again more carefully and relevant parts of the text were noted

6 The a posteriori validation of the prototype AERT version 1

for answering the questions. Reading monitoring skills involved in the process include mainly translation and re-reading.

The difference between the top and bottom group readers in their performance of careful reading of the text was found mainly in the speed of text processing. Top group candidates were able to read the text carefully but at a speed considerably faster and with far fewer pauses than the bottom group, who were plodding through the text word by word. While the top group could finish reading the text and complete the 5 items in 10 minutes (half the time limit), the bottom group were often found to be unable to finish the text and the tasks within the time limit. Monitoring skills were observed to have been used less frequently by the bottom group than by the top or the middle group.

In task completion, understanding explicitly stated main ideas seems to be a skill automatically employed by all readers once the reading process starts. Most students were observed to be able to look for relevant parts of the text for answering EXMI questions, although the bottom group sometimes could not arrive at the right part of the text or failed to understand the text even though the question area was correctly located. More time was spent on IPROP items than on EXMI items. Students were observed to pause for relatively longer times at the located part of the text, reading, re-reading and translating occasionally. This was interpreted as the process when inferences were taking place.

The differences between the top and bottom groups in their performance of task completion in this section lie in the time spent on an item and their confidence in their answers. The top group could locate relevant information fairly quickly and put down their answers confidently. By contrast, it took bottom group readers much longer to locate the question areas and they often hesitated for a long time before they put down the answers.

Example: Question 11 – EXMI (H18: 18 points)
The candidate read the text carefully but at a very fast speed. The process of reading is very smooth with no translation, no re-reading and very few pauses. There seem to be no unknown words in the text for her. After the first reading of the text, which was completed in 6 minutes, she read the five questions carefully and went back to locate answers for each question in the text. Question 11 asks about the ultimate wish of some scientists working on the 5th generation computers. Making use of the topic '5th generation computers' (she reported looking for the 5th generation computers), she quickly located the answer in the last sentence of paragraph 6. Then both the question and the sentence were read again carefully to make sure the sentence answers the question.

6 The a posteriori validation of the prototype AERT version 1

Performance NOT in line with the purpose of reading carefully for EXMI and IPROP
There are students who did not read the text from beginning to end carefully, instead, they read the first question and then went back to the first several paragraphs of the text to look for the answer. When they completed the first item, they went to the second question and looked for the answer in the following several paragraphs of the text. The text was not read once as a continued discourse for the general discourse topic and main ideas. This is not authentic reading, but typical test specific reading, which was not the type of reading expected to be performed in this section of the test.

In task completion, some students were observed to have particular difficulty in making inferences while they had no difficulty in understanding explicitly stated main ideas. They could get the first two EXMI items correct but the following three IPROP items (based on the same text) were answered incorrectly. There were examples where relevant parts of the text were located for an IPROP item but the student failed to answer the question because only the surface meaning of the text was comprehended. There were also examples where the reader comprehended the surface meaning of one part of the text but failed to grasp the meaning implied in the next part of the text where transition of the argument was clearly indicated by the discourse marker 'however'.

Example 1: Passage 3 (J25: 11 points)
The student read the first question and then went to the text looking for the answer. When he located the answer in the 6th paragraph, he went on with the second question and looked for the answer in the following several paragraphs of the text. The whole text had not been read once continuously for a general idea, and he failed two IPROP items.

Example 2: Question 15 – IPROP (J20: 17 points)
This is a top group candidate who correctly answered the other two IPROP items in the section but failed Question 15. The question asks readers to judge the statement that 'The author of the passage concludes that computers are likely to beat humans at chess.' Paragraph 10 of the text tells us that some tasks of human experts could be readily accomplished by a higher-powered computer. But the text went on in paragraph 11 to argue that we are now convinced that most expertise depends on unique human qualities that can never be mimicked by a machine. The candidate read paragraph 10 carefully and made the judgment that the statement was true. He failed to notice the transition of the argument which was clearly indicated by the discourse marker 'however' at the beginning of paragraph 11.

6 The a posteriori validation of the prototype AERT version 1

Section 2: Skimming

Typical performance in line with the purpose of skimming
The strategy of skimming was found to have the most obvious effect on the performance of middle group readers, who did not have enough time to read the text carefully. The test was so designed that test takers would only identify the discourse topic of the text within the time limit through using skimming. The typical performance was observed to be reading the title, and the first and the last paragraphs carefully. If time permitted, the first one or two sentences of each paragraph were also read to confirm the idea they got from reading the opening and concluding paragraphs.

Example: Passage 4 (Question 16) – skimming (J16: 11 points)
The candidate read the title carefully and tried hard to understand the meaning of the word 'apart' in the title. Then he read the first and the last paragraphs for 2 minutes after which he reported to have got some idea of the text. But since he had sufficient time, he quickly moved on to the first one or two sentences of the remaining paragraphs for about 2 minutes to confirm the idea. He spent the remaining 1.5 minutes on the summarising sentence.

Performance NOT in line with the purpose of skimming
Some readers were unaware of the strategy and read the text carefully as they did in the first careful reading section. They stopped whenever they felt they had got the idea or when time did not allow them to go further. This type of performance often resulted in the middle and bottom group readers' failure to arrive at the summarising sentence within the time limit.

By contrast, taking advantage of their fast reading speed, some top group readers performed speeded careful reading with occasional skipping of details (e.g., numbers, names, examples etc.). This performance, though not wholly in line with the purpose of reading in this part of the test, often led to top group readers' satisfactory fulfilment of the task.

Example 1: Passage 6 (Question 18) – skimming (H18: 18 points)
The student is a linguistically very proficient reader, whose careful word by word reading is extremely fast. The strategy of skimming seems unnecessary for her in this section because she finished reading the text in 4.5 minutes. Her comprehension of the text is clear from her summarising sentence which covered the major points of the text.

Example 2: Passage 6 (Question 18) – skimming (M1: 6 points)
The student read the passage from the very beginning, slowly, carefully, skipping only those unknown words and translating quite a lot. He only managed to finish less than half of the text within the time limit and had no time for completing the summarising sentence. Only a short phrase was provided, which has unclear meaning and is irrelevant to the text.

6 The a posteriori validation of the prototype AERT version 1

Section 3: Search reading

Typical performance in line with the purpose of search reading
The typical performance in this section was observed to be reading the questions before the text was processed. With the topic of one question in mind, the reader went to the text to search for relevant information. Often one or two sentences in each paragraph were read to determine its relevance. When a relevant paragraph was located, it was read more carefully before the answer was arrived at.

Example: Question 24 – search reading (H2: 12 points)
The question asks about the solution for biodegradable polymer breaking into large pieces in drug delivery. The candidate looked for information in the text using the idea of limitations of biodegradable polymer, which were located in paragraph 8 and 9. He then read the two paragraphs carefully. In paragraph 9, he found the information that 'many biodegradable polymers can crumble suddenly into chunks'. He immediately reported that this was the limitation of the biodegradable polymer because he comprehended 'crumble suddenly into chunks' as the same idea as 'break into large pieces'. The candidate went on to read the following sentence, which tells us that the research group overcame the problem using a polymer that is water soluble. The candidate reported that he found the answer.

Performance NOT in line with the purpose of search reading
In the questionnaire survey to candidates carried out after the October main trial, search reading was perceived as the strategy that has received least training (see 5.2.2 for the questionnaire data analysis). In this introspection study, search reading was found indeed to constitute a big problem for some of the middle group and most of bottom group candidates.

It was noticed these students were either unaware of the strategy or not sure how to search read. They reported having difficulty locating answers for items in this section of the test. Since search reading items were deliberately worded to avoid exact matching of words in the question with those in the text, the decision on the relevance of a part of the text would have to be based on the words or phrases in the same semantic field. These candidates were observed simply trying to match words in the questions with those in the text. This led to their failure in answering search reading questions. Failure of some middle group candidates was also found sometimes to be caused by a lack of careful reading when the relevant part of the text was located.

One other type of performance in this section was not expected by the test developers. Since search reading was based on the same passage as the one that had just been skimmed, the performance of search reading by the top group students was often contaminated by the more than necessary amount of text covered in the skimming section. Some top group students were observed

6 The a posteriori validation of the prototype AERT version 1

to be able to answer the search reading questions using their memory of what had been read in the skimming section without referring back to the passage. So they did not need to search for information in this section.

Example 1: Questions 27 – 30 – search reading (J20: 17 points)
This is a top group candidate, who is linguistically very competent. He read passage 6 in a speeded careful reading manner for 5 minutes in the skimming section, from which he derived a good summarising sentence. In the search reading section, he read the questions first and then he started to read the text from the very beginning quickly but word by word. When he got to paragraph 3, he arrived at the answer for Question 27. Key words in the questions were born in mind while he was reading the text. So when he got to paragraphs 13 and 14, which talk about 'gene banks', he slowed down and answered Question 29. Therefore, although the student got all the four search reading items correct, it was not achieved through selective search reading as intended by the test developers.

Example 2: Questions 19 – 21: search reading (M14: 6 points)
This is an example of candidates who are unable to search for information in the text or who are employing the wrong strategy, i.e., scanning. Questions 19 to 21 ask about the three ways in which working women in Japan are discriminated against in their jobs. Instead of searching with the topic of 'discrimination in jobs' in mind, the student was looking for the word 'discrimination'. But he found only 'sexual discrimination in education' in paragraph 7 and without further reading he put this down as an answer. He actually reported in the study that it was very difficult to find the answers for items in this section because no words could be matched.

Example 3: Question 24 – search reading (J3: 6 points)
This is the same question as the one we cited in the typical search reading example by candidate H2. The question asks about the solution for the limitation of biodegradable polymer breaking into large pieces in drug delivery. Using the topic of 'biodegradable polymer', the student correctly located the answer in paragraphs 8 and 9. However, the wording in the question has been deliberately paraphrased to avoid direct matching with that in the text and the student had no time left in this section to read the two paragraphs carefully, so she had to give up and left the question unanswered.

Section 4: Scanning

Typical performance in line with the purpose of scanning
Time is an important factor determining the performance in the section. Even top group students must scan otherwise they would be short of time for the last one or two questions. Passages were read more selectively than in the search reading section. Comprehension was not needed for answering questions in this section. As long as one or several words in a question were

6 The a posteriori validation of the prototype AERT version 1

matched with those in the text, correct answers would be arrived at. The speed of matching by top group readers was noticeably faster than both middle group and bottom group ones. Failure in this section was caused either by the unawareness of the strategy for all the three groups or by the slow scanning speed for the middle or bottom group.

Example 1: Questions 31 – 35 – scanning (M2: 12 points)
The student read the five questions quickly first. Without reading the text, he started with the first question by looking for 'biological materials' in the text. He quickly located them in paragraph 3 and got the answer. For the other four items, he matched 'nacre, mother of pearl', 'wood, load-bearing', 'synthetic nacre' and 'turbine blades' with those in the text and got the answers quickly. He processed this text more selectively than the text in the search reading section.

Example 2: Questions 41– 45 – scanning (J16: 11 points)
The candidate made good use of subtitles for items in this section. For each question, he reported to be looking for the information in a section under a particular subtitle. Question 41, for example, asks 'Without advertising you cannot exercise complete control over (blank).' He reported that this should be located in the paragraph under the subtitle 'Why advertise?' He read the first paragraph under that subtitle and matched the words 'exercise complete control over' and arrived at the key quickly.

Performance NOT in line with the purpose of reading
Some candidates were observed to be reading the text in a careful manner. However, unlike the search reading section where some top group readers could get the answers not by search reading, in the scanning section, even top group candidates had to scan in order to get all the five items. If they read carefully they could not finish all the items. This is because a) the text in the search reading section was based on the same one as the text in the skimming section whereas the text in the scanning section was a new one; b) the time limit is one minute shorter in the scanning section than the search reading section and c) there are 5 questions in the scanning section but only 4 in the search reading section. So in this section, candidates either got the answers through scanning or failed at least the last two items due to insufficient time.

Example: Questions 36 – 40 – scanning (M22: 17 points)
This is a top group candidate, linguistically very competent. He got 17 out of 20 but he failed two scanning items because he did not use the strategy properly. In the scanning section, he read the questions first and then started to read the text word by word quickly with a lot of translation, suggesting his good comprehension. He slowed down at places where he felt an answer might be. He read these parts slowly and got the answers for Question 36 after he finished paragraph 3, Question 37 from paragraph 4 and Question 38 from

6 The a posteriori validation of the prototype AERT version 1

paragraph 5. But there was no time left for Questions 39 and 40. Therefore, though proficient, he failed on the last two items of this section.

Section 5: Careful reading for understanding lexical meaning

Typical performance in line with the purpose of reading carefully for understanding lexical meaning

All students seemed to be aware of the necessity for careful reading in order to complete the tasks in this section. Most of them read the text carefully from beginning to the end. Top group students were often able to fill in some of the blanks during this first reading. They were also observed to hesitate between the pair of words designed for each blank (one distractor and the other key) and tried to make decisions on one of the two. Further reading was for the purpose of confirming the answers.

The most popular means reported by introspectors to eliminate distractors employed in this section was to try to identify which words in the list exhibited the correct part of speech. This, however, did not help eliminate the intended distractor which was deliberately chosen to meet the requirement of the correct part of speech for the blank. Therefore, the intended distractor could only be eliminated through comprehension of the context where the word was deleted.

Example: Questions 46 – 50 – ILEX (H12: 17 points)
The student read the text carefully in 3.5 minutes concentrating on the comprehension of the text instead of filling in the blanks. Then she returned to the blanks and read one or two sentences around each blank before making decisions. For Question 46, she hesitated between the pair of words 'denounced' and 'approved', which were designed to be the distractor and the key for this item. When she read the whole paragraph and the following one, she rejected 'denounced' confidently.

Performance NOT in line with the purpose of reading carefully for understanding lexical meanings

Bottom group students were also observed to be reading the passage carefully and paused for a long time where there was a blank. However, they failed the items in this section because a) they did not understand the context in the text; and/or b) words in the bank (either distractors or keys) were unknown words. They were observed to be playing a guessing game trying randomly (or sometimes, grammatically appropriate) words in the bank one by one before making a decision.

Example: Questions 46 – 50: ILEX (H9: 5 points)
This student read the text carefully word by word at a very slow speed and tried to fill in the blanks in this first reading. He tried every word that was correct in terms of the part of speech for each blank. For Question 48, for example, the key is 'unanimity'. He knew it must be a noun for this blank, so

6 The a posteriori validation of the prototype AERT version 1

he tried 'evidence, sensitivity, source, unanimity' before he made a wrong guess of 'sensitivity'.

The use of skills/strategies and the performance on the test tasks

In addition to the description of students' performance in text processing and task completion, the data from the 27 verbal reports were also quantified in terms of the number of items that were:
- correctly answered using the expected skill/strategy – CES
- correctly answered using the unexpected skill/strategy – CUES
- incorrectly answered using the expected skill/strategy – WES
- incorrectly answered using the unexpected skill/strategy – WUES

The detailed record of each candidate is included in Appendix 6.3.3. The following two tables (Table 6.11 and 6.12) summarise the results of the analysis.

Table 6.11

Use of skills/strategies and item responses (for the whole sample)

Section (items)		For the whole sample N=27			
		CES	CUES	WES	WUES
EXMI	2 items n=54	39	0	13	2
IPROP	3 items n=81	32	0	12	37
SKIM	1 item n=27	7	8	4	8
SEARCH	4 items n=108	34	27	14	33
SCAN	5 items n*=135	66	23	15	29
ILEX	5 items n**=135	58	4	29	42
Total	20 items n=540	236	62	87	151

*: including 2 cases of wrong answers through means not clear to us
**: including 2 cases of wrong answers through means not clear to us

6 The a posteriori validation of the prototype AERT version 1

Table 6.12

**Use of skills/strategies and item responses
(for groups at the three levels)**

Section (items)		TOP GROUP* From 14 to 18 points N=9				MIDDLE GROUP** From 10 to 12 points N=9				BOTTOM GROUP From 2 to 8 points N=9			
		CES	CUES	WES	WUES	CES	CUES	WES	WUES	CES	CUES	WES	WUES
EXMI	2 items n=54	15	0	3	0	16	0	2	0	8	0	8	2
IPROP	3 items n=81	21	0	4	2	9	0	6	12	2	0	2	23
SKIM	1 item n=27	3	6	0	0	3	2	1	3	1	0	3	5
SEARCH	4 items n=108	16	16	3	1	14	5	7	10	4	6	4	22
SCAN*	5 items n=135	29	10	3	3	30	3	8	2	7	10	4	24
ILEX**	5 items n=135	29	1	10	4	21	0	10	13	8	3	9	25
Total	20 items n=540	113	33	23	10	93	10	34	40	30	19	30	101

*: including 2 cases of wrong answer through means not clear to us.
**: including 2 cases of wrong answers through means not clear to us.

From Table 6.11, it can be seen that 52 (39 + 13) out of 54 answers to the EXMI items in the global level careful reading section were completed using the expected skill. The only exceptional case was a linguistically extremely poor student who has no comprehension of the text at all and had to guess the answers to the two EXMI items.

However, only about half of the IPROP items (32 + 12 = 44 items, out of 81) were completed using the expected skill. From Table 6.12, it is clear that bottom group students have particular difficulty in making inferences. For the 9 bottom group students (27 IPROP items), 23 were not completed using the expected skill of inferring propositional meanings from the context. They failed to understand even the surface meanings, so they were guessing for these IPROP items.

Table 6.11 shows that out of the total 27 skimming item answers, 8 were correctly answered but not through the use of skimming strategy. From Table 6.12, we can see that 6 were from top group readers. This confirms the idea that the amount of the text covered in the skimming section by top group students was more than we expected because of their fast reading speed.

The search reading strategy was used in a similar way to that of skimming. Table 6.12 tells us clearly that the use of the search reading strategy by top group students was to some degree contaminated by more than the expected amount of the text covered in the skimming section. For the 9 top group students (36 search reading items), 16 were correctly answered through careful not through search reading.

6 The a posteriori validation of the prototype AERT version 1

In the scanning section, by contrast, the correct use of the strategy has an obvious effect on the successful completion of the items. Out of a total of 89 correct answers, only 23 were arrived at through means other than scanning. For middle group students, the effect is clearer. Table 6.12 tells us that for the 9 middle group readers (45 scanning answers), only 3 were arrived at successfully through means other than scanning.

In the local level careful reading section, bottom group students failed to arrive at correct answers because their linguistic proficiency is so poor that they either could not understand the context or they did not know the words in the bank. In both cases, the skill of understanding lexical meaning from the context cannot be employed. From Table 6.12, we can see that out of the 45 answers to ILEX items for the bottom group of 9 candidates, only 8 were correctly answered through the use of the skill of inferring lexical meanings from the context.

Conclusions

The introspection study offered us a chance to look closely into the process of taking the AERT test by students of different levels and from different disciplinary backgrounds. Although the results could not demonstrate the construct being tested in the AERT as clearly as the quantitative data, the validity of the test was evidenced to some degree in the following senses:

1. The description of the typical performances in each section of the test suggests that there are separable and different skills and strategies, which can be employed to achieve different purposes of reading. The use of the skills/strategies in the careful global, careful local and expeditious local sections shows this clearly. The picture is more mixed in the skimming and search reading sections particularly at top and bottom levels owing largely to their either above average or below average linguistic proficiency.
2. Intended skills and strategies on the part of test developers seem to match the performance of middle group readers, i.e., employment of the expected skills/strategies was seen most often in middle group students' performance in the test, noticeably in the expeditious reading sections.
3. Top group readers often out-perform what was expected by test designers in terms of the amount of the text covered in the time available because of their very fast speed of text processing. However, if the time limit for the expeditious global part of the test was set with this group of readers in mind, i.e., should this group of readers be obliged to read expeditiously for main ideas, then this would be placing unfair demands on the middle group. It looks as though highly competent readers, through sheer speed of reading, or highly developed automaticity of word recognition, can

6 The a posteriori validation of the prototype AERT version 1

process a large amount of text and do not need to be as selective in the time available. They constitute in fact a new category of fast careful readers.
4. Bottom group students failed the test for two reasons. First, some of them were unaware of different skills/strategies and were reading carefully throughout the five sections of the test. Second, some of them were aware of the importance of skills/strategies but their poor linguistic proficiency hampered the proper employment of skills/strategies, suggesting a linguistic threshold for the effectiveness of reading skills and strategies.
5. Background knowledge was not found to have an effect on the performance of the three subtests by these students. A few top group medical science students who did the medical subtest were found to be using their medical knowledge to further explain the text, but this was not tested by the items. A few bottom group students tended to use their background knowledge in answering questions on the text on Japanese women, which is a very familiar topic. But they failed these questions because items could only be answered from information in the text.
6. Overall using introspection as a tool for test development has a number of limitations. First, the time needed for data transcription is very long. In this study, the whole transcription process took the research group more than 10 days. Secondly, the sampling is very difficult. The size and the randomness of the sample is limited by the lengthy data collection and transcription process. The representativeness of the sample is difficult to predict before the data is transcribed. Thirdly, the reliability of the data depends largely on the willingness to cooperate on the part of the informants. Fourthly, there exists the possible contamination of the employment of skills/strategies from the use of test taking strategies by test takers in an attempt to arrive at correct answers. However, introspection is the only method available to find out what test takers are actually doing in taking the test. Therefore, efforts need to be made to deal with these problems so as to improve the validity and reliability of the qualitative data available to the test developers.

7 Conclusions and recommendations

Conclusions

There is evidence in both the *a priori* and *a posteriori* validation of the AERT to support the case for maintaining separate testing of the skills in the four parts of the test. The *a priori* studies, the needs analysis, the teaching and test task analyses all evidence the separability of reading skills/strategies for teaching and testing purposes. The theoretical literature on processing supports a componential view of reading as does the empirical research into the divisibility of reading.

The *a posteriori* empirical studies lend further support to a componential view of reading. Both the factor analysis and the cross tabulations in the first and second trials indicate the separable nature of these skills/strategies. The retrospection data and the introspection data offer further support for this position. The introspection data show that for most of the medium level students and above in our study different styles of reading are promoted in accordance with the different sections of the test. The weakest students, however, appear to have only one style, of slow careful reading whatever the skill/strategy being tested.

This has important ramifications for the ways scores should be reported in the AERT. Spolsky (1994) has succinctly adumbrated the complex and multidimensional nature of comprehension and stressed the need for full description in reporting results as against a single grade or score. He argues (1995:151)

> *...we will need to design and use a variety of reading assessment procedures to allow us to report on a variety of aspects of the student's ability to understand, and to establish some systematic way of reporting the results on all of them. The differences the student shows across this range of results will inform us at least as much as will the result of adding them together. However good our tests are, a single score will always mislead.*

Given the likelihood that different skills and strategies can be taught and then tested through the AERT, then some form of profiling of these abilities is essential rather than collapsing scores into a single score or grade for reporting purposes.

7 Conclusions and recommendations

What is to be done? Recommendations

1. There is still more work to be done in improving the way the test is administered. We need to find a way of ensuring that candidates spend an equal amount of time on each passage in each section. This will enable us to further investigate the componentiality issue. The global versus local dimension is apparent in our data set with candidates doing significantly better on the former. There is also some evidence to suggest that candidates do not perform as well on the expeditious as against the careful reading sections of the test.

    However, the data in both trials suggest that the lack of time spent on the third passage in each of the first three sections has unintended effects. When we remove the items set on the third passage in each section, the factor analyses carried out on the first two passages show a clear set of loadings which neatly mirror the structure of the test (Appendix 5 2.22). To operationalise our specification even more faithfully we might give more time to the first careful reading section to ensure that all candidates have sufficient time to demonstrate their ability in this. The greatest challenge lies in testing the expeditious strategies of skimming, search reading and scanning (Sections 2 through 4). We have to find ways of more strictly controlling the time spent on each passage to maintain the integrity of the strategy being tested. At the moment too much time is spent on the first two out of the three passages making these more like tests of careful reading.

2. Consideration might be given to cutting down the size of the test to 40 items. On the whole we have been successful in our attempts to reduce the background knowledge effect by using passages of medium to low subject specificity and high to medium topic familiarity. We could improve on this by eliminating 4 passages that show a slight background knowledge effect according to the ANOVA analyses we carried out (see Appendix 5.2.23 – 31). We could take out TOTCARE 3 (items 11 – 15), TOTSKCH 1 items 16, 19 – 22, TOTSCAN 1 (items 31 – 35) and TOTLEXI3 (items 56 – 60).

    The excisions would only slightly reduce the alphas for the overall test and the 4 parts.

Overall	.80 (40 items)	.85 (60 items)
Part 1	.60 (10 items 1 – 10)	.65 (15 items)
Part 2	.62 (10 items 17,18, 23 – 30)	.65 (15 items)
Part 3	.66 (10 items 36 – 45)	.69 (15 items)
Part 4	.55 (10 items 46 – 55)	.65 (15 items)

    This strategy would retain the highest set of alphas for a 40 item test (see Appendix 5.2.21). The reduction in test size would have many benefits. The biggest advantages would accrue in terms of practicality. It would reduce the test time and marking by a third and substantially reduce costs.

7 Conclusions and recommendations

It might also make it easier to control the time spent on each passage within the sections. It opens up the possibility of collecting answer sheets passage by passage. The first and second passage in each section might also be printed in two different colours and so facilitate closer control of test taking by the invigilators.

In terms of validity reducing the test in this way would be the best scenario. It means that we have a reading test with three Arts (passages 1, 9 and 10), two Science (passages 6 and 11) and three Life Science passages (passages 2,5,8). In seven out of eight of these passages, the ANOVA analyses show that there was no significant difference in the performance of the three discipline groups on the items set on that passage. In the case of the eighth passage the difference is only .38 of a mark. These passages are face valid in that they have been perceived as belonging to a discipline area but accessible to all according to the qualitative data in the feed back questionnaire.

The alternative scenario of taking out just the Life Science passages (2, 5, 8) has some merit. Overall there is no significant difference in the performance of the test population on the items set on the Arts and Science passages. The easier Life Science items occasion a significant difference with the Arts and Science items. If we took out the Life Science passages, only two of the remaining passages (1 and 4) would exhibit significant differences between the discipline groups on the items set. Similar positive points accrue as in the first scenario with regard to time and cost.

However, the real problem with the second scenario is that the passages would be broadly speaking Arts and Physical Sciences. The life scientists might feel aggrieved. In addition the whole test population has performed better on the Life Science passages and the cross tabulation data clearly show that in this test population many more would fail the test if the Life Science passages were removed.

Despite all the care we took at the *a priori* validation stage, it was not possible to produce parallel tests. If the Life Scientists took their own twenty items and the other groups their own it would be inequitable. One cannot predict the difficulty level of performance tests in advance. We had tried to select appropriate texts and to write valid items in line with the systematic procedures outlined in this work. It would seem unfortunate to make the test more difficult at a stroke by eliminating all the Life Science passages. It is a further argument for all students to take the same test irrespective of background discipline, with the proviso that test developers have empirically demonstrated that they have been able to minimalise the effect of background knowledge.

7 Conclusions and recommendations

On balance, therefore, we would recommend scenario one: eliminating the four passages where there is a slight difference in the scores attributable to disciplines and establishing a forty-item test to be taken by all.

3. It is essential that the work already begun on preparing a second version of the test is continued and when this is available it might be released as a practice test or as part of a training manual for the test.
4. To ensure the parallelness of future versions a baseline measure must be established through a random sampling on a wider test population. Only in this way will statistical equating of future versions of the AERT be possible.
5. The AERT test in both the first and second trials clearly demonstrates that a large number of students in Chinese Universities are not yet meeting the requirements of the syllabus. They are not yet able to process English texts carefully let alone expeditiously.

On the positive side the development of the AERT has led to a clear specification of what is involved in EAP reading both in terms of activities and in terms of the performance conditions that must be addressed in text selection. This is a major step forward and it should facilitate the preparation of courses materials for teaching reading and enhance the mediational advice that can be provided by teachers to their students. The AERT is a blueprint for the future development of academic reading in English in China.

It is our view that such development should be cross disciplinary as experience in other countries round the world suggests that in training teachers to teach reading and to develop materials or tests efficiently the focus needs to be generic. The greatest potential for improvement at the national level lies in developing core courses and materials for all. Preparing a course or materials for a very specific discipline is extremely time consuming and of no advantage to anybody outside of that discipline. Experience of pre and in-sessional English courses at tertiary level in many countries supports an EAP as against an ESP approach.

This research study has shown how we can develop a specification of EAP reading skills and strategies for all Chinese undergraduates at least in terms of common reading activities and categories of description for performance conditions. Most crucially we have developed a valid and reliable EAP reading test which is fair to all students and discriminates against nobody whatever their discipline. The AERT has the potential to provide useful and usable information on a person's ability to read in English for different purposes in an academic setting.

References

Adkins, A. and McKean, I. (1983) *Text to Note – Study Skills for Advanced Learners*. London: Edward Arnold (Publisher) Ltd.

Alderson, J. C. (1990a) Testing reading comprehension skills (part one). *Reading in a Foreign Language* 6: 425–38.

Alderson, J. C. (1990b) Testing reading comprehension skills: getting students to talk about taking a reading test (part two). *Reading in a Foreign Language* 7: 465 – 503.

Anderson, N. J., Bachman, L., Perkins, K. and Cohen, A. (1991) An exploratory study into the construct validity of a reading comprehension test: triangulation of data sources. *Language Testing* 8: 41 – 66.

Arnaudet, M. L. and Barrett, M. E. (1984) *Approaches to Academic Reading and Writing*. Washington DC: Prentice-Hall, Inc.

Bachman, L. F., Vanniarjan, A. K. S. and Lynch, B. (1988) Tasks and ability analysis as a basis for examining content and construct comparability in two EFL proficiency batteries. *Language Testing* 5: 128 – 59.

Barr, P., Clegg, C. and Wallace, C. (1981) *Advanced Reading Skills*. London: Longman.

Barr, R., Kamil, M. L., Mosenthal, P. and Pearson, P. D. (eds.) (1991) *Handbook of Reading Research* Vol II. New York: Longman.

Berg, P. C. (1973) Evaluating reading abilities. In McGinitie, W. H. (ed.): 27 – 34.

Berkoff, N. A. (1979) Reading skills in extended discourse in English as a Foreign Language. *Journal of Research in Reading*. 2/2: 95 – 107.

Bernhardt, E. B. (1991a) *Reading Development in Second Language: Theoretical, Empirical and Classroom Perspectives*. New Jersey: Ablex Publishing Corporation.

Bernhardt, E. B. (1991b) A psycholinguistic perspective on Second Language literacy. In Hulstijn, J. H. and Matter, J. F. :31 – 44.

British Council. (1980) *Reading and Thinking in English*. Oxford University Press.

Brutten, S. R., Perkins, K. and Upshur, J. A. (1991) Measuring growth in ESL reading. *Paper presented at the 13th Annual Language Testing Research Colloquium*. Princeton, N J.

Carrell, P. L. (1984) The effects of rhetorical organisation on ESL readers. *TESOL Quarterly* 18: 441 – 69.

References

Carver, R. P. (1992) What do standardized tests of reading comprehension measure in terms of efficiency, accuracy and rate? *Reading Research Quarterly* 27: 347 – 59.

Chikalanga I. W. (1990) *Inferencing in the Reading Process*. Unpublished PhD thesis. University of Reading.

Chikalanga, I. W. (1992) A suggested taxonomy of inferences for the reading teacher. *Reading in a Foreign Language* 8: 697 – 710.

Clapham, C. (1994) *The Effect of Background Knowledge on EAP Reading Test Performance*. Unpublished PhD thesis. Lancaster University.

Clapham, C. (1996) *The Development of IELTS: A study of the effect of background knowledge on reading comprehension*. Cambridge: Cambridge University Press.

Coady, J. (1979) A psycholinguistic model of the ESL reader. In Mackay, R. *et al.* (eds.): 5 – 12.

Davis, F. B. (1944) Fundamental factors of comprehension in reading. *Psychometrika* 9: 185 – 97.

Davis, F. B. (1968) Research in comprehension in reading. *Reading Research Quarterly* 3: 499 – 545.

Davis, F. B. (1972) Psychometric research on comprehension in reading. *Reading Research Quarterly* 7: 628 – 78.

Dornic, S. (ed.) (1977) *Attention and Performance VI*. New York: Academic Press.

Drahozal, E. C. and Hanna, G. S. (1979) Reading comprehension subscores: pretty bottles for ordinary wine. *Journal of Reading* 21/5: 416 – 20.

Faerch, C. and Kasper, G. (ed.) (1987) *Introspection in Second language Research*. Multilingual Matters Ltd. England.

Farr, R. C. (1968) The convergent and discriminant validity of several upper level reading tests. *Yearbook of the National Reading Conference* 17: 181 – 91.

Farr, R. C., Carey, R. and Tone, B. (1986) Recent theory and research into the reading process: implications for reading assessment. In Orasanu, J. (ed.): 134 – 49.

Foll, D. (1990) *Contrasts: Developing Awareness*. London: Longman.

Fries, C. C. (1962) *Linguistics and Reading*. New York: Holt, Rinehart and Winston.

Glendinning, E. and Holmstrom, B. (1992) *Study Reading – A Course in Reading Skills for Academic Purpose*. Cambridge: Cambridge University Press.

Goodman, K. S. (1967) Reading: a psycholinguistic guessing game. *Journal of the Reading Specialist* 6: 126 – 35.

Gough, P. B. (1972) One second of reading. In Kavanagh and Mattingly (eds.): 331 – 58.

References

Gough, P. B. and Tunmer, W. E. (1986) Decoding, reading and reading disability. *Remedial and Special Education* 7: 6 – 10.

Grabe, W. (1991) Current developments in second language reading research. *TESOL Quarterly* 25: 375 – 406.

Greenall, S. and Pye, D. (1994) *Reading 4*. Cambridge: Cambridge University Press.

Greenall, S. and Swan, M. (1986) *Effective Reading-reading Skills for Advanced Students*. Cambridge: Cambridge University Press.

Grellet, F. (1981) *Developing Reading Skills*. Cambridge: Cambridge University Press.

Grotjahn, R. (1987) On the methodological basis of introspective methods. In Faerch, C. and Kasper, G. (ed.): 54 – 81.

Guthrie, J. T. (ed.) (1977) *Cognition, Curriculum, and Comprehension*. Newark, Delaware: International Reading Association.

Guthrie, J. T. and Kirsch, I. S. (1987) Distinctions between reading comprehension and locating information in text. *Journal of Educational Psychology* 79: 220–97.

Harrison, M. (1994) *Key Reading Skills for CAE*. Cambridge: Cambridge University Press

Hoover, W. A. and Tunmer, W. E. (1993) The components of reading. In Thompson, J. B. *et al.*: 1 – 19.

Hulstijn, J. H. and Matter, J. F. (eds.) (1991) Reading in two languages. *AILA Review* 8. Amsterdam.

Just, M. A. and Carpenter, P. A. (1980) A theory of reading: from eye fixation to comprehension. *Psychological Review* 87: 329 – 54.

Just, M. A. and Carpenter, P. A. (1987) *The Psychology of Reading and Language Comprehension*. Boston, Mass.: Allyn and Bacon.

Kaplan, R. B. and Shaw, P. A. (1983) *Exploring Academic Discourse: A textbook for Advanced Level ESL Reading and Writing Students*. Massachusetts: Newbury House Publishers, Inc.

Kavanagh, F. J. and Mattingly, G. (eds.) (1972) *Language by Ear and by Eye*. Cambridge, Mass: MIT Press.

Khalifa, H. (1997) *A Study in the Construct Validation of the Reading Module of an EAP Proficiency Test Battery: Validation from a Variety of Perspectives*. PhD thesis. University of Reading.

Kintsch, W. and van Dijk, T. A. (1978) Toward a model of text comprehension and production. *Psychological Review* 85: 363 – 94.

Klare, G. M. (1984) Readability. In Pearson *et al.*: 681 – 744.

LaBerge, D. and Samuels, S. J. (1974) Towards a theory of automatic information processing in reading. *Cognitive Psychology* 6: 293 – 323.

Long, M. H. *et al.* (1980) *Reading English for Academic Study*. Massachusetts: Newbury House publishers, Inc.

References

Lumley, T. J. N. (1993) Reading comprehension sub-skills: teachers' perceptions of content in an EAP test. *Melbourne Papers in Applied Linguistics* 2: 25 – 55.

Lunzer, E. and Gardner, K. (eds.) (1979) *The Effective Use of Reading*. London: Heinemann Educational.

Lunzer, E., Waite, M. and Dolan, T. (1979) Comprehension and comprehension tests. In Lunzer, E. and Gardner, K. (eds): 37–71.

Lynch, E. S. (1988) *Reading for Academic Success – Selections from Across the Curriculum*. Collier Macmillan Canada, Inc.

McGinitie, W. H. (1973) *Assessment Problems in Reading*. Newark, Del.: International Reading Association.

McGovern, D., Mathews, M. and Mackay, S. E. (1994) *English for Academic Study: Reading*. Prentice Hall International (UK) Ltd.

Mackay, R., Barhman, B. and Jordan, R. R (eds.) (1979) *Reading in a Second Language*. Massachusetts: Rowley Mass.

Meyer, B. J. F. (1975) *The Organization of Prose and its Effect on Memory*. Amsterdam: North-Holland.

Meyer, B. J. F. and Freedle, R. O. (1984) The effects of different discourse types on recall. *American Educational Research Journal* 21: 121 – 43.

Munby, J. (1978) *Communicative Syllabus Design*. Cambridge: Cambridge University Press.

Nation, P. (1997) The language learning benefits of extensive reading. *The Language Teacher* 21: 13 – 16.

Nevo, N. (1989) Test-taking strategies on a multiple-choice test of reading comprehension. *Language Testing* 6: 199 – 215.

Nolan-Woods, E. and Foll, D. (1986) *Penguin Skills Series – Penguin Advanced Reading Skills*. England: Penguin Books Ltd.

Nuttall, C. (1982/1996) *Teaching Reading Skills in a Foreign Language*. London: Heinemann Educational.

Orasanu, J. (ed.) (1986) *Reading Comprehension: From Research to Practice*. Hillsdsale, N.J.: Erlbaum.

Paran, A. (1991) *Reading Comprehension*. Limassol, Cyprus: Burlington Books Ltd.

Paris, S. G., Wasik, B. A. and Turner, J. C. (1991) The development of strategic readers. In Pearson, P. D. *et al.* (eds.): 609 – 40.

Perfetti, C. A. (1977) Language comprehension and fast decoding: some psycholinguistic prerequisites for skilled reading comprehension. In Guthrie, J. T. (ed.): 141 – 83.

Pugh, A. K. (1978) *Silent Reading*. London: Heinemann Educational.

Rathmell, G. (1984) *Bench Marks in Reading*. Hayward, California: Alemany Press.

References

Rayner, K. and Pollatsek, A. (1989) *The Psychology of Reading*. Englewood Cliffs N.J.: Prentice Hall.

Ridgway, T. (1996) Reading theory and foreign language reading comprehension. *Reading in a Foreign Language* 10: 55 – 76

Ridgway, T. (1997) Thresholds of the background knowledge effect in foreign language reading. *Reading in a Foreign Language* 11: 151 – 68.

Rosenshine, B. V. (1980) Skill hierarchies in reading comprehension. In Spiro, R. J. *et al.*: 535 – 54.

Rost, D. H. (1993) Assessing the different components of reading comprehension: fact or fiction. *Language Testing* 10: 79 – 92.

Rumelhart, D. E. (1977) Toward an interactive model of reading. In Dornic, S. (ed.): 573 – 603.

Salimbene, S. (1988) *Interactive Reading*. Cambridge: Newbury House Publishers.

Silberstein, S. (1994) *Techniques and Resources in Teaching Reading*. New York: Oxford University Press.

Sim, D. D. and Laufer-Dvorkin, D. (1982) *Reading Comprehension Course: Selected Strategies, Collins Study Skills in English*. Glasgow: William Collins Sons and Co Ltd.

Singer, H. and Ruddell, R. B. (eds.) (1970) *Theoretical Models and Processes of Reading*. Newark Del: International Reading Association.

Smith, F. (1971) *Understanding Reading: A Psycholinguistic Analysis of Reading and Learning to Read*. New York: Holt, Rinehart & Winston.

Spearritt, D. (1972) Identification of subskills in reading comprehension by maximum likelihood factor analysis. *Reading Research Quarterly* 8: 92 – 111.

Spiro, R. J., Bruce, B. C. and Brewer, W. F. (eds.) (1980) *Theoretical Issues in Reading Comprehension*. Hillsdale, N.J: Lawrence Erlbaum Association, Publishers.

Spolsky, B. (1994) Comprehension testing, or can understanding be measured? in Brown, G. *et al.* (eds.) *Language and Understanding*: 141 – 152.

Spolsky, B. (1994) *Measured Words*. Oxford University Press: Oxford.

Stanovich, K. E. (1980) Toward an interactive compensatory model of individual differences in the development of reading fluency. *Reading Research Quarterly* 16: 32 – 71.

Thompson, G. B., Tunmer, W. E. and Nicholson, T. (1993) *Reading Acquisition Processes*. Clevedon: Multilingual Matters Ltd.

Tomlinson, B. and Ellis, R. (1988) *Reading Advanced*. Oxford: Oxford University Press.

Urquhart A. H. and Weir C. J. (1998) *Reading in a Second Language*. London: Longman.

Venezky, R. L. and Calfee, R. C. (1970) The reading competency model. In Singer, H. and Ruddell, R. B. (eds.): 273 – 91.
Wallace, J. M. (1980) *Study Skills in English*. Cambridge: Cambridge University Press
Wallace, C. (1992a) *Reading*. Oxford: Oxford University Press.
Weaver, C. A. and Kintsch, W. (1991) Expository text. In Barr R. *et al.* (eds): 230 – 45.
Weakley, S. (1993) *Procedures In the Content Validation of an EAP Proficiency Test of Reading Comprehension*. Unpublished MATEFL Dissertation. CALS. University of Reading.
Weir, C. J. (1983) *Identifying the Language Needs of Overseas Students in Tertiary Education in the United Kingdom*. PhD Thesis: University of London, Institute of Education.
Weir, C. J. (1990) *Communicative Language Testing*. London: Prentice Hall.
Weir, C. J. (1993) *Understanding and Developing Language Tests*. London:Prentice Hall.
Weir, C. J. (1994) Reading as multi-divisible or unitary: between scylla and charybdis. *Paper presented at RELC*. Singapore. April.
Weir, C. J., Hughes, A. and Porter, D. (1990) Reading skills: hierarchies, implicational relationships and identifiability. *Reading in a Foreign Language* 7: 505 – 10.
Weir, C. J. and Porter, D. (1996) The multi-divisible or unitary nature of reading: the language tester between Scylla and Charybdis. *Reading in a Foreign Language* 10: 1 – 19.
Williams, E. (1984) *Reading in the Language Classroom*. London: Macmillan.
Yang H. Z. and Weir C. J. (forthcoming) *The Validation Report of the College English Test*.
Zhou, S., Weir, C. J. and Green, R. 1998 The Test for English Majors Validation Project. Shanghai: Foreign Language Education Press.

Appendices

Chapter 2

2.2 A needs analysis for the Advanced English Reading Test   129
2.3 Analysis of texts and tasks in published EAP teaching materials and tests   132

Chapter 4

4.1 Subject tutors' questionnaire survey on text suitability   171
4.2 Text mapping instructions and notes   173

Chapter 5

5.1 Test data and questionnaire data analysis of the AERT prototype version 1 – First trial in April 1997   179
5.2 Test data and questionnaire data analysis of the AERT prototype version 1 – Main trial in October 1997   207

Chapter 6

6.1 Expert judgment/Student retrospection questionnaire   276
6.2 Student perception of skills/strategies being tested in each section   278
6.3 Student introspection on the AERT prototype version 1   281

Appendices - Chapter 2

Appendix 2.2 Needs analysis for the Advanced English Reading Test

Institution: _____

Discipline area: _____

Dear colleague:

College English Teaching Syllabus stipulates that there should be a post-foundation stage of academic reading, which, however, has been neglected by both school authorities and students. To promote the teaching of academic reading, we intend to develop an academic reading test, which, we hope, will exert a positive washback effect on the post-CET teaching of academic reading. We designed this questionnaire to invite your opinions on the teaching of academic reading in universities. Thank you for your co-operation.

01 — 02 Please indicate the degree of importance of each item by putting a tick in the appropriate box and fill in the blank if there are any other alternatives.

H: high importance
M: medium importance
L: low importance
N: no importance

01   Nature of academic texts: Please tick the appropriate box for degree of importance

	H	M	L	N
a) journal articles				
b) newspaper articles				
c) abstracts				
d) research reports				
e) chapters from books				
f) manuals				
g) business documents				

Please write other types of academic texts if any and indicate their degree of importance by ticking an appropriate box.

h) _____				
i) _____				
j) _____				

Appendices - Chapter 2

02   Topics of reading materials:

	H	M	L	N
a) science and technology				
b) biology and medical science				
c) arts and humanities				

Please write other topics of reading materials if any and indicate their importance by ticking an appropriate box.

d) _____				
e) _____				

03—05 Choose one of the figures and tick the corresponding box

03: Requirements of vocabulary for academic reading:

	a	b	c	d
a) 4000 — 5000				
b) 5000 — 6000				
c) 6000 — 7000				
d) 7000 — 8000				

Notes: The vocabulary requirement for CET-4 is 4000.
       The vocabulary requirement for CET-6 is 5300.

04   Average length for each type of the text

a) less than 1000 words
b) 1000 —2000 words
c) 2000 —3000 words
d) more than 3000 words

	a	b	c	d
journal articles				
newspaper articles				
abstracts				
research reports				
chapters from books				
manuals				
business documents				
_____				
_____				

Appendices - Chapter 2

05   **Average speed of academic reading**

a)   70 — 90 wpm
b)   90 — 120 wpm
c)   120 — 150 wpm
d)   above 150 wpm

a	b	c	d

06—18   **Please indicate the degree of importance of the following reading skills used in academic reading by ticking the appropriate box.**

H: high importance   M: medium importance   L: low importance   N: no importance

			H	M	L	N
06	survey for gist	06				
07	scan for specifics	07				
08	understand explicitly stated main ideas	08				
09	understand inferred meanings	09				
10	distinguish main idea from supporting detail	10				
11	obtain information conveyed through non-verbal forms (charts, diagrams etc.)	11				
12	summarise by extracting salient points or rejecting redundant or irrelevant information	12				
13	evaluate critically author s viewpoints	13				
14	use reference skills, e.g., bibliography, index, footnotes, etc.	14				
15	deduce meanings of unfamiliar lexical items using contextual clues	15				
16	understand sentences through their grammatical structures	16				
17	understand relations between parts of text by using discourse markers	17				
18	understand relations between parts of text by use grammatical cohesion devices	18				

Please write other skills if any used in academic reading and indicate their degree of importance by ticking the appropriate box.

19	_____	19				
20	_____	20				
21	_____	21				

Appendix 2.3 Analysis of texts and tasks in published EAP teaching materials and tests

2.3.1.1	Lists of EAP reading coursebooks being analysed
2.3.1.2	Lists of coursebooks and books about EGP reading being analysed
2.3.2	Lists of EAP reading tests being analysed
2.3.3.1	A taxonomy of teaching tasks in EAP reading coursebooks
2.3.3.2	A taxonomy of teaching tasks in books about EGP reading
2.3.3.3	A taxonomy of teaching tasks in EGP reading coursebooks
2.3.4	An analysis of skills/strategies and item types in EAP reading tests
2.3.5	A breakdown of skills/strategies tested in EAP reading tests
2.3.6	Rhetorical organisations (Meyer and Freedle 1984 Quoted in P. L. Carrell 1984)
2.3.7.1	An analysis of conditions of EAP reading teaching tasks: D. McGovern *et al.*
2.3.7.2	An analysis of conditions of EAP reading teaching tasks: E. S. Lynch
2.3.7.3	An analysis of conditions of EAP reading teaching tasks: E. H. Glendinning and B. Holmstrom
2.3.7.4	An analysis of conditions of EAP reading teaching tasks: B. Tomlinson and R. Ellis
2.3.7.5	An analysis of conditions of EAP reading teaching tasks: S. Salimbene
2.3.7.6	An analysis of conditions of EAP reading teaching tasks: M. L Arnaudet and M. E. Barrett
2.3.8	Summary of conditions of EAP reading coursebooks
2.3.9.1	An analysis of conditions of EAP reading tests: UETESOL June 1996
2.3.9.2	An analysis of conditions of EAP reading tests: UETESOL February 1996
2.3.9.3	An analysis of conditions of EAP reading tests: IELTS April 1995
2.3.9.4	An analysis of conditions of EAP reading tests: TOEFL 1991

Appendices - Chapter 2

2.3.9.5	An analysis of conditions of EAP reading tests: TEEP TB II A 1986
2.3.9.6	An analysis of conditions of EAP reading tests: ELTS (GA/l) UCLES 1979
2.3.9.7	An analysis of conditions of EAP reading tests: ELTS (SS/l) UCLES 1979
2.3.9.8	An analysis of conditions of EAP reading tests: ELTS (T/l) UCLES 1979
2.3.9.9	An analysis of conditions of EAP reading tests: EPTB short form D 1977
2.3.9.10	An analysis of conditions of EAP reading tests: ELBA 1967
2.3.10	Summary of conditions of EAP reading tests
2.3.11.1	Classification of EAP reading texts according to Meyer and Freedle's expository description
2.3.11.2	Breakdown of skills/strategies by rhetorical organisation
2.3.12	Glossary of EAP reading test formats
2.3.13.1	A breakdown of test formats used in EAP reading tests
2.3.13.2	A breakdown of test formats against skills/strategies tested in EAP reading tests
2.3.13.3	A summary table of levels vs. test formats vs. skills/strategies used in EAP reading tests
2.3.13.4	A summary table of expeditious vs. careful reading vs. test formats used in EAP reading tests

Appendices - Chapter 2

Appendix 2.3.1.1
List of EAP reading coursebooks being analysed

Author(s)	Title of the book	Date of publication
1 Yorkey, R. C.	Study Skills	1970
2 British Council	Reading and Thinking in English	1980
3 Long, M. H. *et al.*	Reading English for Academic Study	1980
4 Morrow, K.	Skills for Reading	1980
5 Wallace, M. J.	Study Skills in English	1980
6 Sim, D. D. & Laufer-Dovrkin, B.	Reading Comprehension Course - Selected Strategies	1982
7 Adkins, A. & McKean.	Text to Note-Study Skills for Advanced Learners	1983
8 Kaplan, R. & Shaw, P. A.	Exploring Academic Discourse	1983
9 Arnaudet, M. L. & Barrett, M. E.	Approaches to Academic Reading & Writing	1984
10 Salimbene, S.	Interactive Reading	1986
11 Ellis, R. & Tomlinson, B.	Reading-Advanced	1988
12 Lynch, E. S.	Reading for academic success-Selections from Across the Curriculum	1988
13 Glendinning, E. H. & Holmstrom, B.	Study Reading –A course in reading skills for academic purposes	1992
14 McGovern, D. *et al.*	Reading	1994

Appendices - Chapter 2

Appendix 2.3.1.2
Lists of EGP reading coursebooks being analysed

Author(s)	Title of the book	Date of publication
Barr, Clegg and Wallace	Advanced Reading Skills	1981
Nolan-Woods and Foll	Penguin Advanced Reading Skills	1986
Foll, D.	Contrast: Developing Text Awareness	1990
Paran, A.	Reading Comprehension	1991
Greenall, S. & Pye, D.	Reading 4	1993
Harrison, M.	Key Reading Skills for CAE	1994

Lists of books about EGP reading being analysed

Author(s)	Title of the book	Date of publication
1 Grellet, F.	Developing Reading Skills	1981
2 Williams, E.	Reading in the classroom	1984
3 Rathmell, G.	Bench Marks in Reading	1984
4 Greenall, S. & Swan, M.	Effective Reading-reading Skills for Advanced Students	1986
5 Silberstein, S.	Techniques and Resources in Teaching Reading	1994
6 Nuttall, C.	Teaching Reading Skills in a Foreign Language	1996

Appendices - Chapter 2

Appendix 2.3.2
Lists of EAP reading tests being analysed

Acronym	Name	Developer(s)	The paper analysed
UETESOL	University Entrance Test in English for Speakers of Other Languages	NEAB (Northern Examinations and Assessment Board) starting from 1990	UETESOL • February 1996 • June 1996
IELTS	International English Language Testing System	BC, UCLES and IDP starting from 1989	IELTS specimen materials • April 1995
TOEFL	Test of English as a Foreign Language	ETS Educational Testing Service starting from 1964	Reading for TOEFL Workbook • 1991 ETS
TEEP	Test in English for Educational Purposes	AEB (The Associated Examining Board) CALS (from 1991: Centre for Applied Language studies) starting from 1984	TEEP • 1986
ELTS	English Language Testing Service	BC & UCLES (The British Council & University of Cambridge Local Examinations Syndicate) starting from 1980	ELTS 1979 • general academic • social science • technology
EPTB	English Proficiency Test Battery	BC Alan Davies starting from 1964	EPTB • short version form D 1977
ELBA	English Language Battery	University of Edinburgh Department of Applied Linguistics by Elisabeth Ingram (The Ingram Test) One form only: 1967	ELBA • 1967

Appendices - Chapter 2

Appendix 2.3.3.1

A taxonomy of teaching tasks in EAP Reading Coursebooks

References	Pre-reading		Expeditious Reading			While Reading		Careful Reading		Summary
	PV	PD	SKM quick & global	SCH	SCN quick & local	EXMI	IPROP careful & global	IPRAG	ILEX careful & local	SYN	WS
Yorkey, R.C. (1970), Study Skills	X		X	X	X	X			X	X	X
British Council (1980). Reading and Thinking in English		X		X			X	X	X	X	X
Long, M.H. et al. (1980). Reading English for Academic Study			X		X				X		
Morrow, K.(1980). Skills for reading		X		X	X	X	X		X	X	
Wallace, M.J. (1980). Study Skills in English	X	X	X	X	X						X
Sim, D.D. & Laufer-Dovrkin, B. (1982). Reading Comprehension Course - Selected Strategies		X	X	X	X		X	X	X	X	
Adkins, A. & McKean. (1983). Text to Note-Study Skills for Advanced Learners		X	X	X	X	X	X		X	X	
Kaplan, R. & Shaw, P. A. (1983), Exploring Academic Discourse		X	X	X	X	X	X	X	X	X	X
Arnaudet, M.L. & Barrett, M.E. (1984). Approaches to Academic Reading & Writing	X	X	X	X	X	X	X			X	X
Salimbene, S. (1986). Interactive Reading		X	X	X	X	X	X	X	X	X	
Ellis, R. & Tomlinson, B. (1988). Reading-Advanced		X	X	X	X	X	X	X	X		
Lynch, E. S. (1988). Reading for academic success- Selections from Across the Curriculum	X	X	X	X	X	X	X	X	X	X	X
Glendinning, E. H. & Holmstrom, B. (1992), Study Reading - A course in reading skills for academic purposes	X	X	X	X	X	X	X	X	X	X	
McGovern, D. et al. (1994). Reading		X	X	X	X	X	X	X	X		

137

Appendices - Chapter 2

Appendix 2.3.3.2

A taxonomy of teaching tasks in books about EGP reading

Reference books	Pre-reading		While reading									Summary
			Expeditious Reading				Careful Reading					
			quick & global		quick & local				careful & global	Careful	Reading careful & local	
	PV	PD	SKM	SCH	SCN	EXM	IPROP	IPRAG	ILEX	SYN	WS
Grellet, F. (1981). Developing Reading Skills	X	X	X	X	X	X	X					
Williams, E. (1984). Reading in the classroom		X	X									
Rathmell, G. (1984). Bench Marks in Reading					X	X	X				X	
Greenall, S. & Swan, M. (1986). Effective Reading-reading skills for advanced students		X			X	X	X	X	X	X		X
Silberstein, S. (1994). Techniques and Resources in Teaching Reading	X	X	X		X	X	X	X	X	X		
Nuttall, C. (1996). Teaching Reading Skills in a Foreign Language	X	X	X		X	X	X	X	X	X		

Appendices - Chapter 2

Appendix 2.3.3.3

A taxonomy of teaching tasks in EGP reading coursebooks

Reference books	Pre-reading		While reading								Summary
			Expeditious Reading			Careful Reading					
			quick & global		quick & local		careful & global		careful & local		
	PV	PD	SKM	SCH	SCN	EXMI	IPROP	IPRA G	I LEX	SYN	WS
Barr, Clegg, and Wallace (1981). Advanced Reading Skills		X	X	X	X			X	X		X
Nolan-Woods & Foll, D. (1986). Penguin Advanced Reading skill	X	X	X		X	X	X	X	X	X	
Foll, D. (1990). Contrast: Developing Text Awareness		X	X	X	X	X	X	X	X		
Paran, A. (1991). Reading Comprehension		X	X	X	X	X	X	X	X		X
Greenall, S & Pye, D. (1993) Reading 4		X	X			X	X	X	X		X
Harrison, M. (1994). Key Reading Skills for CAE.		X	X	X	X	X	X	X	X		

139

Appendices - Chapter 2

Appendix 2.3.4

An analysis of skills/strategies and item types in EAP reading tests

UETESOL (June 96)

Test Formats	Reading Expeditiously			Reading Carefully			Reading at the Microlinguistic Level	
	SCAN	SEARCH	SKIM	EXMI	IPROP	IPRAG	ILEX	SYN
T/F/NG				3A4 a, b, d, e, f, g	3A4 c			
MATCH			3A1					
GF				3A5				
TABLE	3A3 a+c=1 3B1 3B2 (4 parts)	3A3 b+d=1 3B2 (5 parts)						
SEQ	3A2							

UETESOL (Feb. 96)

Test Formats	Reading Expeditiously			Reading Carefully			Reading at the Microlinguistic Level	
	SCAN	SEARCH	SKIM	EXMI	IPROP	IPRAG	ILEX	SYN
MCQ			3B1	3A1a, 3A1d	3A1b, 3A1c			
T/F/NG	3A2c	3A2a, 3A2d		3A2b, 3B2/ a, b, d, e, f	3B2c			
MATCH					3B3			
TABLE	3A3							

Appendix 2.3.4 (cont.)

IELTS (April 95 specimen)

Test Formats	Reading Expeditiously			Reading Carefully			Reading at the Microlinguistic Level	
	SCAN	SEARCH	SKIM	EXMI	IPROP	IPRAG	ILEX	SYN
MCQ				11				
T/F/NG					17, 18, 19, 20, 21, 22, 26, 27, 28, 29			
SAO	3, 4							
MATCH		1, 2		12, 13, 14, 15, 16				
GF	23, 24	25		5, 6, 7, 8				
TABLE	9, 10	35, 36, 37, 38						
ITRN	30	31, 32, 33, 34						

TOEFL (Reading for TOEFL 1991 workbook)

Test Formats	Reading Expeditiously			Reading Carefully			Reading at the Microlinguistic Level	
	SCAN	SEARCH	SKIM	EXMI	IPROP	IPRAG	ILEX	SYN
MCQ	31, 37, 45, 47, 51, 58	33	55	35, 39, 41, 42, 44, 50	32, 34, 36, 40, 43, 46, 48, 53, 54, 56, 57, 59, 60	46, 49, 52	38, 49, 52	

TEEP 1986

Test Formats	Reading Expeditiously			Reading Carefully			Reading at the Microlinguistic Level	
	SCAN	SEARCH	SKIM	EXMI	IPROP	IPRAG	ILEX	SYN
SAQ	task2/2			task 2/ 3, 8, 9	task 2/ 5, 7		task 2/ 1, 4, 6	
TEXTC							task 1/ 1 – 17	task 1/ 1 – 17
SEQ					task 2/ 10			(task2/ 10)

Appendices - Chapter 2

Appendix 2.3.4 (cont.)

ELTS (GA/1)

Test Formats	Reading Expeditiously			Reading Carefully			Reading at the Microlinguistic Level	
	SCAN	SEARCH	SKIM	EXMI	IPROP	IPRAG	ILEX	SYN
MCQ	10, 32, 33, 34, 35, 36	2, 11, 37, 38, 39, 40		3, 4, 12	1, 5, 6, 13, 14, 15, 16, 17, 18, 19, 20, 21, 22, 23, 24, 25, 26, 27, 28, 29, 30, 31		8, 9	7

ELTS (SS/1)

Test Formats	Reading Expeditiously			Reading Carefully			Reading at the Microlinguistic Level	
	SCAN	SEARCH	SKIM	EXMI	IPROP	IPRAG	ILEX	SYN
MCQ	15, 16, 17, 18, 33, 34, 35, 36, 37	38, 39, 40		13, 14, 22, 26, 30	1, 2, 3, 4, 5, 6, 7, 8, 9, 10, 11, 12, 19, 20 21, 24		23, 25, 27, 28, 29, 31, 32	

ELTS (T/1)

Test Formats	Reading Expeditiously			Reading Carefully			Reading at the Microlinguistic Level	
	SCAN	SEARCH	SKIM	EXMI	IPROP	IPRAG	ILEX	SYN
MCQ	3, 4, 5, 13, 14, 15, 17, 25, 32, 33, 35, 36	6, 7, 8, 9, 37, 38, 39, 40		1, 2, 11, 16, 19, 21, 29, 31	10, 12, 20, 22, 23, 24, 26, 27, 28, 30, 34		18	

Appendices - Chapter 2

Appendix 2.3.4 (cont.)

EPTB (Short version Form D 1977)

Test Formats	Reading Expeditiously			Reading Carefully			Reading at the Microlinguistic Level	
	SCAN	SEARCH	SKIM	EXMI	IPROP	IPRAG	ILEX	SYN
CTEST							Part 1 test 2	Part 1 test 2
CLOZEL				Part 2 test 4			Part 2 test 4	Part 2 test 4

ELBA (1967)

Test Formats	Reading Expeditiously			Reading Carefully			Reading at the Microlinguistic Level	
	SCAN	SEARCH	SKIM	EXMI	IPROP	IPRAG	ILEX	SYN
MCQ				1, 2, 5, 6, 9, 10, 11, 12, 13, 18, 19, 20	3, 4, 7, 8, 14, 15, 16, 17			

Appendices - Chapter 2

Appendix 2.3.5

A breakdown of skills/strategies tested in EAP reading tests

	No of Items	Reading	Expenditiously			Reading Carefully			Reading at the Microlinguistic Level	
		SKIM	SEARCH	SCAN	EXMI	IPROP	IPRAG		SYN
UETESOL JUNE 96	30	1 = 3.3%	6 = 20.0%	8 = 26.7%		1 = 3.3%			
UETESOL FEB 96	30	1 = 3.3%	2 = 6.7%		8 = 26.7%	8 = 26.7%			
IELTS APRIL 95	38			7 = 18.4%					
TOEFL 1991	30	1 = 3.3%	1 = 3.3%	6 = 20.0%	6 = 20.0%		1 = 3.3%*	2 = 6.7%*	
TEEP 1986	17 10			TASK 2 1 = 10%	TASK2 3 = 30%	TASK 2 3 = 30%		TASK 1 : 17 = 100% * TASK 2 : 3 = 30%	TASK 2 : 1 = 10%
ELTS [GA] 1979	40		6 = 15.0%	6 = 15.0%	3 = 7.5%				
ELTS [SS] 1979	40		3 = 7.5%	9 = 22.5%	5 =12.5%			7 = 17.5%	1 = 2.5%
ELTS [T] 1979	40		8 = 20.0%	12 = 30.0%	8 = 20.0%			1 = 2.5%	
EPTB 1977	50 180				PART 2 = 180 =100%**			PART 1 = 50 =100%* PART 2 = 80 =100%**	
ELBA 1967	20				12 = 60%	8 = 40%			

*= both skills are being tested;   ** = all skills are being tested

Appendices - Chapter 2

Appendix 2.3.6

Rhetorical organisations
[Meyer & Freedle 1984 quoted in Carrell, P. L. 1984 TQ 18/3 pp 441–69]

TYPE	DESCRIPTION	EXAMPLE	TOP-LEVEL STRUCTURE	EAP READING TEST EXAMPLE
COLLECTION OF DESCRIPTIONS	When a number or collection of attributes, specifications or settings are given about a topic, the structures of collection and description are combined to form a collection of descriptions	*Our 25th high school reunion was held last year. We saw many old friends, danced until dawn, and agreed to meet again in five years.*	TOPIC — 25th high school reunion / Saw old friends, Danced until dawn, Agreed to meet again	UETESOL JUNE 96 — Tennis racquets
CAUSATION	Represents ideas which are grouped not only chronologically but which are also causally related e.g. if—then statements of logic or cause—effect statements.	*Sally wasn't eating well, exercising or resting enough. As a result, she felt weak and run-down and never wanted to do anything.*	TOPIC — Sally's health / Antecedent [Sally not eat well] — Consequence [Sally feel weak]	IELTS 1995 — People & Organisations: The Selection Issue
PROBLEM/ SOLUTION	Contains all the features of cause/effect, with additional feature of overlapping content between propositions in the problem and solution e.g. scientific texts, also experimental psychological research reports [problem, method, results and discussion].	*Pollution is a problem; polluted rivers are health hazards and eyesores. One solution is to bar the dumping of industrial wastes.*	TOPIC — Pollution / Problem [Pollution is a problem] — Solution [Bar dumping of industrial wastes]	ELTS [T] 1979 — Trouble-shooting small engine
COMPARISON	Organised on the basis of opposing viewpoints [either alternate views giving equal weight to two sides, or adversative views clearly favouring one side]. E.g. political essays particularly adversative sub-type.	*Despite evidence that smoking is harmful, many people claim this is not so. Although smoking has been related to lung and heart disease, for some people smoking may relieve tension.*	TOPIC — Smoking / One view [Smoking harmful, related to lung and heart disease] — Opposing view [Smoking may relieve tension]	ELBA 1967 — Academic politics

145

Appendices - Chapter 2

Appendix 2.3.7.1

An analysis of conditions of EAP reading teaching tasks

CONDITIONS	D. McGOVERN *et al.* - READING
STATED PURPOSES FOR READING	Looking quickly through a text for specific details, locating information on a predetermined topic, processing a text selectively to get the main idea(s) as efficiently as possible, reading carefully for explicitly stated main idea(s), inferring propositional meaning related to a text, inferring meaning of lexical items and understanding the syntactical structure of a sentence.
NATURE OF THE TEXTS	Texts cover a variety of topics which are of general interest. They contain sub-technical vocabulary common to many fields. Extracts are taken from newspapers e.g. THES; journals e.g. New Scientist, The Economist; from academic journals e.g. Finance & Development; The Oxford Review of Education; from books e.g. The Humane City; as well as one abstract from the academic journal – International Affairs.
RHETORICAL ORGANISATION	Collection of descriptions, causation, comparison, problem/solution.
LEXICAL RANGE	Not stated
TOPIC AREAS	Academic success; counselling overseas students; urban development; global warming; education in Asia; international diplomacy; development and cultural values in Africa.
BACKGROUND KNOWLEDGE	The book is designed for students in a wide range of academic subjects —arts, social sciences, and sciences. Thus common denominator subjects have been chosen which should be of general interest to an educated readership.
ILLOCUTIONARY FEATURES	To describe, to inform, to persuade, to explain, to instruct
CHANNEL OF PRESENTATION	Textual and graphics
SIZE OF INPUT / LENGTH OF TEXT (approx.)	Ch 1 = 250 + 550; Ch 2 = 250 + 550; Ch 3 = 250 + 550 (split into 2 pieces); Ch 4 = 290 + 600 + 150; Ch 5 = 600 + 600; Ch 6 = 130 + 500 +1200; Ch 7 = 350 + 600.
SPEED OF PROCESSING	No guidelines provided.
CONTROL OVER READING SKILLS BEING USED	None indicated other than rubrics (read the following passage quickly) though the teacher may impose some in terms of time allocations. Each text is used to exploit a variety of reading skills/strategies.
AMOUNT OF HELP	Examples given where task involves unusual exercise-type/question e.g. p14 Find 3 generalisations – one is given.
METHOD FACTOR/ RESPONSE MODE	SAQ, MCQ (3 options), answers requiring full sentences; MATCH ; SEQ.; T/F; sentence completion, outline summary completion, information transfer (pp. 58 & 85).
QUESTION/ANSWER IN L1/TL	TL
RECEPTIVE/ PRODUCTIVE	Both

Appendix 2.3.7.2
An analysis of conditions of EAP reading teaching tasks

CONDITIONS	E. S. LYNCH - READING FOR ACADEMIC SUCCESS
STATED PURPOSES FOR READING	Previewing/Skimming; Finding the Main and Supporting Ideas; Outlining, Annotating, Summarizing, Note-taking Vocabulary in Context, Vocabulary Study; Close Reading; Looking at Sentence Structure; Putting It All Together. Occasional exercises on scanning; tone; definitions; using quotation marks and ellipses; and understanding figures, charts and tables. (vii–viii)
NATURE OF THE TEXTS	8 units each treating a different academic discipline. Each unit contains unedited conceptually complete readings on closely related subjects drawn, with few exceptions, from basic textbooks and from other books which might be assigned in college classes. The readings are of general interest rather than of interest only to students planning to major in the field. (vii) Extracts are all taken from academic books.
RHETORICAL ORGANISATION	Collection of descriptions, causation, comparison, problem/solution.
LEXICAL RANGE	Not stated
TOPIC AREAS	History and Immigration; Home Economics –Nutrition; Biology - Ecology; Communications –The Media and Politics; Sociology – Technology; Psychology – The Split Brain; Economics – Oil; Physics –Optics and Vision
BACKGROUND KNOWLEDGE	The book is designed for advanced students of English as a second language with academic aspirations, as well as for students in college developmental reading classes (iv).
ILLOCUTIONARY FEATURES	To describe, to inform, to persuade, to explain, to instruct
CHANNEL OF PRESENTATION	Textual with graphics
SIZE OF INPUT / LENGTH OF TEXT (approx.)	Ch 1 = 750; Ch 2 = 1100; Ch 3 = 570; Ch 4 = 300; Ch 5 = 750; Ch 6 = 1400; Ch 7 = 1200+ tables/graphs; Ch 8 = 630; Ch 9 = 1400; Ch 10 = 1000; Ch 11 = 1700 + tables/graphs; Ch 12 = 660; Ch 13 = 800; Ch 14 = 1100; Ch 15 = 1700 + table; Ch 16 = 900; Ch 17 = 1200; Ch 18 = 1500; Ch 19 = 1800; Ch 20 = 900 + diagrams; Ch 21 = 1500; Ch 22 = 1300; Ch 23 = 1300; Ch 24 = 2400 + diagrams; Ch 25 = 1900 + tables; Ch 26 = 900 + diagrams; Ch 27 = 1500 + diagrams; Ch 28 = 1400 + diagrams.
SPEED OF PROCESSING	No guidelines provided.
CONTROL OVER READING SKILLS BEING USED	None indicated other than rubrics though the teacher may impose some in terms of time allocations. Each text is used to exploit a variety of reading skills/strategies.
AMOUNT OF HELP	Dictionary is encouraged at times.
METHOD FACTOR/ RESPONSE MODE	SAQ, MCQ (2 or 3 options), MATCH; T/F; sentence completion, outline summary completion, ITRN; banked cloze (exact no); chart completion; gap-filling (correct form of word) sentence transformation; summary; supplying synonyms for words in passage; taking notes.
QUESTION/ANSWER IN L1/TL	TL
RECEPTIVE/ PRODUCTIVE	Both

Appendices - Chapter 2

Appendix 2.3.7.3

An analysis of conditions of EAP reading teaching tasks

CONDITIONS	E. H. GLENDINNING & B. HOLMSTROM - STUDY READING
STATED PURPOSES FOR READING	*Study Reading* aims to develop the reading skills you need to find information quickly, to identify what is important in a text, and to compare different source of information. (p1)
NATURE OF THE TEXTS	*Study Reading* uses passages from textbooks, journals, reference works and study guides which have been drawn from current reading lists in a range of college/university disciplines and from a variety of higher educational institutions (p3). Sources include extracts/index/content pages are taken from books e.g. Ascent of Man; extracts from journals e.g. New Internationalist, New Scientist; encyclopaedia and dictionary extracts; bibliographies.
RHETORICAL ORGANISATION	Collection of descriptions, causation, comparison, problem/solution.
LEXICAL RANGE	Not stated
TOPIC AREAS	The Spirit of Enquiry; The Developing World; The Natural World; The Physical World; Into the Future; The Individual and Society; Work.
BACKGROUND KNOWLEDGE	*Study Reading* includes texts from the humanities, social sciences and science. The texts are appropriate to the needs of students requiring reading skills for study purposes. For students who have to use textbooks, reference materials and other sources written in English for study purposes.
ILLOCUTIONARY FEATURES	To describe, to inform, to persuade, to explain, to instruct
CHANNEL OF PRESENTATION	Textual and graphics
SIZE OF INPUT / LENGTH OF TEXT (approx.)	Ch 1 = 420 + one index + short extracts [4-5 lines] + 190 + 270; Ch 2 = contents page + 315 + 135 + 150 x 2 + 600; Ch 3 = 90 + 500 + 50 + 190; Ch 4 = charts/ graphics + 250 + 150 + 100 + 400 (in 4 parts); Ch 5 = 110 x 2 + 750 + 350 + 300; Ch 6 = graphics + 300 + 500 +400; Ch 7 = graphics with short texts + 100 + 280 + 270 + 350; Ch 8 = 80 + 150 x 2 + 100 x 2 + 150 + graphics + 150 + 200; Ch 9 = 150 x 2 + 350 + 250 + 7 x 50-80 word texts x 2; Ch 10 = 350 x 2 + graphics/bibliographies/encyclopaedic entries + 450 + 550; Ch 11 = index (1 page) + abstracts of 150-200 words x 4.
SPEED OF PROCESSING	No guidelines provided.
CONTROL OVER READING SKILLS BEING USED.	None indicated other than rubrics though the teacher may impose some in terms of time allocations. Different passages/chunks of passage used to exploit different reading skills/strategies.
AMOUNT OF HELP	Some examples given.
METHOD FACTOR/ RESPONSE MODE	MATCH; text completion; sentence completion; selective deletion; MCQ (3 options); guided summary writing; summary writing; gap-filling; ITRN; table completion; SEQ; SAQ; answers requiring complete sentences
QUESTION/ANSWER IN L1/TL	TL
RECEPTIVE/ PRODUCTIVE	Both

Appendices - Chapter 2

Appendix 2.3.7.4

An analysis of conditions of EAP reading teaching tasks

CONDITIONS	B. TOMLINSON & R. ELLIS - READING - ADVANCED
STATED PURPOSES FOR READING	To develop the students ability to read for study purposes, and in particular assist them in identifying the discourse structure of fairly long texts; to enable the students to identify authorial stance (i.e. the attitude the writer takes to the content of a passage); to encourage the students to respond imaginatively to what they read.
NATURE OF THE TEXTS	Section 1: semi-academic in nature and chosen to illustrate a particular type of discourse, such as argument or a report. Section 2: fictional text. Section 3: texts appropriate for review and evaluation tasks. Extracts are taken from novels e.g. *Watership Down, The Tenth Man;* letters e.g. from *The Color Purple;* journals e.g. *The Economist, New Society, TES;* books e.g. *Contrastive Analysis, Teaching Reading Skills in a Foreign Language;* dialogue e.g. *Educating Rita.*
RHETORICAL ORGANISATION	Collection of descriptions, causation, comparison, problem/solution.
LEXICAL RANGE	Not stated
TOPIC AREAS	Sexism, Comprehension, Animal Language, Rules, English Accents and Arguing.
BACKGROUND KNOWLEDGE	This book assumes that students will already have had extensive practice of traditional reading skills [for example, skimming and scanning] and that they have a fairly high level of linguistic competence.
ILLOCUTIONARY FEATURES	To describe, to inform, to persuade, to explain, to instruct
CHANNEL OF PRESENTATION	Textual and graphics
SIZE OF INPUT / LENGTH OF TEXT (approx.)	Unit 1 = 2500 + 290; Unit 2 = c.4000 + 200 + 200 +140 + 140 +1200 + 700; Unit 3 = 100 +1000 + 1100; Unit 4 = 900 + 190 + 300 + 380 +1300 (divided into 8 extracts); Unit 5 = 400 + 700 + 500 + 720; Unit 6 = 700 + 700 +250 + 550
SPEED OF PROCESSING	No guidelines provided.
CONTROL OVER READING SKILLS BEING USED.	None indicated other than rubrics (read the following passage quickly etc.) though the teacher may impose some in terms of time allocations. Each text is used to exploit a variety of reading skills/strategies.
AMOUNT OF HELP	Some guidance given in how to approach various exercises.
METHOD FACTOR/ RESPONSE MODE	True/false; MCQ (3 or 4 options); ITRN; table/text/list/diagram completion; quizzes; jumbled sentences for reordering; SAQ and/or complete sentences; taking notes; questionnaire; MATCH; summary writing/outline; plus preceding/follow-up oral and written work.
QUESTION/ANSWER IN L1/TL	TL
RECEPTIVE/ PRODUCTIVE	Both

Appendices - Chapter 2

Appendix 2.3.7.5
An analysis of conditions of EAP reading teaching tasks

CONDITIONS	S. SALIMBENE - INTERACTIVE READING
STATED PURPOSES FOR READING	To develop more effective and efficient reading habits. (ix)
NATURE OF THE TEXTS	The reading selection is taken from university textbooks, source books and periodicals suitable for college/university level. The texts are neither shortened nor simplified. (ix) Extracts are taken from books e.g. *How to develop your thinking ability* which also appear in dialogue form; journals e.g.*Time, Harvard Business Review;* extracts from books also include prefaces e.g. from *Planets, Stars & Galaxies.*
RHETORICAL ORGANISATION	Collection of descriptions, causation, comparison, problem/solution.
LEXICAL RANGE	Not stated
TOPIC AREAS	Your Verbal Maps; New Light On Adult Life Cycles; Perception and Human Understanding; The Water We Drink ... And Dump Our Wastes In; The Nature of Statistical Methods; Man and the Heavens; Crowds; Marriage, Divorce and the Family; What Do You Mean I Can t Write? How to Mark a Book.
BACKGROUND KNOWLEDGE	College/university level
ILLOCUTIONARY FEATURES	To describe, to inform, to persuade, to explain, to instruct
CHANNEL OF PRESENTATION	Textual some with graphics
SIZE OF INPUT/ LENGTH OF TEXT (approx.)	Ch 1 = 1500 (divided into 22 chunks used for different exercises, chunks vary from 24 to 150 words); Ch 2 = 920 (divided into 11 chunks used as a whole for skimming, then in chunks for subsequent exercises, chunks vary from 60 to 150 words); Ch 3 = 1500 plus graphics [divided into 17 chunks used for different exercises, chunks vary from 40 to 210 words); Ch 4 = 14Ω pages include 2Ω graphics with 20 - 44 lines x 13 words each; Ch 5 = 7 pages with 37 lines x 13 words each; Ch 6 = 7 pages with 37 lines x 13 words; Ch 7 = 5Ω pages with 37 lines x 13 words; Ch 8 = 11 pages with 38 lines x 13 words; Ch 9 = 12Ω pages include 2 pages of graphics with 37 lines x 13 words; Ch 10 = 3Ω pages with 40 lines @ 13 words.
SPEED OF PROCESSING	Occasional suggestion e.g. *This task should take no more than 15 minutes.* (p54)
CONTROL OVER READING SKILLS BEING USED.	None indicated other than rubrics e.g. *Quickly scan the text for unknown words* (p81) Each part of a text (chunk - see above) may be used to exploit a variety of reading skills/strategies.
AMOUNT OF HELP	Occasional advice given in approaching tasks.
METHOD FACTOR/ RESPONSE MODE	SAQ; CAQ; paraphrase sentences; ITRN; summary writing; dialogue completion and creation; outline completion; paragraph writing; question writing; gap filling; list completion; note taking; plus oral work based on some of the above.
QUESTION/ANSWER IN L1/TL	TL
RECEPTIVE/ PRODUCTIVE	Both

Appendices - Chapter 2

Appendix 2.3.7.6

An analysis of conditions of EAP reading teaching tasks

CONDITIONS	M. L. ARNAUDET & M. E. BARRETT - APPROACHES TO ACADEMIC READING & WRITING
STATED PURPOSES FOR READING	To guide students toward intensive analytical reading of academic prose ... The reading sections of this book are designed to help students recognize the elements of organization, basic thought relationships, and textual coherence devices common to academic writing. (vii)
NATURE OF THE TEXTS	Texts are taken from academic books e.g. *Organizational Behaviour*, *Psychology*, *Essentials of Management*, *Political Ideologies*; journals e.g. *Psychology Today*;
RHETORICAL ORGANISATION	Collection of descriptions, causation, comparison, problem/solution.
LEXICAL RANGE	A basic academic vocabulary. (vii)
TOPIC AREAS	Identifying Controlling Ideas; Recognizing Major Thought Relationships; The Short Paper; Coping with Longer Texts; The Summary; The Critical Review; The Essay Examination; The Research Paper.
BACKGROUND KNOWLEDGE	Intended for advanced learners of English as a foreign language whose goal is mastery of written English as it is used in an academic environment. The text assumes a high level of proficiency in English usage and a TOEFL score of 550 or above to successfully handle the material in this book. (vii)
ILLOCUTIONARY FEATURES	To describe, to inform, to persuade, to explain, to instruct
CHANNEL OF PRESENTATION	Mainly textual with occasional graphics
SIZE OF INPUT / LENGTH OF TEXT (approx.) (Some texts are used more than once, or appear in slightly modified form)	Ch 1 = 170 + 180 + 180 + 140 + 210 + 240 + 100 + 230 + 50 + 80 + 180 + 300 + 120 + 130 + 200 + 300 + 50 + 90 + 100 + 230 + 50 + 200 + 250; Ch 2 = 200 + 130 + 180 + 220 + one-page chart + 300 + 180 + 200 + 120 + 130 + 290; Ch 3 = 130 + 160 + 210 + 190 + 290 + 850; Ch 4 = 150 + 200 + 100 + 230 + 180 + 280 + 90 + 320 + 190 + 480; Ch 5 = 350 + 200 + 330; Ch 6 = 120 + 250 + 350 + 750 + 760; Ch 7 = no reading passages; Ch 8 = indices x 2 (one-page long) + 180 + 1400; plus Research Chapters A, B & C = 16 pages, 15 pages, 12.5 pages long respectively.
SPEED OF PROCESSING	No guidelines provided
CONTROL OVER READING SKILLS BEING USED.	None indicated. Each text is used to exploit a specific reading skill/strategy, though the same passage may appear later in a slightly modified format, or with additional text, for a different purpose.
AMOUNT OF HELP	N/A
METHOD FACTOR/ RESPONSE MODE	ITRN; MATCH; guided summary writing; SAQ; CAQ; essay writing based on a chart; guided essay writing; sentence transformation (pp.75/95); categorize statements (3 groups); writing an outline; proofreading.
QUESTION/ANSWER IN L1/TL	TL
RECEPTIVE/ PRODUCTIVE	Both

Appendices - Chapter 2

Appendix 2.3.8

Summary of conditions of EAP reading coursebooks

Test paper	No of texts	Length [words]	Control over skill/ strategy used	Control over time spent	Rhetorical organisation	Skills/ strategies tested
McGovern, D. et al. Reading 1994	16	250-1200	None	None	C of descriptions Causation Comparison Problem/solution	PD, SKIM, SEARCH, SCAN, EXMI, IPROP, IPRAG, ILEX
Glendinning, E. H. & Holmstrom, B. Study Reading 1992	62	50-750	None	None	C of descriptions Causation Comparison Problem/solution	PV, PD, SKIM, SEARCH, SCAN, EXMI, IPROP, IPRAG, ILEX, SYN
Lynch, E. S. Reading for Academic Success 1988	28	300-2400	None	None	C of descriptions Causation Comparison Problem/solution	PV, PD, SKIM, SCAN, EXMI, IPROP, IPRAG, ILEX, SYN, WS
Ellis, R. & Tomlinson, B. Reading-Advanced 1988	25	100-4000	None	None	C of descriptions Causation Comparison Problem/solution	PD, SEARCH, SCAN, EXMI, IPROP, IPRAG
Salimbene, S. Interactive Reading 1986	10	920-5400 divided into chunks of varying length	None	Suggested	C of descriptions Causation Comparison Problem/solution	PV, PD, SKIM, SEARCH, SCAN, EXMI, IPROP, ILEX, SYN
Arnaudet, M. L. & Barrett, M. E. Approaches to Academic Reading & Writing 1984	59	50-850	None	None	C of descriptions Causation Comparison Problem/solution	PD WS

Appendices - Chapter 2

Appendix 2.3.9.1

An analysis of conditions of EAP reading tests

Test paper:	UETESOL (June 96) (Reference: Syllabus for 1997 and 1998)
Conditions	**Descriptions**
Stated purposes for reading	Test paper: Not stated. syllabus pp2: To scan for particular information; To extract, summarise and manipulate information; To make inferences; To apply the information to the solution of a related problem.
Nature of the texts	Of an academic but non-literary nature at the level of an introductory text for an educated reader. (*syllabus p 2*)
Rhetorical organisation	Including collection of descriptions and causation.
propositional features — Lexical range	No information given.
Topic areas	Of general interest, dealing with issues which are interesting, recognisably appropriate. Avoids as far as possible passages the subject of which would clearly place some candidates at an advantage over others. (*syllabus p 2*)
Background knowledge	Accessible to candidates entering undergraduate study.
Illocutionary features	To describe and to explain.
Channel of presentation	Normally textual. Question format includes tables.
Size of input/ length of text	2 passages totalling approximately 1400 words. passage 1: 820 passage 2: 570
Speed of processing	Candidates have 2.5 hours for the written paper which comprises 3 tests: writing, editing and reading.
Control over skills/strategies	No control.
Control over time spent	No control.
Amount of help	Questions can be read in advance; no recourse to dictionary.
Method factor/ response mode	Formats include: GF, MATCH, T/F/NG, SEQ, TABLE. 'Care will be taken not to create problems for candidates in the expression of their answers. Questions therefore will usually involve the use of graphical, tabular or other summarising frameworks to identify the main and supporting ideas in the text... candidates may also be asked to produce short written responses. In these cases marks will be awarded for the content of answers rather than the accuracy of language so long as the meaning can be clearly determined.' (*syllabus p 3*)
Question/ answer in L1/TL	All in TL.
Receptive/ productive	Receptive/productive.
Number and ordering of tasks	30 items. There are separate booklets for questions and texts. Questions can be read in advance.
Explicitness of weighting	Provided clearly on the test paper. All items carry 1 mark though more than 1 piece of information may be required from the candidate in order to obtain that mark.

153

Appendices - Chapter 2

Appendix 2.3.9.2

An analysis of conditions of EAP reading tests

Test paper:	UETESOL (Feb. 96) (Reference: Syllabus for 1997 and 1998)	
Conditions	**Descriptions**	

Stated purposes for reading	Test paper: Not stated.
	syllabus p 2: To scan for particular information;
	     To extract, summarise and manipulate information;
	     To make inferences;
	     To apply the information to the solution of a related problem.	

Nature of the texts	Of an academic but non-literary nature at the level of an introductory text for an educated reader. *(syllabus p 2)*	
Rhetorical organisation	Including comparison and causation.	
propositional features	Lexical range	No information given.
	Topic areas	Of general interest, dealing with issues which are interesting, recognisably appropriate. Avoids as far as possible passages the subject of which would clearly place some candidates at an advantage over others. *(syllabus p 2)*
	Background knowledge	Accessible to candidates entering undergraduate study.
Illocutionary features	To persuade and to explain.	
Channel of presentation	Normally textual. Question format includes diagrams and/or tables.	
Size of input/ length of text	2 passages totalling approximately 1400 words. passage 1: 620 passage 2: 790	
Speed of processing	Candidates have 2.5 hours for the written paper which comprises 3 tests: writing, editing and reading.	
Control over skills/strategies	No control.	
Control over time spent	No control.	
Amount of help	Questions can be read in advance; no recourse to dictionary.	
Method factor/ response mode	Formats include: MCQ, GF, MATCH, T/F/NG, TABLE. 'Care will be taken not to create problems for candidates in the expression of their answers. Questions therefore will usually involve the use of graphical, tabular or other summarising frameworks to identify the main and supporting ideas in the text... candidates may also be asked to produce short written responses. In these cases marks will be awarded for the content of answers rather than the accuracy of language so long as the meaning can be clearly determined.' *(syllabus p 3)*	
Question/ answer in L1/TL	All in TL.	
Receptive/ productive	Receptive/productive.	
Number and ordering of tasks	30 items. There are separate booklets for questions and texts. Questions can be read in advance.	
Explicitness of weighting	Provided clearly on the test paper. All items carry 1 mark though more than 1 piece of information may be required from the candidate in order to obtain that mark.	

154

Appendices - Chapter 2

Appendix 2.3.9.3

An analysis of conditions of EAP reading tests

Test paper:	IELTS (Specimen materials: April 1995) Module: Academic Reading (Reference: The IELTS Handbook April 1995)
Conditions	**Descriptions**
Stated purposes for reading	Test paper: Not stated. Handbook p 6: ... assess whether a candidate is ready to study or train in the medium of English at an undergraduate or postgraduate level.
Nature of the texts	Texts written for a non-specialist audience: chapters from books, articles from journals, etc. (Handbook p 12)
Rhetorical organisation	Including collection of descriptions and causation.
propositional features — Lexical range	If texts contain technical terms then a simple glossary is provided.
Topic areas	Of a general academic nature, dealing with issues which are interesting/ recognisably appropriate, e.g., the eruption of a volcano, people and organisations, etc.
Background knowledge	Accessible to candidates entering undergraduate or postgraduate courses. (Reference: The IELTS Handbook April 1995 p 12)
Illocutionary features	To describe and to explain.
Channel of presentation	Normally textual but question formats contain diagrams and tables.
Size of input/ length of text	3 passages totalling approximately 2700 words. passage 1: 950 passage 2: 740 passage 3: 1000
Speed of processing	60 minutes for 38 items.
Control over skills/strategies	No control.
Control over time spent	Suggested only: 20 minutes for each passage including tasks.
Amount of help	Questions can be read in advance; no recourse to dictionary.
Method factor/ response mode	Formats include: MCQ, SAQ, GF, MATCH, T/F/NG, ITRN.
Question/ answer in L1/TL	All in TL.
Receptive/ productive	Receptive/productive (maximum 3 words for some items).
Number and ordering of tasks	38 items. Texts and tasks become increasingly difficult as the test progresses. Some of the questions may appear before the text, some may come after, depending on the nature of the questions.
Explicitness of weighting	Marks not explicitly stated. All items equally weighted (1 mark).

Appendices - Chapter 2

Appendix 2.3.9.4

An analysis of conditions of EAP reading tests

Test paper:	TOEFL (Reading for TOEFL: 1991)
Conditions	**Descriptions**
Stated purposes for reading	Stated clearly in the instruction of the reading section. The examinee reads a variety of short passages on academic subjects and answers a number of questions on both factual information and inferred meanings.
Nature of the texts	Of a general academic nature.
Rhetorical organisation	Including collection of description and causation.
propositional features — Lexical range	No information given.
Topic areas	Of general interest, dealing with issues which are interesting and recognisably appropriate.
Background knowledge	Accessible to EFL candidates entering undergraduate or graduate study.
Illocutionary features	To describe and to explain.
Channel of presentation	Normally textual.
Size of input/ length of text	5 passages, totalling approximately 1900 words. passage 1: 400 passage 2: 370 passage 3: 330 passage 4: 360 passage 5: 450
Speed of processing	Candidates have 45 minutes to complete 30 MCQ vocabulary items and 30 MCQ reading items.
Control over skills/strategies	No control.
Control over time spent	No control.
Amount of help	Questions can be read in advance; no recourse to dictionary.
Method factor/ response mode	Format: MCQ
Question/ answer in L1/TL	No writing is involved.
Receptive/ productive	Receptive.
Number and ordering of tasks	30 MCQ items. Questions appear after texts but can be read before should the candidate so desire.
Explicitness of weighting	Not explicitly stated on the paper. All items equally weighted.

156

Appendices - Chapter 2

Appendix 2.3.9.5
An analysis of conditions of EAP reading tests

Test paper:	TEEP 1986 (TB II A) (Reference: TEEP handbook)
Conditions	**Descriptions**
Stated purposes for reading	Test paper: Not stated. Handbook: p 3: To read academic texts both intensively and extensively.
Nature of the texts	Of a general academic nature.
Rhetorical organisation	Including causation and comparison.
propositional features — Lexical range	No information given.
Topic areas	Of general interest, dealing with issues which are interesting, recognisably appropriate, e.g., unemployment among university graduates, changes in the position of women, student—tutor relationship etc.
Background knowledge	Accessible to candidates entering undergraduate and graduate study.
Illocutionary features	To explain and to persuade.
Channel of presentation	Normally textual.
Size of input/ length of text	Task 1: 1 passage of approximately 500 words. Task 2: 1 passage of approximately 1030 words.
Speed of processing	Task 1: 20 minutes Task 2: 30 minutes
Control over skills/strategies	No control.
Control over time spent	Suggested only: 20 mins for task 1 30 mins for task 2.
Amount of help	In task 1, the topic of the text is introduced in the instructions and four examples are given; Candidates are advised to read questions before the text for Task 2; No recourse to dictionary.
Method factor/ response mode	Formats include: TEXTC, SAQ.
Question/ answer in L1/TL	All in TL.
Receptive/ productive	Mostly receptive but involves some writing. Task 1: Candidates are asked to complete a text by identifying the position of some missing words and by supplying them. Task 2: Candidates are asked to produce short written responses.
Number and ordering of tasks	Task 1: 17 missing words Task 2: 10 SAQ. Information needed to answer questions follows the sequence of the text. Texts and questions appear in separate booklets but testees are recommended to read questions before the text.
Explicitness of weighting	Marks are not explicitly stated. In this version of the TEEP, all items are equally weighted.

Appendices - Chapter 2

Appendix 2.3.9.6
An analysis of conditions of EAP reading tests

Test paper:	ELTS (GA/1): UCLES 1979 (reference: ELTS Validation Project Report: BC UCLES 1988 by C. Criper and A. Davies ELTS Research Report 1 (i).)
Conditions	**Descriptions**
Stated purposes for reading	Test paper: Not stated. Validation report p 95: * Understanding the communicative value (function) of sentences and utterances * Understanding relations between parts of a text through grammatical cohesion devices * Distinguishing the main idea from supporting details * Extracting salient points to summarise * Basic reference skills * Scanning to locate specifically required information
Nature of the texts	Texts written for a non-specialist audience: chapters from books, articles from journals, research reports, contents pages, bibliographies, appendices, indices etc.
Rhetorical organisation	Including collection of descriptions and comparison.
propositional features — Lexical range	No information given.
Topic areas	Of a general academic nature, dealing with issues which are interesting/ recognisably appropriate, e.g., adult literacy in the world today, agricultural development in India etc.
Background knowledge	Accessible to candidates entering undergraduate or postgraduate courses.
Illocutionary features	To describe and to persuade.
Channel of presentation	Normally textual, but one text is longer and includes graphics, e.g., tables, charts, etc.
Size of input/ length of text	4 passages plus one bibliography and one index, totalling approx. 3880 words. passage 1: 250 passage 2: 1100 passage 3: 690 passage 4: 690 passage 5: 750 passage 6: 400
Speed of processing	55 minutes for 40 items.
Control over skills/strategies	No control.
Control over time spent	No control.
Amount of help	Questions can be read in advance; no recourse to dictionary.
Method factor/ response mode	Format: MCQ
Question/ answer in L1/TL	All in TL.
Receptive/ productive	Receptive. No writing involved.
Number and ordering of tasks	40 items. The source booklet contains a brief introduction to the passages used in the test and a brief description of the purpose of reading. The question booklet is separate from the source booklet. Questions can be read before the text.
Explicitness of weighting	No information given.

158

Appendices - Chapter 2

Appendix 2.3.9.7
An analysis of conditions of EAP reading tests

Test paper:	ELTS (SS/1): UCLES 1979
	(reference: ELTS Validation Project Report: BC UCLES 1988 by C. Criper and A. Davies ELTS Research Report 1 (i).)
Conditions	**Descriptions**
Stated purposes for reading	Test paper: Not stated. Validation report p 96: * Understanding relations between parts of text through grammatical cohesion devices * Distinguishing the main idea from supporting details * Scanning to locate specifically required information
Nature of the texts	Texts written for a non-specialist audience: chapters from books, articles from journals, research reports, contents pages, bibliographies, appendices, indices etc.
Rhetorical organisation	Including collection of descriptions and causation.
propositional features — Lexical range	No information given.
Topic areas	Of social studies, dealing with issues which are interesting and recognisably appropriate, e.g., public administration, demographic studies, prisons and prison life etc.
Background knowledge	Accessible to candidates entering undergraduate or postgraduate courses.
Illocutionary features	To describe and to explain.
Channel of presentation	Normally textual, but one text is longer and includes graphics, e.g., tables, charts, etc.
Size of input/ length of text	3 passages plus one bibliography and one index, totalling approx. 3920 words passage 1: 690 passage 2: 1330 passage 3: 760 passage 4: 750 passage 5: 390
Speed of processing	55 minutes for 40 items.
Control over skills/strategies in passages	No control.
Control over time spent	No control.
Amount of help	Questions can be read in advance; no recourse to dictionary.
Method factor/ response mode	Format: MCQ
Question/ answer in L1/TL	All in TL.
Receptive/ productive	Receptive. No writing involved.
Number and ordering of tasks	40 items. The source booklet contains a brief introduction to the passages used in the test and a brief description of the purpose of reading. The question booklet is separate from the source booklet. Questions can be read before the text.
Explicitness of weighting	No information given.

Appendices - Chapter 2

Appendix 2.3.9.8
An analysis of conditions of EAP reading tests

Test paper:	ELTS (T/1): UCLES 1979 (reference: ELTS Validation Project Report: BC UCLES 1988 by C. Criper and A. Davies ELTS Research Report 1 (i).)
Conditions	**Descriptions**
Stated purposes for reading	Test paper: Not stated. Validation report p 96: * Basic reference skills * Scanning to locate specifically required information
Nature of the texts	Texts written for a non-specialist audience: chapters from books, articles from journals, research reports, contents pages, bibliographies, appendices, indices etc.
Rhetorical organisation	Including problem/solution, collection of descriptions and causation.
propositional features — Lexical range	No information given.
Topic areas	From the field of engineering and workshop technology, ranging from more abstract to more practical levels, e.g., guide to trouble-shooting the small engine, tensile test, lenses, etc.
Background knowledge	Accessible to candidates entering undergraduate or postgraduate courses.
Illocutionary features	To explain and to describe.
Channel of presentation	Both textual and graphic. Four of the five passages contain tables and charts.
Size of input/ length of text	5 passages plus one glossary and one index, totalling approx. 2800 words passage 1: 700 passage 2: 400 passage 3: 450 passage 4: 370 passage 5: 360 passage 6: 530
Speed of processing	55 minutes for 40 items.
Control over skills/strategies	No control.
Control over time spent	No control.
Amount of help	Questions can be read in advance; no recourse to dictionary.
Method factor/ response mode	Format: MCQ
Question/ answer in L1/TL	All in TL.
Receptive/ productive	Receptive. No writing involved.
Number and ordering of tasks	40 items. The source booklet contains a brief introduction to the passages used in the test and a brief description of the purpose of reading. The question booklet is separate from the source booklet. Questions can be read before the text.
Explicitness of weighting	No information given.

Appendix 2.3.9.9

An analysis of conditions of EAP reading tests

Test paper:	EPTB (short version form D 1977)
Conditions	**Descriptions**
Stated purposes for reading	Test paper: Part 1: This is a Test of your understanding of written English. Part 2: This is a Test of Reading Speed. Part 2 is an optional speed reading test.
Nature of the texts	Of a general academic nature.
Rhetorical organisation	Including only comparison.
propositional features — Lexical range	No information given.
propositional features — Topic areas	Of general interest, dealing with issues which are interesting and recognisably appropriate.
propositional features — Background knowledge	Accessible to candidates entering tertiary level (degree, diploma, certificate) study.
Illocutionary features	To persuade.
Channel of presentation	Textual only.
Size of input/ length of text	Part 1: two short passages, totalling approximately 100 words (containing an additional 50 incomplete words). Part 2: one passage of approximately 900 words containing 180 superfluous foreign or irrelevant words.
Speed of processing	Part 1: 5 minutes Part 2: 10 minutes
Control over skills/strategies	Part 1: careful reading (2 short passages) Part 2: speed reading (1 long passage)
Control over time spent	Part 1: suggested 5 minutes but paper not physically removed Part 2: suggested 10 minutes and paper then collected in after 10 mins
Amount of help	No recourse to dictionary.
Method factor/ response mode	Formats include: C-test and Cloze elide.
Question/ answer in L1/TL	TL.
Receptive/ productive	Receptive/productive (Some spelling of words is involved.)
Number and ordering of tasks	Part 1: 50 incomplete words Part 2: 180 foreign/irrelevant words
Explicitness of weighting	No information given.

Appendices - Chapter 2

Appendix 2.3.9.10
An analysis of conditions of EAP reading tests

Test paper:	ELBA (1967)
Conditions	**Descriptions**
Stated purposes for reading	Not stated.
Nature of the texts	Of a general academic nature.
Rhetorical organisation	Including comparison and problem/solution.
propositional features — Lexical range	No information given.
propositional features — Topic areas	Of general interest, dealing with issues which are interesting and recognisably appropriate.
propositional features — Background knowledge	Accessible to candidates entering tertiary level study.
Illocutionary features	To persuade and to explain.
Channel of presentation	Textual only.
Size of input/ length of text	4 short passages, totalling approximately 430 words. passage 1: 80 passage 2: 100 passage 3: 150 passage 4: 100
Speed of processing	20 minutes for 20 MCQ items.
Control over skills/strategies	No control.
Control over time spent	No control.
Amount of help	No recourse to dictionary.
Method factor/ response mode	Format: MCQ
Question/ answer in L1/TL	No writing is involved.
Receptive/ productive	Receptive.
Number and ordering of tasks	4-7 items per passage, total 20 items.
Explicitness of weighting	No information given.

162

Appendices - Chapter 2

Appendix 2.3.10
Summary of conditions of EAP reading tests

Test Paper	No of Texts	No of Test Formats	No of Items	Time	Length [words]	Control over s/s** used	Control over time spent	Rhetorical Organisation	Skills/ Strategies tested
UETESOL JUNE 96	2	5	30	2.5 hrs*	820/570	None	None	C of descriptions Causation	SKIM, SCAN, SEARCH, EXMI, IPROP
UETESOL FEB 96	2	4	30	2.5 hrs*	620/790	None	None	Comparison Causation	SKIM, SEARCH, SCAN, EXMI, IPROP
IELTS APR 95	3	7	38	60 mins.	950/740 1000	None	Suggested	C of descriptions Causation	SEARCH, SCAN, EXMI, IPROP
TOEFL 1991	5	1	30	45 mins. 330/360	400/370 450	None	None Causation	C of descriptions	SKIM, SEARCH, SCAN, EXMI, IPROP, ILEX IPROP/ IPRAG, IPROP/ILEX,
TEEP 1986	2	3	17 10	50 mins.	500 1030	None	Suggested	Causation Comparison	SCAN, EXMI, IPROP, ILEX, ILEX/SYN, SYN
ELTS [GA] 1979	6	1	40	55 mins.	250/690 1100/400 690/750	None	None	C of descriptions Comparison	SEARCH, SCAN, EXMI, IPROP, ILEX, SYN
ELTS [SS] 1979	5	1	40	55 mins.	690/760 1330 750/390	None	None	C of descriptions Causation	SEARCH, SCAN, EXMI, IPROP, ILEX
ELTS [T] 1979	6	1	40	55 mins.	700/400 450/370 360/530	None	None	Problem/solution C of descriptions Causation	SEARCH, SCAN EXMI, IPROP, ILEX,
EPTB 1977	3	2	50 180	15 mins.	50/50 900	Yes	Suggested/ Yes	Comparison	EXMI/ILEX/SYN ILEX/SYN
ELBA 1967	2	1	20	20 mins.	80/100 150/100	None	None	Comparison Problem/solution	EXMI, IPROP

* paper comprises 3 tests: writing, editing and reading   ** skills/strategies

163

Appendices - Chapter 2

Appendix 2.3.11.1
Classification of EAP reading tests according to Meyer & Freedle's expository description

PAPER	TITLE	LENGTH [WORDS]	RHETORICAL ORGANISATION	SKILLS/ STRATEGIES TESTED
UETESOL JUNE 96	1. Tennis racquets 2. Waterborne disease	820 570	C of descriptions Causation	2 SCAN 1 SEARCH 1 SKIM 14 EXMI 1 IPROP 6 SCAN 5 SEARCH
UETESOL FEB 96	1. Coffee farming methods 2. Weather in the UK	620 790	Comparison Causation	11 SCAN 2 SEARCH 3 EXMI 2 IPROP 1 SKIM 5 EXMI 6 IPROP
IELTS APR 95	1. Mount St Helen's 2. People & Organisations 3. The Rollfilm Revolution	950 740 1000	C of descriptions Causation C of descriptions	4 SCAN 2 SEARCH 5 EXMI 2 SCAN 1 SEARCH 5 EXMI 6 IPROP 1 SCAN 8 SEARCH 4 IPROP
TOEFL 1991	1. Julia Morgan, the architect 2. Residents of the bayou waters 3. Market prices 4. Cholecystokinin hormones 5. One-room schools	400 370 330 360 450	C of descriptions C of descriptions Causation Causation C of descriptions	1 SCAN 1 SEARCH 1 EXMI 2 IPROP 1 SCAN 3 EXMI 3 IPROP 1 ILEX 2 SCAN 1 EXMI 1 IPROP 1 IPROP/G 1 IPROP/X 1 SCAN 1 EXMI 2 IPROP 1 IPROP/ILEX 1 SCAN 1 SKIM 4 IPROP
TEEP 1986	1. British tutors 2. Experiences of unemployment	500 1030	Causation Comparison	17 ILEX/SYN 1 SCAN 3 EXMI 3 IPROP 3 ILEX 1 SYN
ELTS [GA]* 1979	1. Postgraduate courses 2. Literacy in the world 3. Girls behind bars 4. The violent harvest 5. Note on prison literature 6. Index [book on imprisonment]	250 1100 690 690 750 400	C of descriptions Comparison C of descriptions Comparison C of descriptions C of descriptions	1 SEARCH 2 EXMI 1 IPROP 1 SCAN 1 SEARCH 1 EXMI 3 IPROP 2 ILEX 1 SYN 12 IPROP 6 IPROP 2 SCAN 3 SCAN
ELTS [SS]** 1979	1. Girls behind bars 2. Human population 3. Control of public admin 4. Note on prison literature 5. Index [book on imprisonment]	690 1330 760 750 390	C of descriptions Causation Causation C of descriptions C of descriptions	12 IPROP 4 SEARCH 3 EXMI 4 IPROP 1 ILEX 2 EXMI 6 ILEX 2 SCAN 3 SCAN
ELTS [T]*** 1979	1. Trouble-shooting small engine 2. Tensile test 3. Tests for form/relationship 4. Lenses 5. Electricity 6. Glossary/bib/index	700 400 450 370 360 530	Problem/solution Problem/solution Problem/solution C of descriptions Causation C of descriptions	3 SCAN 2 EXMI 3 SCAN 4 SEARCH 2 EXMI 2 IPROP 1 SCAN 1 EXMI 1 IPROP 1 ILEX 1 SCAN 1 EXMI 4 IPROP 2 EXMI 3 IPROP 2 SCAN / 1 IPROP / 2 SCAN
EPTB 1977	1. Crystal Palace 2. Emotional dev/t of an infant 3. Britain's univs/polys	50 50 900	Comparison Comparison Comparison	28 ILEX/SYN 22 ILEX/SYN 180 EXMI/ILEX/SYN
ELBA 1967	1. Fine Italian hand 2. Academic politics 3. Thinking is silent speech 4. Outside exchange call	80 100 150 100	Comparison Comparison Problem/solution Problem/solution	2 EXMI 2 IPROP 2 EXMI 2 IPROP 5 EXMI 3 EXMI 4 IPROP

* 4 items based on collection of passages [search];   ** 3 items based on collection of passages [search];
*** 4 items based on collection of passages [search]

Appendices - Chapter 2

Appendix 2.3.11.2

Breakdown of skills/strategies by rhetorical organisation

Skill/strategy	Collection of descriptions	Causation	Comparison	Problem/Solution
SKIM	2 passages	1 passage		
SEARCH	5 passages	3 passages	2 passages	1 passage
SCAN	13 passages	4 passages	3 passages	3 passages
EXMI	6 passages	6 passages	7 passages	2 passages
IPROP	10 passages	6 passages	6 passages	2 passages
ILEX	1 passage	4 passages	5 passages	1 passage
SYN		1 passage	5 passages	

Total number of passages = 40

Appendix 2.3.12
Glossary of EAP reading test formats

Acronym	Name	Description
MCQ	Multiple Choice Question	Testees are required to select the best choice from several options (usually four, could be three or five) for each question or incomplete statement based on the understanding of the text. Questions/incomplete statements may appear before or after the text.
T/F/NG	True / False / Not Given	Testees are required to decide whether each of a number of statements, which are related to a given text, is true (agrees with what the writer has said), false (disagrees with what the writer has said) or not given (no information is given in the text).
SAQ	Short Answer Question	Testees are required to answer questions using several key words based on the information provided in a text. Questions may appear before or after the text.
MATCH	Matching	Testees are required to match lists or phrases based on the information given in a text. In multiple matching, testees are required to choose the most suitable headings from a given heading bank for identified paragraphs or sections of a text, or for several texts. Alternatively, testees are required to choose from a list of passages or paragraphs the one(s) that contains the necessary information for answering the questions.
GF	Gap-Filling	Testees are required to fill in the gaps in notes or summary paragraphs of the text by using their own words, words from the text, or a bank of optional words according to the information provided in the text.
TABLE	Table Completion	Testees are required to complete a table in their own words or words from the text by using the information provided in the text.
TEXTC	Text Completion	Testees are required to complete a text by identifying the positions where words have been deliberately omitted and by inserting all the missing words.
CTEST	C-test	Testees are required to read through a text and complete every incomplete word in the text indicated by one or more initial letter(s) and some dots.
CLOZEL	Cloze Elide	Testees are required to read through a passage and underline all the foreign or irrelevant words which do not belong to the passage.
ITRN	Information Transfer	Testees are required to transfer the textual information provided in a text into a non-verbal form by labelling or completing a diagram.
SEQ	Sequencing	Testees are required to put headings, paragraphs, statements etc. into the correct sequential order according to text or chronological order. Alternatively, testees are required to reorder some statements to form a new paragraph.

Appendices - Chapter 2

Appendix 2.3.13.1
A breakdown of test formats used in EAP reading tests

TEST PAPERS	No of items	MCQ	T/F/NG	SAQ	MATCH	GF	TABLE	ITRN	SEQ	TEXTC	CTEST	CLOZEL
UETESOL JUNE 96	30		7 = 23.3%		1 = 3.3%	8 = 26.7%	13 = 43.3%		1 = 3.3%			
UETESOL FEB 96	30	5 = 16.7%	10 = 33.3%		5 = 16.7%		10 = 33.3%					
IELTS APR 95	38	1 = 2.63%	10 = 26.3%	2 = 5.26%	7 = 18.4%	7 = 18.4%	6 = 15.8%	5 = 13.1%				
TOEFL 1991	30	30 = 100%										
TEEP 1986	17 10			9 = 90%					1 = 10%	17 = 100%		
ELTS [GA] 1979	40	40 = 100%										
ELTS [SS] 1979	40	40 = 100%										
ELTS [T] 1979	40	40 = 100%										
EPTB 1977	50 180										50 = 100%	180 = 100%
ELBA 1967	20	20 = 100%										

Appendices - Chapter 2

Appendix 2.3.13.2
A breakdown of test formats against skills/strategies tested in EAP reading tests

SKILLS/STRATEGIES	MCQ	T/F/NG	SAQ	MATCH	GF	TABLE	ITRN	SEQ	TEXTC	CTEST	CLOZEL
SCAN	33	1	3		2	19	1	1			
SEARCH	18	2		2	1	10	4				
SKIM	2			1							
EXMI	37	11	3	5	12			1			180**
IPROP	71—2	12	2	5							
IPRAG	0—3		3								
ILEX	11—13							1	17*	50*	180**
SYN	1										
TOTALS	176	26	11	13	15	29	5	3	17	50	180

Total no. of items from 10 test papers = 525.   min—max no. of items

* tests both skills   ** tests all three skills

168

Appendices - Chapter 2

Appendix 2.3.13.3

A summary table of levels vs. test formats vs. skills/strategies used in EAP reading tests

LEVEL	TEST FORMAT	SKILLS/STRATEGIES	
GLOBAL	MATCH	SEARCH	2
		SKIM	1
		EXMI	5
		IPROP	5
GLOBAL/ LOCAL	TABLE	SCAN	19
		SEARCH	10
	ITRN	SCAN	1
		SEARCH	4
	GF	SCAN	2
		SEARCH	1
		EXMI	12
	T/F/NG	SCAN	1
		SEARCH	2
		EXMI	11
		IPROP	12
	MCQ	SCAN	33
		SEARCH	18
		SKIM	2
		EXMI	37
		IPROP	71 — 2
		IPRAG	0 — 3
		ILEX	11 — 13
		SYN	1
	SAQ	SCAN	3
		EXMI	3
		IPROP	2
	CLOZEL	EXMI ILEX SYN	180**
	SEQ	SCAN	1
		IPROP	1
		SYN	1
LOCAL	TEXTC	ILEX SYN	17*
	CTEST	ILEX SYN	50*

Total no. of items from 10 test papers = 525.   * tests both skills   ** tests all three skills   min—max no. of items

Appendices - Chapter 2

Appendix 2.3.13.4
A summary table of expeditious vs. careful reading vs. test formats used in EAP reading tests

SKILLS AND STRATEGIES	TEST FORMAT	SKILLS/ STRATEGIES	
EXPEDITIOUS	TABLE	SCAN	19
		SEARCH	10
	ITRN	SCAN	1
		SEARCH	4
EXPEDITIOUS AND CAREFUL	MATCH	SEARCH	2
		SKIM	1
		EXMI	5
		IPROP	5
	GF	SCAN	2
		SEARCH	1
		EXMI	12
	T/F/NG	SCAN	1
		SEARCH	2
		EXMI	11
		IPROP	12
	MCQ	SCAN	33
		SEARCH	18
		SKIM	2
		EXMI	37
		IPROP	71 — 2
		IPRAG	0 — 3
		ILEX	11 — 13
		SYN	1
	SAQ	SCAN	3
		EXMI	3
		IPROP	2
	SEQ	SCAN	1
		IPROP	1
		SYN	1
CAREFUL	CLOZEL	EXMI	
		ILEX	180**
		SYN	
	TEXTC	ILEX	17*
		SYN	
	CTEST	ILEX	50*
		SYN	

Total no. of items from 10 test papers = 525.   * tests both skills   ** tests all three skills   min—max no. of items

170

Appendix 4.1.1 Subject tutors' questionnaire survey on text suitability – Instruction sheet

---

The aim of the session is to identify items that can be used to test expeditious reading at the global level, that is those which test the strategies of:

    i]   search reading to locate information on a predetermined topic (i.e., not exact words but words in the same semantic field)

    ii]   skimming to quickly establish a discourse topic or an outline summary of the text

A : INDIVIDUAL WORK

Stage I :   8.5 minutes
- Read the text quickly to establish the outline summary, the main ideas and any important supporting details.

Stage II: 3 minutes
- Without looking back at the text, write out these ideas and important details as clearly as you can on a sheet of paper.
- Try as far as possible to organise the points in the order they appeared in the text.
- Number the points you have made.

B : GROUP WORK

- On a master sheet of paper, list the main ideas and any supporting details that the group members agree on.
- Write the number of people who agreed on them e.g., 4/5 (four out of 5 agreed)
- Normally agreement of n — 1is necessary i.e.,if there are 5 people in the group at least 4 must have included the point for a consensus.

Appendices - Chapter 4

Appendix 4.1
Subject tutors' questionnaire
survey on text suitability – Questionnaire

Questionnaire to Subject Teachers

Name: _____

Department: _____

Area of specialisation: _____

Please give us your assessment of the topic familiarity, subject specificity and language difficulty of each text for the students you teach by ticking the appropriate boxes.

Key:
H = high   M = medium   L = low   N = not at all

Text	Topic familiarity				Subject specificity				Language difficulty			
	H	M	L	N	H	M	L	N	H	M	L	N
1												
2												
3												
4												
5												
6												
7												
8												
9												
10												
11												
12												
13												
14												
15												

Appendix 4.2
Text mapping instructions and notes

4.2.1 Expeditious reading at the global level
4.2.2 Expeditious reading at the local level
4.2.3 Careful reading at the global level
4.2.4 Careful reading at the local level
4.2.5 AERT items and text mapping notes

Appendices - Chapter 4

Appendix 4.2.21
Text mapping
Expeditious reading at the local level

The aim of the session is to identify items that can be used to test expeditious reading at the local level, that is those which test the strategy of:

    i]   scanning for specific details

A   :   INDIVIDUAL WORK

Stage I :   8.5 minutes
- Read the text quickly to identify important specific information

Stage II: 3 minutes
- Without looking back at the text, write out this detailed information as clearly as you can on a sheet of paper.
- Try as far as possible to organise the points in the order they appeared in the text.
- Number the points you have made.

B   :   GROUP WORK

- On a master sheet of paper, list the detailed ideas that the group members agree on.
- Write the number of people who agreed on them e.g., 4/5 (four out of 5 agreed)
- Normally agreement of n — 1 is necessary i.e., if there are 5 people in the group at least 4 must have included the point for a consensus.

Appendix 4.2.3
Text mapping
Careful reading at the global level

The aim of the session is to identify items that can be used to test careful reading at the global level, that is those which test the skills of:

    i]   understanding explicitly stated main ideas (EXMI)
    ii]   understanding implicitly stated main ideas (IPROP)

A   :   INDIVIDUAL WORK

Stage I :   12.5 minutes
- Read the text carefully to establish the main ideas and any important supporting details.

Stage II: 3 minutes
- Without looking back at the text, write out these main ideas and detailed information as clearly as you can on a sheet of paper.
- Try as far as possible to organise the points in the order they appeared in the text.
- Number the points you have made.

B   :   GROUP WORK

- On a master sheet of paper, list the main ideas and any supporting details that the group members agree on.
- Write the number of people who agreed on them e.g., 4/5 (four out of 5 agreed)
- Normally agreement of n – 1 is necessary i.e., if there are 5 people in the group at least 4 must have included the point for a consensus.

[Source: Reading in a Second Language, Urquhart A. H. and Weir C. J. (1998). Longman]

Appendices - Chapter 4

Appendix 4.2.4
Text mapping
Careful reading at the local level

he aim of the session is to identify items that can be used to test careful reading at he local level, that is those which test the skill of:

    i]   understanding contextualised meanings of academic vocabulary

:   INDIVIDUAL WORK

tage I: 7 minutes
- Read the text carefully to establish the main ideas and any important supporting details.

tage II: 3 minutes
- Highlight these words that are considered as academic and that bear important contextualised meanings.

:   GROUP WORK

- On a master sheet of paper, list the words that the group members agree on.
- Write the number of people who agreed on them e.g., 4/5 (four out of 5 agreed)
- Normally agreement of n – 1 is necessary i.e., if there are 5 people in the group at least 4 must have included the word for a consensus.

Appendices - Chapter 4

Appendix 4.2.5
AERT items and text mapping notes

Section I: Careful Reading for EXMI and IPROP

Item no.	Skill/ strategy	Text mapping points	Agreement
1	EXMI	rise of Asia, gross world product (economic growth)	4/4
2		middle-class Asia	3/4
3	IPROP	the idea of modernisation	3/4
4		governments + democracy - West	4/4
5		governments + democracy - East	4/4
6	EXMI	fewer side-effects than other cancer treatment	3/4
7		not sure of level of effectiveness (cure/prevent/halt growth)	3/4
8	IPROP	block signal to stop flow of blood + oxygen to tumour	4/4
9		successful on mice (not yet on humans)	4/4
10		other uses: old people/blind from diabetes	3/4
11	EXMI	5th generation (software)	4/4
12		computers will never surpass humans (in expertise)	4/4
13	IPROP	applications of computers, e.g., expert systems	4/4
14		expertise (humans) = rules + intuition - successful	4/4
15		expertise (computers) = rules - not successful	4/4

Section II: Skimming

Item no.	Text mapping points	Agreement
16	traditional attitudes at home and work	4/4
17	problems with delivery system	4/4
18	dwindling diversity of staple crops	4/4

Section III: Search Reading

Item no.	Text-mapping points	Agreement
19	discrimination against women in jobs (less pay)	4/4
20	discrimination against women in jobs (low position/social status)	4/4
21	discrimination against women in jobs (few at managerial level)	4/4
22	divorce rate increases, instigated 60% by women	3/4
23	first polymers problematic (swept away, rate fell)	4/4
24	biodegradable polymer	3/4
25	promising development (greater survival rate)	3/4
26	other applications: e.g., transplant (liver)	3/4
27	disease can resist potato genes (mutates, blight)	4/4
28	modern commercial agriculture (profitability)	3/4
29	gene banks: problems and solutions	4/4
30	gene banks: problems and solutions	4/4

Appendices - Chapter 4

Appendix 4.2.5
AERT items and text mapping notes

Section IV: Scanning

Item no.	Text mapping points	Agreement
31	natural materials - disadvantage: inconvenience	3/4
32	mother of pearl - nacre: strength of the structure	3/4
33	special structure of wood	3/4
34	synthetic materials - improved heat resistance	3/4
35	use of synthetic materials: e.g., turbine blades of aeroplanes	3/4
36	hierarchy of nature	4/4
37	biologists tend to specialise	3/4
38	emergent properties	3/4
39	reductionism: down to basics	3/4
40	the example of DNA	3/4
41	reasons for ad	4/4
42	making decisions: choose media	3/4
43	making decisions: purposes	3/4
44	what to ad?	3/4
45	ad cannot sell poor quality products/bad services/...	3/4

Section V: Careful Reading for Understanding Contextualised Lexical Meanings (ILEX)

Item no.	Text mapping points	Agreement
46	approved	4/4
47	revealed	4/4
48	unanimity	4/4
49	evidence	3/4
50	compelled	3/4
51	constitute	3/4
52	equivalent	4/4
53	model	3/4
54	characteristics	3/4
55	mechanism	4/4
56	constrain	3/4
57	solution	3/4
58	variables	4/4
59	equilibrium	4/4
60	reduction	3/4

Appendix 5.1
Test data and questionnaire data analysis of the AERT prototype version 1 – First trial in April 1997

1   Descriptive of item01 to item60 (variable order)
2   Reliability analysis – scale (alpha) item01 to item60
3   Number of non-responses – item01 to item60
4   Reliability analysis – scale (alpha) section 1 to section 5
5   Descriptive of subtotals and the total for the whole population
6   Descriptive of subtotals and the total in terms of disciplines
7   Histogram of the total score
8   Summary of cross-tabulations for the whole population
9   Correlation Coefficients between subtests
10 Factor analysis – passage totals
11 Factor analysis – careful global vs. quick global
12 Factor analysis – careful global vs. careful local
13 Factor analysis – quick local vs. careful local
14 Factor analysis – 10 'real' careful global vs. 7 'real' quick global
15 Questionnaire to students (first trial in April 1997)
16 Summary of returns to feedback questionnaire on the April 1997 trial of the AERT prototype version 1

Appendices - Chapter 5

Appendix 5.1.1
Descriptive statistics of item01 to item60 (variable order)

Number of valid observations (listwise) = 303.00

Variable	Mean	Std Dev	Minimum	Maximum	Valid N	Label
ITEM01	.73	.45	.00	1.00	303	
ITEM02	.72	.45	.00	1.00	303	
ITEM03	.36	.48	.00	1.00	303	
ITEM04	.67	.47	.00	1.00	303	
ITEM05	.57	.50	.00	1.00	303	
ITEM06	.87	.33	.00	1.00	303	
ITEM07	.71	.45	.00	1.00	303	
ITEM08	.71	.45	.00	1.00	303	
ITEM09	.51	.50	.00	1.00	303	
ITEM10	.48	.50	.00	1.00	303	
ITEM11	.64	.48	.00	1.00	303	
ITEM12	.61	.49	.00	1.00	303	
ITEM13	.26	.44	.00	1.00	303	
ITEM14	.25	.43	.00	1.00	303	
ITEM15	.69	.46	.00	1.00	303	
ITEM16	.57	.50	.00	1.00	303	
ITEM17	.46	.50	.00	1.00	303	
ITEM18	.20	.40	.00	1.00	303	
ITEM19	.65	.48	.00	1.00	303	
ITEM20	.39	.49	.00	1.00	303	
ITEM21	.36	.48	.00	1.00	303	
ITEM22	.63	.48	.00	1.00	303	
ITEM23	.64	.48	.00	1.00	303	
ITEM24	.65	.48	.00	1.00	303	
ITEM25	.49	.50	.00	1.00	303	
ITEM26	.73	.45	.00	1.00	303	
ITEM27	.66	.47	.00	1.00	303	
ITEM28	.31	.46	.00	1.00	303	
ITEM29	.54	.50	.00	1.00	303	
ITEM30	.48	.50	.00	1.00	303	
ITEM31	.87	.34	.00	1.00	303	
ITEM32	.77	.42	.00	1.00	303	
ITEM33	.47	.50	.00	1.00	303	
ITEM34	.81	.39	.00	1.00	303	
ITEM35	.46	.50	.00	1.00	303	
ITEM36	.60	.49	.00	1.00	303	
ITEM37	.74	.44	.00	1.00	303	
ITEM38	.66	.47	.00	1.00	303	
ITEM39	.53	.50	.00	1.00	303	
ITEM40	.76	.43	.00	1.00	303	
ITEM41	.69	.46	.00	1.00	303	
ITEM42	.46	.50	.00	1.00	303	
ITEM43	.34	.47	.00	1.00	303	
ITEM44	.42	.49	.00	1.00	303	
ITEM45	.39	.49	.00	1.00	303	
ITEM46	.62	.49	.00	1.00	303	
ITEM47	.58	.49	.00	1.00	303	
ITEM48	.31	.46	.00	1.00	303	
ITEM49	.35	.48	.00	1.00	303	
ITEM50	.30	.46	.00	1.00	303	
ITEM51	.53	.50	.00	1.00	303	
ITEM52	.13	.33	.00	1.00	303	
ITEM53	.56	.50	.00	1.00	303	
ITEM54	.50	.50	.00	1.00	303	
ITEM55	.40	.49	.00	1.00	303	
ITEM56	.47	.50	.00	1.00	303	
ITEM57	.84	.37	.00	1.00	303	
ITEM58	.56	.50	.00	1.00	303	
ITEM59	.66	.48	.00	1.00	303	
ITEM60	.58	.49	.00	1.00	303	

[Source: Reading in a Second Language, Urquhart A. H. and Weir C. J. (1998). Longman]

Appendix 5.1.2
Reliability analysis – scale (alpha)

Statistics for SCALE	Mean 32.8878	Variance 98.2655	Std Dev 9.9129	No. of Variables 60

Item-total Statistics

	Scale Mean if Item Deleted	Scale Variance if Item Deleted	Corrected Item-Total Correlation	Alpha if Item Deleted
ITEM01	32.1617	95.3347	.3131	.8789
ITEM02	32.1683	96.3855	.1899	.8804
ITEM03	32.5248	94.8595	.3383	.8786
ITEM04	32.2145	94.9638	.3365	.8786
ITEM05	32.3135	95.2623	.2853	.8793
ITEM06	32.0132	96.9402	.1860	.8803
ITEM07	32.1782	95.2529	.3161	.8789
ITEM08	32.1782	95.5112	.2866	.8792
ITEM09	32.3729	96.3075	.1738	.8808
ITEM10	32.4059	94.1559	.3973	.8777
ITEM11	32.2442	94.7547	.3513	.8784
ITEM12	32.2805	94.9707	.3205	.8788
ITEM13	32.6304	95.1013	.3480	.8785
ITEM14	32.6403	95.8536	.2629	.8795
ITEM15	32.2013	94.7640	.3632	.8782
ITEM16	32.3135	95.6928	.2402	.8799
ITEM17	32.4257	94.2254	.3910	.8778
ITEM18	32.6898	94.8836	.4144	.8778
ITEM19	32.2376	96.0957	.2073	.8803
ITEM20	32.5017	94.4760	.2677	.8795
ITEM21	32.5281	95.2103	.3010	.8791
ITEM22	32.2574	95.8739	.2279	.8800
ITEM23	32.2475	94.8624	.3387	.8786
ITEM24	32.2409	94.7265	.3552	.8783
ITEM25	32.3960	94.8161	.3280	.8787
ITEM26	32.1617	95.7519	.2647	.8795
ITEM27	32.2277	94.9513	.3341	.8786
ITEM28	32.5743	95.5698	.2729	.8794
ITEM29	32.3432	94.4646	.3663	.8782
ITEM30	32.4059	95.3744	.2701	.8795
ITEM31	32.0198	96.7811	.2053	.8801
ITEM32	32.1155	96.2085	.2282	.8799
ITEM33	32.4224	94.1852	.3950	.8778
ITEM34	32.0759	96.0969	.2626	.8795
ITEM35	32.4323	95.5906	.2487	.8798
ITEM36	32.2838	95.6543	.2475	.8798
ITEM37	32.1485	94.9746	.3614	.8783
ITEM38	32.2244	95.2409	.3031	.8790
ITEM39	32.3531	94.2358	.3897	.8778
ITEM40	32.1320	95.6183	.2925	.8792
ITEM41	32.1947	95.0845	.3294	.8787
ITEM42	32.4323	93.1535	.5050	.8762
ITEM43	32.5512	93.5595	.4895	.8765
ITEM44	32.4719	93.7666	.4451	.8771
ITEM45	32.4950	94.6283	.3570	.8783
ITEM46	32.2706	94.9663	.3227	.8788
ITEM47	32.3102	93.9564	.4237	.8774
ITEM48	32.5809	95.6880	.2616	.8796
ITEM49	32.5347	96.0973	.2066	.8803
ITEM50	32.5875	95.3690	.2995	.8791
ITEM51	32.3597	94.7940	.3308	.8787
ITEM52	32.7624	96.6188	.2356	.8798
ITEM53	32.3300	96.1622	.1902	.8806
ITEM54	32.3927	96.5241	.1515	.8811
ITEM55	32.4917	95.0984	.3064	.8790
ITEM56	32.4158	94.1775	.3955	.8778
ITEM57	32.0462	95.9118	.3099	.8790
ITEM58	32.3267	94.9955	.3120	.8789
ITEM59	32.2310	94.2312	.4124	.8776
ITEM60	32.3069	94.8028	.3344	.8786

Reliability Coefficients:

No. of Cases = 303.0

No. of Items = 60

Alpha = .8807

Appendices - Chapter 5

Appendix 5.1.3
Number of non-responses for each item in the first trial in April 1997

Section 1 Item No	No. of non-responses	Section 2 Item No.	No. of non-responses	Section 3 Item No.	No. of Non-responses	Section 4 Item No.	No of non responses	Section 5 Item No.	No. of non-responses
1	2	16	0	19	4	31	2	46	1
2	2	17	6	20	6	32	4	47	1
3	14	18	17	21	14	33	9	48	1
4	12			22	6	34	13	49	0
5	13			23	13	35	73	50	1
6	1			24	19	36	18	51	0
7	6			25	18	37	47	52	1
8	6			26	14	38	33	53	2
9	8			27	22	39	57	54	2
10	20			28	39	40	51	55	2
11	36			29	67	41	49	56	1
12	56			30	72	42	120	57	2
13	78					43	136	58	3
14	75					44	143	59	2
15	67					45	140	60	1

Appendices - Chapter 5

Appendix 5.1.4
Reliability analysis – scale (alpha) of sections

Section 1 - Careful (global)

Statistics for	Mean	Variance	Std Dev	No. of Variables
SCALE	8.7888	8.8095	2.9681	15

Item-total Statistics

	Scale Mean if Item Deleted	Scale Variance if Item Deleted	Corrected Item-Total Correlation	Alpha if Item Deleted
ITEM01	8.0627	7.9331	.2690	.6711
ITEM02	8.0693	8.1442	.1802	.6820
ITEM03	8.4257	7.8148	.2832	.6695
ITEM04	8.1155	7.8177	.2935	.6681
ITEM05	8.2145	7.6128	.3481	.6605
ITEM06	7.9142	8.3039	.2069	.6776
ITEM07	8.0792	7.8215	.3072	.6663
ITEM08	8.0792	7.7354	.3429	.6618
ITEM09	8.2739	7.8684	.2459	.6748
ITEM10	8.3069	7.5843	.3536	.6597
ITEM11	8.1452	7.7868	.2960	.6677
ITEM12	8.1815	7.8643	.2573	.6730
ITEM13	8.5314	7.8459	.3146	.6656
ITEM14	8.5413	7.9776	.2642	.6717
ITEM15	8.1023	7.6021	.3869	.6558

Reliability Coefficients
No. of Cases = 303.0   No. of Items = 15
Alpha = .6836

[Source: Reading in a Second Language, Urquhart A. H. and Weir C. J. (1998). Longman]

Appendices - Chapter 5

Section 2 and 3 - Skimming and Search reading

Statistics for	Mean	Variance	Std Dev	No. of Variables
SCALE	7.7657	9.6833	3.1118	15

Item-total Statistics

	Scale Mean if Item Deleted	Scale Variance if Item Deleted	Corrected Item-Total Correlation	Alpha if Item Deleted
ITEM16	7.1914	8.6718	.2627	.6807
ITEM17	7.3036	8.5102	.3171	.6737
ITEM18	7.5677	8.7032	.3485	.6715
ITEM19	7.1155	8.6919	.2710	.6795
ITEM20	7.3795	8.6932	.2616	.6807
ITEM21	7.4059	8.7122	.2608	.6808
ITEM22	7.1353	8.9783	.1626	.6928
ITEM23	7.1254	8.3153	.4101	.6619
ITEM24	7.1188	8.4494	.3610	.6682
ITEM25	7.2739	8.4181	.3491	.6695
ITEM26	7.0396	8.8196	.2503	.6817
ITEM27	7.1056	8.6312	.2966	.6763
ITEM28	7.4521	8.7121	.2753	.6789
ITEM29	7.2211	8.4509	.3391	.6708
ITEM30	7.2838	8.5616	.2975	.6762

Reliability Coefficients
No. of Cases = 303.0   No. of Items = 15
Alpha = .6913

Section 4 - Scanning

Statistics for	Mean	Variance	Std Dev	No. of Variables
SCALE	8.9637	10.5185	3.2432	15

Item-total Statistics

	Scale Mean if Item Deleted	Scale Variance if Item Deleted	Corrected Item-Total Correlation	Alpha if Item Deleted
ITEM31	8.0957	10.0736	.1533	.7466
ITEM32	8.1914	9.6454	.2670	.7388
ITEM33	8.4983	9.3700	.2939	.7373
ITEM34	8.1518	9.7517	.2510	.7399
ITEM35	8.5083	9.3832	.2901	.7377
ITEM36	8.3597	9.3834	.2983	.7367
ITEM37	8.2244	9.3667	.3561	.7307
ITEM38	8.3003	9.4956	.2739	.7389
ITEM39	8.4290	9.0736	.3971	.7262
ITEM40	8.2079	9.3772	.3628	.7302
ITEM41	8.2706	9.3106	.3527	.7309
ITEM42	8.5083	8.8269	.4868	.7163
ITEM43	8.6271	8.7975	.5331	.7121
ITEM44	8.5479	8.9439	.4507	.7204
ITEM45	8.5710	9.1464	.3829	.7278

Reliability Coefficients
No. of Cases = 303.0   No. of Items = 15
Alpha = .7450

Appendices - Chapter 5

Section 5 - Careful (local)

Statistics for	Mean	Variance	Std Dev	No. of Variables
SCALE	7.3696	9.5715	3.0938	15

Item-total Statistics

	Scale Mean if Item Deleted	Scale Variance if Item Deleted	Corrected Item-Total Correlation	Alpha if Item Deleted
ITEM46	6.7525	8.2531	.3866	.6727
ITEM47	6.7921	8.2712	.3709	.6746
ITEM48	7.0627	8.6418	.2637	.6879
ITEM49	7.0165	8.7977	.1918	.6967
ITEM50	7.0693	8.5945	.2846	.6855
ITEM51	6.8416	8.3920	.3208	.6810
ITEM52	7.2442	8.9335	.2662	.6882
ITEM53	6.8119	8.5903	.2516	.6899
ITEM54	6.8746	8.6730	.2196	.6940
ITEM55	6.9736	8.4364	.3146	.6818
ITEM56	6.8977	8.2114	.3874	.6723
ITEM57	6.5281	8.8063	.2909	.6854
ITEM58	6.8086	8.3473	.3402	.6785
ITEM59	6.7129	8.3378	.3668	.6754
ITEM60	6.7888	8.4784	.2949	.6843

Reliability Coefficients
No. of Cases = 303.0   No. of Items = 15
Alpha = .6981

Appendix 5.1.5
Descriptive of subtotals and total score for the whole population

Number of valid observations (listwise) = 303.00

Variable	Mean	Std Dev	Minimum	Maximum	Valid N	Label
TOTCARE1	3.06	1.33	.00	5.00	303	
TOTCARE2	3.29	1.26	.005	.00	303	
TOTCARE3	2.44	1.41	.00	5.00	303	
TOTSCH1	2.03	1.18	.00	4.00	303	
TOTSCH2	2.50	1.28	.00	4.00	303	
TOTSCH3	2.00	.29	.004	.00	303	
TOTSKCH1	2.60	1.35	.005	.00	303	
TOTSKCH2	2.97	1.46	.005	.00	303	
TOTSKCH3	2.20	1.46	.005	.00	303	
TOTSCAN1	3.37	1.21	.00	5.00	303	
TOTSCAN2	3.30	1.46	.005	.00	303	
TOTSCAN3	2.29	1.72	.005	.00	303	
TOTLEXI1	2.16	1.36	.005	.00	303	
TOTLEXI2	2.10	1.31	.005	.00	303	
TOTLEXI3	3.11	1.43	.005	.00	303	
TOTCARE	8.79	2.971	.001	5.00	303	
TOTSKIM	1.23	.96	.00	3.00	303	
TOTSKSCH	7.77	3.11	.001	5.00	303	
TOTSCAN	8.96	3.24	.001	5.00	303	
TOTLEXI	7.37	3.09	.00	14.00	303	
TOTQUICK	16.73	5.492	.00	29.00	303	
TOTSLOW	16.16	5.153	.00	28.00	303	
TOTGLOB	16.55	5.383	.00	28.00	303	
TOTLOCAL	16.33	5.573	.00	29.00	303	
TOT1ART	10.11	3.992	.00	19.00	303	
TOT2SCIE	10.12	3.531	.00	18.00	303	
TOT3LIFE	12.67	3.912	.00	20.00	303	
TOTSCORE	32.89	9.917	.00	56.00	303	

Appendices - Chapter 5

Appendix 5.1.6
Descriptive statistics of subtotals and the total in terms of disciplines

Discipline = 1 (arts/humanities/business/management):

Number of valid observations (listwise) = 56.00

Variable	Mean	Std Dev	Minimum	Maximum	Valid N	Label
TOT1ART	7.86	3.38	2.00	17.00	56	
TOT2SCIE	7.50	2.98	1.00	16.00	56	
TOT3LIFE	10.11	3.57	3.00	19.00	56	
TOTSCORE	25.46	8.23	8.00	49.00	56	

Discipline = 2 (science and technology):

Number of valid observations (listwise) = 151.00

Variable	Mean	Std Dev	Minimum	Maximum	Valid N	Label
TOT1ART	11.93	3.66	2.00	19.00	151	
TOT2SCIE	11.77	3.15	5.00	18.00	151	
TOT3LIFE	14.38	3.26	4.00	20.00	151	
TOTSCORE	38.09	8.33	17.00	56.00	151	

Discipline = 3 (biology/medical/life science):

Number of valid observations (listwise) = 96.00

Variable	Mean	Std Dev	Minimum	Maximum	Valid N	Label
TOT1ART	8.54	3.48	2.00	16.00	96	
TOT2SCIE	9.03	3.02	1.00	17.00	96	
TOT3LIFE	11.46	3.80	2.00	20.00	96	
TOTSCORE	29.03	8.54	7.00	47.00	96	

Appendix 5.1.7
Histogram of the total score of the whole population

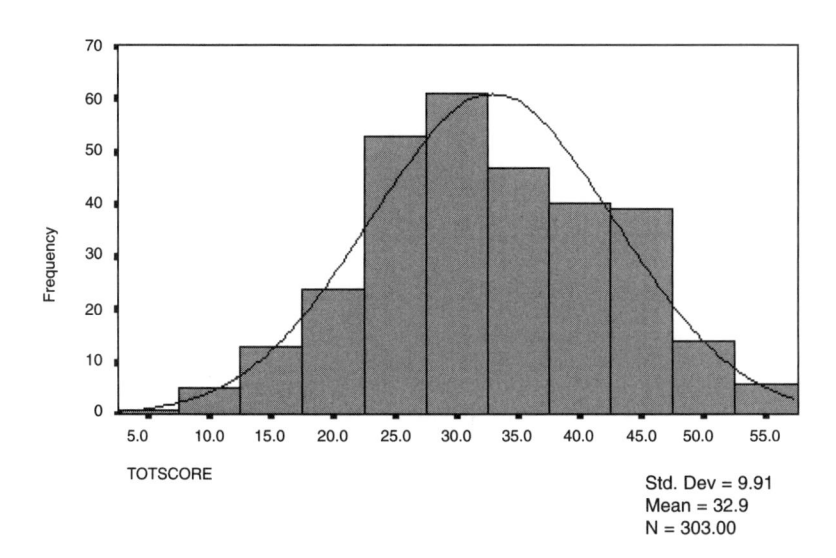

TOTSCORE

Std. Dev = 9.91
Mean = 32.9
N = 303.00

[Source: Reading in a Second Language, Urquhart A. H. and Weir C. J. (1998). Longman]

Appendices - Chapter 5

Appendix 5.1.8
Summary of cross-tabulations

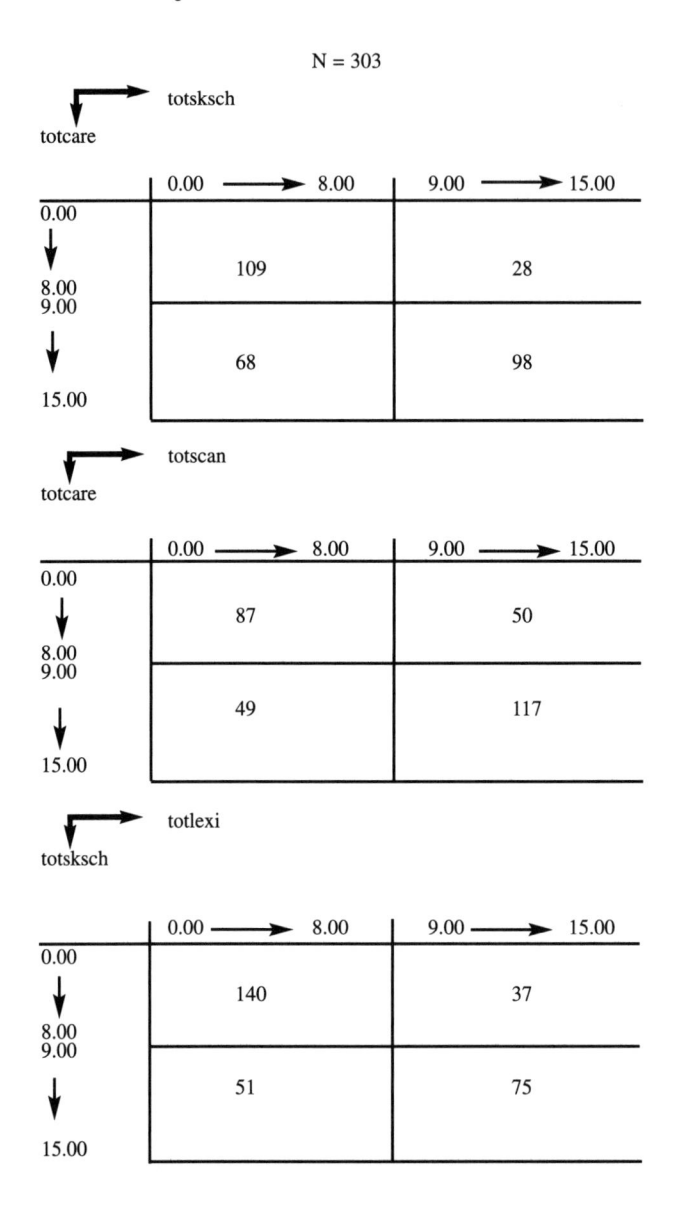

N = 303

totcare → totksch

	0.00 → 8.00	9.00 → 15.00
0.00 ↓ 8.00	109	28
9.00 ↓ 15.00	68	98

totcare → totscan

	0.00 → 8.00	9.00 → 15.00
0.00 ↓ 8.00	87	50
9.00 ↓ 15.00	49	117

totsksch → totlexi

	0.00 → 8.00	9.00 → 15.00
0.00 ↓ 8.00	140	37
9.00 ↓ 15.00	51	75

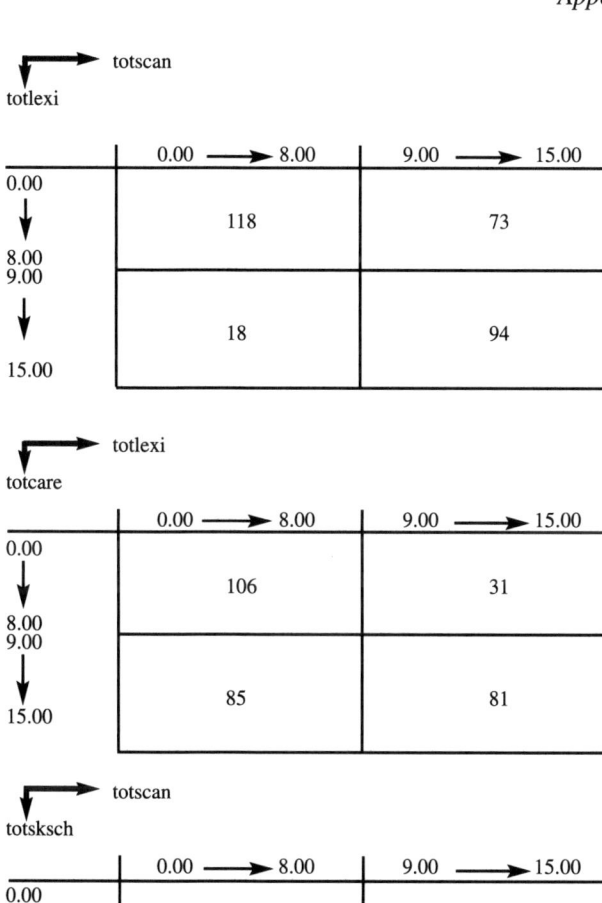

Appendices - Chapter 5

            totscan
totlexi

	0.00 ⟶ 8.00	9.00 ⟶ 15.00
0.00 ↓ 8.00	118	73
9.00 ↓ 15.00	18	94

            totlexi
totcare

	0.00 ⟶ 8.00	9.00 ⟶ 15.00
0.00 ↓ 8.00	106	31
9.00 ↓ 15.00	85	81

            totscan
totsksch

	0.00 ⟶ 8.00	9.00 ⟶ 15.00
0.00 ↓ 8.00	105	72
9.00 ↓ 15.00	31	95

Appendices - Chapter 5

Appendix 5.1.9

Correlation Coefficients between Subtests

	TOTCARE	TOTSKSCH	TOTSCAN	TOTLEXI	TOTQUICK	TOTSLOW	TOTGLOB	TOTLOCAL	TOTSCORE
TOTCARE	1.0000 (303) P= .	.5654 (303) P= .000	.5489 (303) P= .000	.4423 (303) P= .000	.6452 (303) P= .000	.8423 (303) P= .000	.8788 (303) P= .000	.5655 (303) P= .000	.7945 (303) P= .000
TOTSKSCH	.5654 (303) P= .000	1.0000 (303) P= .	.4900 (303) P= .000	.5060 (303) P= .000	.8570 (303) P= .000	.6300 (303) P= .000	.8904 (303) P= .000	.5666 (303) P= .000	.8014 (303) P= .000
TOTSCAN	.5489 (303) P= .000	.4900 (303) P= .000	1.0000 (303) P= .	.5439 (303) P= .000	.8692 (303) P= .000	.6433 (303) P= .000	.5863 (303) P= .000	.8846 (303) P= .000	.8151 (303) P= .000
TOTLEXI	.4423 (303) P= .000	.5060 (303) P= .000	.5439 (303) P= .000	1.0000 (303) P= .	.6086 (303) P= .000	.8560 (303) P= .000	.5368 (303) P= .000	.8724 (303) P= .000	.7813 (303) P= .000
TOTQUICK	.6452 (303) P= .000	.8570 (303) P= .000	.8692 (303) P= .000	.6086 (303) P= .000	1.0000 (303) P= .	.7377 (303) P= .000	.8517 (303) P= .000	.8444 (303) P= .000	.9365 (303) P= .000
TOTSLOW	.8423 (303) P= .000	.6300 (303) P= .000	.6433 (303) P= .000	.8560 (303) P= .000	.7377 (303) P= .000	1.0000 (303) P= .	.8292 (303) P= .000	.8503 (303) P= .000	.9276 (303) P= .000
TOTGLOB	.8788 (303) P= .000	.8904 (303) P= .000	.5863 (303) P= .000	.5368 (303) P= .000	.8517 (303) P= .000	.8292 (303) P= .000	1.0000 (303) P= .	.6398 (303) P= .000	.9020 (303) P= .000
TOTLOCAL	.5655 (303) P= .000	.5666 (303) P= .000	.8846 (303) P= .000	.872 (303) P= .000	.8444 (303) P= .000	.8503 (303) P= .000	.6398 (303) P= .000	1.0000 (303) P= .	.9089 (303) P= .000
TOTSCORE	.7945 (303) P= .000	.8014 (303) P= .000	.8151 (303) P= .000	.7813 (303) P= .000	.9365 (303) P= .000	.9276 (303) P= .000	.9020 (303) P= .000	.9089 (303) P= .000	1.0000 (303) P= .

(Coefficient / (Cases) / 2-tailed Significance)   " . " is printed if a coefficient cannot be computed

Appendices - Chapter 5

Appendix 5.1.10
Factor analysis of passage totals

Analysis number 1 Listwise deletion of cases with missing values
Extraction 1 for analysis 1, Principal Components Analysis (PC)

Initial Statistics:

Variable	Communality	Factor	Eigenvalue	Pct of Var	Cum Pct
TOTCARE1	1.00000	1	4.18454	34.9	34.9
TOTCARE2	1.00000	2	1.04561	8.7	43.6
TOTCARE3	1.00000	3	1.01069	8.4	52.0
TOTSKCH1	1.00000	4	.82949	6.9	58.9
TOTSKCH2	1.00000	5	.74245	6.2	65.1
TOTSKCH3	1.00000	6	.73801	6.2	71.3
TOTSCAN1	1.00000	7	.70759	5.9	77.2
TOTSCAN2	1.00000	8	.68537	5.7	82.9
TOTSCAN3	1.00000	9	.57282	4.8	87.6
TOTLEXI1	1.00000	10	.55142	4.6	92.2
TOTLEXI2	1.00000	11	.47454	4.0	96.2
TOTLEXI3	1.00000	12	.45746	3.8	100.0

PC extracted 4 factors.

Factor Matrix:

	Factor 1	Factor 2	Factor 3	Factor 4
TOTCARE1	.59661	.41260	-.00128	-.13894
TOTCARE2	.57844	.48131	-.15600	-.00330
TOTCARE3	.60298	-.15660	-.34395	.40190
TOTSKCH1	.52091	.33170	.35784	.38271
TOTSKCH2	.62868	.33099	.03976	.09638
TOTSKCH3	.58850	-.18434	-.33310	.28161
TOTSCAN1	.56936	.06692	-.14645	-.54760
TOTSCAN2	.57145	-.09757	-.33277	-.28954
TOTSCAN3	.64332	-.44645	-.06445	.07682
TOTLEXI1	.61276	-.26759	.36445	-.06820
TOTLEXI2	.49851	-.16412	.58500	-.06997
TOTLEXI3	.65493	-.23190	.12686	-.12020

Appendices - Chapter 5

Final Statistics:

Variable	Communality	Factor	Eigenvalue	Pct of Var	Cum Pct
TOTCARE1	.54548	1	4.18454	34.9	34.9
TOTCARE2	.59060	2	1.04561	8.7	43.6
TOTCARE3	.66793	3	1.01069	8.4	52.0
TOTSKCH1	.65589	4	.82949	6.9	58.9
TOTSKCH2	.51566				
TOTSKCH3	.57057				
TOTSCAN1	.64996				
TOTSCAN2	.53064				
TOTSCAN3	.62324				
TOTLEXI1	.58456				
TOTLEXI2	.62256				
TOTLEXI3	.51325				

VARIMAX rotation 1 for extraction 1 in analysis 1 - Kaiser Normalization.
VARIMAX converged in 7 iterations.

Rotated Factor Matrix:

	Factor 1	Factor 2	Factor 3	Factor 4
TOTCARE1	.62663	.06843	.14628	.35600
TOTCARE2	.68429	.18215	-.02032	.29792
TOTCARE3	.24659	.77317	.07610	.05948
TOTSKCH1	.66732	.14945	.35875	-.24400
TOTSKCH2	.63147	.22176	.20415	.16141
TOTSKCH3	.19237	.70827	.10002	.14803
TOTSCAN1	.23178	.05967	.20672	.74158
TOTSCAN2	.13408	.36250	.11138	.60733
TOTSCAN3	-.00418	.59897	.45727	.23528
TOTLEXI1	.13906	.20804	.70249	.16867
TOTLEXI2	.18398	-.01130	.76645	.03382
TOTLEXI3	.15465	.31186	.53667	.32259

Factor Transformation Matrix:

	Factor 1	Factor 2	Factor 3	Factor 4
Factor 1	.54015	.52551	.51022	.41443
Factor 2	.80834	-.41859	-.41375	-.01339
Factor 3	.10596	-.52168	.74765	-.39704
Factor 4	.20880	.52580	-.09753	-.81880

Appendices - Chapter 5

Appendix 5.1.11
Factor analysis

– Careful global (Section 1) vs. quick global (Section 2 and 3)

Extraction 1 for analysis 1, Principal Components Analysis (PC)
PC extracted 3 factors.
Factor Matrix:

	Factor 1	Factor 2	Factor 3
ITEM01	.35844	.27370	-.05325
ITEM02	.24690	.20022	.28014
ITEM03	.38788	.19564	.13207
ITEM04	.42515	.15713	.03260
ITEM05	.37780	.16581	.50634
ITEM06	.23188	.30214	.33360
ITEM07	.39451	.20359	.30837
ITEM08	.40870	.00678	.08191
ITEM09	.28193	-.02318	.32395
ITEM10	.49366	.01570	.06398
ITEM11	.40740	-.02358	-.05849
ITEM12	.40052	-.39898	.27995
ITEM13	.40172	-.21805	-.07847
ITEM14	.32518	-.23729	-.05698
ITEM15	.47762	-.25485	-.21617
ITEM16	.31409	-.09419	-.03184
ITEM17	.46244	-.16589	.15687
ITEM18	.49330	-.20725	.04067
ITEM19	.31064	.19918	-.49811
ITEM20	.34307	.29354	-.40747
ITEM21	.39256	.27228	-.33790
ITEM22	.25668	.29991	.04751
ITEM23	.46689	.24674	-.21266
ITEM24	.43567	.17708	-.02225
ITEM25	.42966	.27795	-.19310
ITEM26	.34842	.12932	.12362
ITEM27	.39320	-.09736	.13614
ITEM28	.37070	-.27079	-.01136
ITEM29	.41188	-.50700	.09237
ITEM30	.35401	-.56104	.06009

Final Statistics:

Factor	Eigenvalue	Pct of Var	Cum Pct
1	4.47544	14.9	14.9
2	1.87766	6.3	21.2
3	1.50321	5.0	26.2

Appendices - Chapter 5

Appendix 5.1.12
Factor analysis

– Careful global (section 1) vs. careful local (section 5)

Extraction 1 for analysis 1, Principal Components Analysis (PC)
PC extracted 3 factors.

Factor Matrix:

	Factor 1	Factor 2	Factor 3
ITEM01	.35419	.07147	.24566
ITEM02	.25198	.02516	.32407
ITEM03	.39938	.04971	.32812
ITEM04	.36344	.19864	.09796
ITEM05	.35125	.41042	.43283
ITEM06	.22666	.13507	.46428
ITEM07	.38603	.19247	.20150
ITEM08	.37549	.34387	-.09751
ITEM09	.20756	.48369	.19068
ITEM10	.47791	.09945	-.01514
ITEM11	.41513	.03979	-.05306
ITEM12	.35698	.20657	-.57466
ITEM13	.42686	.12114	-.16013
ITEM14	.31132	.29858	-.26518
ITEM15	.42710	.42185	-.42105
ITEM46	.43179	-.33806	.11272
ITEM47	.50645	-.31203	.11268
ITEM48	.30775	-.09041	.09677
ITEM49	.24747	-.07246	.26668
ITEM50	.33496	-.23607	-.01828
ITEM51	.42613	-.13725	.04570
ITEM52	.32176	-.34385	-.03447
ITEM53	.27668	-.41138	-.06872
ITEM54	.24263	-.14900	.06010
ITEM55	.37222	-.31271	-.14617
ITEM56	.47017	-.11028	-.10293
ITEM57	.38027	-.03741	-.18228
ITEM58	.38288	-.30800	-.01056
ITEM59	.51289	-.01229	-.19782
ITEM60	.41676	-.02467	-.07180

Final Statistics:

Factor	Eigenvalue	Pct of Var	Cum Pct
1	4.19728	14.0	14.0
2	1.77580	5.9	19.9
3	1.60594	5.4	25.3

[Source: Reading in a Second Language, Urquhart A. H. and Weir C. J. (1998). Longman]

Appendix 5.1.13
Factor analysis

– Quick local (section 4) vs. careful local (section 5)

Extraction 1 for analysis 1, Principal Components Analysis (PC)
PC extracted 3 factors.
Factor Matrix:

	Factor 1	Factor 2	Factor 3
ITEM31	.18893	.28262	.04600
ITEM32	.28786	.24083	-.06660
ITEM33	.42854	.17809	.14400
ITEM34	.30137	.27661	-.07745
ITEM35	.34978	.09895	-.16718
ITEM36	.30559	.43120	-.18796
ITEM37	.39786	.47897	-.14380
ITEM38	.38304	.29199	-.03568
ITEM39	.44227	.21125	-.40997
ITEM40	.36703	.24985	-.45002
ITEM41	.46816	-.06191	.01588
ITEM42	.62225	-.33958	-.17039
ITEM43	.65898	-.25165	-.11374
ITEM44	.53830	-.39993	-.37367
ITEM45	.47238	-.45275	-.42235
ITEM46	.40925	.02313	.42706
ITEM47	.50306	.17178	.22969
ITEM48	.32428	-.36926	.08405
ITEM49	.25591	-.26326	-.03529
ITEM50	.38541	.00233	.18296
ITEM51	.37917	.02224	.21610
ITEM52	.32522	.12481	.27892
ITEM53	.24462	-.06104	.24418
ITEM54	.21047	-.17169	.32412
ITEM55	.38249	-.02289	.26833
ITEM56	.45033	-.11359	.29472
ITEM57	.36916	-.08421	.06824
ITEM58	.44744	.03738	.10064
ITEM59	.50376	.22711	.06223
ITEM60	.38239	-.12764	.16480

Final Statistics:

Factor	Eigenvalue	Pct of Var	Cum Pct
1	4.97661	16.6	16.6
2	1.78572	6.0	22.5
3	1.62011	5.4	27.9

Appendices - Chapter 5

Appendix 5.1.14
Factor analysis

– 10 'real' careful reading items and 7 'real' quick reading items

Extraction 1 for analysis 1, Principal Components Analysis (PC)
PC extracted 5 factors.
Factor Matrix:

	Factor 1	Factor 2	Factor 3	Factor 4	Factor 5
ITEM01	.33980	.30213	-.42959	.39310	.00941
ITEM02	.30414	.24455	.35449	.20725	.17944
ITEM03	.42881	.22511	-.35055	.19024	.39294
ITEM04	.41660	.13762	-.30028	.04322	-.27608
ITEM05	.48730	.33886	-.09423	-.36913	-.07391
ITEM06	.27569	.40107	.13037	-.21722	.47566
ITEM07	.41864	.32510	.36321	-.30644	.10341
ITEM08	.42985	.23574	.16546	.00930	-.44112
ITEM09	.32646	.16604	-.28318	-.34636	-.08221
ITEM10	.49856	.06956	.06834	.06809	-.46961
ITEM16	.35932	-.16407	.41519	.32608	-.00875
ITEM17	.50429	-.08255	.39916	.09829	.07862
ITEM18	.52063	-.16912	-.04681	.23618	-.15515
ITEM27	.47097	-.15017	-.14464	-.03406	.19570
ITEM28	.40079	-.29604	-.09279	.35658	.24182
ITEM29	.48836	-.56898	-.12834	-.31633	.10707
ITEM30	.43802	-.63250	.00142	-.26277	.00871

Final Statistics:

Factor	Eigenvalue	Pct of Var	Cum Pct
1	3.06132	18.0	18.0
2	1.58638	9.3	27.3
3	1.17320	6.9	34.2
4	1.10677	6.5	40.8
5	1.06585	6.3	47.0

Appendices - Chapter 5

Appendix 5.1.15

15 Questionnaire to students (First trial in April 1997)

Name _____ University _____
Disciplinary area _____ Class _____
Date of passing CET-4 _____ Date of passing CET-6 _____

I   About the passages

Passages	A1 - A12 language difficulty				B13 - B24 topic familiarity			B13 - B24 disciplinary area				D37 - D48 subject specificity			
	very diff	diff	easy	very easy	very fam	fam	not fam	not fam at all	arts business mngmt	science tech	biology medical life sci		very spec	spec	not spec	not spec at all
1 A billion consumers																
2 Cancer-stranglers																
3 Mindless machine																
4 Japanese women ...																
5 Sugaring the pill																
6 Tomorrow's bitter ...																
7 Trick's of nature																
8 Themes in the study ...																
9 Successful advertising...																
10 Andropov ...																
11 Quark ...																
12 Elephants ...																

Appendices - Chapter 5

II   About the test formats

Formats	E49 - E53 your familiarity with the test format			F54 - F58 your opinion of the test format		
	very familiar	familiar	not familiar	not familiar at all	very good	good	not good	not good at all
1 short-answer questions								
2 true/false judgement								
3 table/flow chart completion								
4 sentence completion								
5 banked cloze								

III   Time sufficiency

Sections	G59 - G63 time sufficiency for each section			
	very sufficient	quite sufficient	just enough	not sufficient
1 careful global reading				
2 skimming				
3 search reading				
4 scanning				
5 careful local reading				

Appendices - Chapter 5

IV Comments on sections

<table>
<tr><th colspan="6">H64 - H67
comments on sections</th></tr>
<tr><th></th><th>Section 1
careful reading
global</th><th>Section 2
skimming</th><th>Section 3
search reading</th><th>Section 4
scanning</th><th>Section 5
careful reading
local</th></tr>
<tr><td>Most difficult section</td><td></td><td></td><td></td><td></td><td></td></tr>
<tr><td>Easiest section</td><td></td><td></td><td></td><td></td><td></td></tr>
<tr><td>Least time pressured section</td><td></td><td></td><td></td><td></td><td></td></tr>
<tr><td>Most time pressured section</td><td></td><td></td><td></td><td></td><td></td></tr>
</table>

V General comments on the test

<table>
<tr><th colspan="5">I68 - I73
general comments on the test</th></tr>
<tr><th></th><th>very good</th><th>good</th><th>average</th><th>not good</th></tr>
<tr><td>Test form</td><td></td><td></td><td></td><td></td></tr>
<tr><td>Test content</td><td></td><td></td><td></td><td></td></tr>
<tr><td>Length of the test</td><td></td><td></td><td></td><td></td></tr>
<tr><td>Total time of the test</td><td></td><td></td><td></td><td></td></tr>
<tr><td>Test layout</td><td></td><td></td><td></td><td></td></tr>
<tr><td>Test rubrics</td><td></td><td></td><td></td><td></td></tr>
</table>

Appendices - Chapter 5

Appendix 5.1.16
Summary of returns to feedback questionnaire on the April 1997 trial of the AERT prototype Version 1

Part I About the passages

A: language difficulty
1: very difficult   2: difficult   3: easy 4: very easy

Number of valid observations (listwise) = 279.00

Variable	Mean	Std Dev	Minimum	Maximum	Valid N Label
A01DIFF	2.60	.59	1.00	4.00	303
A02DIFF	2.39	.61	1.00	4.00	303
A03DIFF	2.35	.64	1.00	4.00	301
A04DIFF	2.82	.58	1.00	4.00	302
A05DIFF	2.20	.68	1.00	4.00	302
A06DIFF	2.52	.65	1.00	4.00	300
A07DIFF	2.35	.66	1.00	4.00	297
A08DIFF	2.21	.61	1.00	4.00	298
A09DIFF	2.71	.61	1.00	4.00	296
A10DIFF	2.29	.68	1.00	4.00	296
A11DIFF	2.30	.67	1.00	4.00	299
A12DIFF	2.78	.58	1.00	4.00	297

B: topic familiarity
1: very familiar   2: familiar   3: not very familiar   4: not familiar at all

Number of valid observations (listwise) = 252.00

Variable	Mean	Std Dev	Minimum	Maximum	Valid N Label
B13FAM	2.30	.62	1.00	4.00	298
B14FAM	2.64	.71	1.00	4.00	300
B15FAM	2.57	.66	1.00	4.00	296
B16FAM	2.09	.60	1.00	4.00	299
B17FAM	2.90	.71	1.00	4.00	298
B18FAM	2.74	.63	1.00	4.00	298
B19FAM	2.83	.62	1.00	4.00	295
B20FAM	2.85	.60	1.00	4.00	291
B21FAM	2.22	.62	1.00	4.00	292
B22FAM	2.76	.66	1.00	4.00	288
B23FAM	2.81	.67	1.00	4.00	293
B24FAM	2.34	.60	1.00	4.00	291

Appendices - Chapter 5

C: disciplinary area
1: arts and humanities   2: science and technology   3: life science

Number of valid observations (listwise) = 266.00

Variable	Mean	Std Dev	Minimum	Maximum	Valid N Label
C25DISP	1.06	.27	1.00	3.00	300
C26DISP	2.97	.18	1.00	3.00	303
C27DISP	1.97	.28	1.00	3.00	301
C28DISP	1.05	.28	1.00	3.00	301
C29DISP	2.90	.35	1.00	3.00	300
C30DISP	2.12	.65	1.00	3.00	302
C31DISP	2.13	.51	1.00	3.00	300
C32DISP	2.26	.83	1.00	3.00	297
C33DISP	1.07	.31	1.00	3.00	296
C34DISP	1.12	.38	1.00	3.00	290
C35DISP	2.01	.37	1.00	3.00	292
C36DISP	1.96	.82	1.00	3.00	290

D: subject specificity
1: very specific   2: specific   3: not very specific   4: not specific at all

Number of valid observations (listwise) = 268.00

Variable	Mean	Std Dev	Minimum	Maximum	Valid N Label
D37SPEC	2.74	.58	1.00	4.00	298
D38SPEC	2.07	.72	1.00	4.00	301
D39SEPC	2.53	.68	1.00	4.00	295
D40SPEC	2.92	.69	1.00	4.00	300
D41SPEC	2.03	.75	1.00	4.00	298
D42SPEC	2.54	.62	1.00	4.00	300
D43SPEC	2.41	.72	1.00	4.00	298
D44SPEC	2.33	.74	1.00	4.00	295
D45SPEC	2.71	.67	1.00	4.00	294
D46SPEC	2.78	.74	1.00	4.00	293
D47SPEC	2.17	.80	1.00	4.00	293
D48SPEC	2.84	.61	1.00	4.00	296

Appendices - Chapter 5

Part II About the formats

E: familiarity
1: very familiar   **2: familiar**   **3: not very familiar**   **4: not familiar at all**

Number of valid observations (listwise) = 299.00

Variable	Mean	Std Dev	Minimum	Maximum	Valid N Label
E49FRFAM	2.47	.63	1.00	4.00	302
E50FRFAM	2.42	.72	1.00	4.00	302
E51FRFAM	2.88	.61	1.00	4.00	300
E52FRFAM	2.31	.61	1.00	4.00	302
E53FRFAM	1.80	.60	1.00	4.00	301

F: attitude towards formats
1: like very much   **2: like**   **3: dislike**   **4: dislike a lot**

Number of valid observations (listwise) = 292.00

Variable	Mean	Std Dev	Minimum	Maximum	Valid N Label
F54FRLIK	2.40	62	1.00	4.00	295
F55FRLIK	2.25	.64	1.00	4.00	297
F56FRLIK	2.36	.68	1.00	4.00	296
F57FRLIK	2.15	.57	1.00	4.00	295
F58FRLIK	1.98	.62	1.00	4.00	296

Part III About time limits

G: time limits
1: very sufficient   **2: quite sufficient**   **3: just enough**   **4: not enough**

Number of valid observations (listwise) = 301.00

Variable	Mean	Std Dev	Minimum	Maximum	Valid N Label
G59TMSUF	2.78	.92	1.00	4.00	303
G60TMSUF	3.23	.75	1.00	4.00	303
G61TMSUF	3.28	.76	1.00	4.00	303
G62TMSUF	3.47	.79	1.00	4.00	301
G63TMSUF	1.96	.83	1.00	4.00	303

Appendices - Chapter 5

Part IV comments on each section

1: careful **2: skim** **3: search** **4: scan** **5: lexical**

H64MSDIF: most difficult section

Value Label	Value	Frequency	Percent	Valid Percent	Cum Percent
	1.00	83	24.4	28.0	28.0
	2.00	91	26.8	30.7	58.8
	3.00	47	13.8	15.9	74.7
	4.00	53	15.6	17.9	92.6
	5.00	22	6.5	7.4	00.0
		44	12.9	Missing	
	Total	340	100.0	100.0	

Valid cases 296   Missing cases 44

H65MSESY: easiest section

Value Label	Value	Frequency	Percent	Valid Percent	Cum Percent
	1.00	41	12.1	14.2	14.2
	2.00	13	3.8	4.5	18.7
	3.00	37	10.9	12.8	31.5
	4.00	73	21.5	25.3	56.7
	5.00	125	36.8	43.3	100.0
		51	15.0	Missing	
	Total	340	100.0	100.0	

Valid cases 289   Missing cases 51

H66TMESY: least time pressured

Value Label	Value	Frequency	Percent	Valid Percent	Cum Percent
	1.00	35	10.3	11.9	11.9
	2.00	6	1.8	2.0	13.9
	3.00	9	2.6	3.1	16.9
	4.00	11	3.2	3.7	20.7
	5.00	234	68.8	79.3	100.0
		45	13.2	Missing	
	Total	340	100.0	100.0	

Valid cases 295   Missing cases 45

Appendices - Chapter 5

H67TMDIF: most time pressured

Value Label	Value	Frequency	Valid Percent	Cum Percent	Percent
	1.00	38	11.2	12.6	12.6
	2.00	73	21.5	24.3	36.9
	3.00	61	17.9	20.3	57.1
	4.00	122	35.9	40.5	97.7
	5.00	7	2.1	2.3	100.0
		39	11.5	Missing	
	Total	340	100.0	100.0	

Valid cases   301   Missing cases   39

Part V: Comments on the whole paper

1: like very much   2: like   3: like a little   4: dislike

I68: formats   I69: content   I70: length
I71: time limits   I72: design   I73: rubrics

Number of valid observations (listwise) = 301.00

Variable	Mean	Std Dev	Minimum	Maximum	Valid N	Label
I68FRLIK	2.48	.88	1.00	4.00	302	
I69CNLIK	2.35	.78	1.00	4.00	302	
I70LNLIK	2.92	.91	1.00	4.00	302	
I71TMLIK	3.04	.89	1.00	4.00	302	
I72DSLIK	2.37	.96	1.00	4.00	301	
I73DRLIK	2.33	.97	1.00	4.00	302	

Appendices - Chapter 5

Appendix 5.2
Test data analysis of the AERT prototype version 1 – Main trial in October 1997

1	Descriptive of item01 to item60 (variable order)
2	Reliability analysis – scale (alpha) item01 to item60
3	Number of non-responses – item01 to item60
4	Reliability analysis – scale (alpha) section 1 to section 5
5	Reliability analysis – scale (alpha) if test reduced
6	Subject discipline of passages
7	Descriptive of subtotals and the total for the whole population
8	Descriptive of each passage by three discipline groups
9	Descriptive of subtotals and the total by the three discipline groups
10	Histogram of the total score for the whole population
11	Summary of cross-tabulations by subtotals for the whole population
12	Summary of cross-tabulations by passage disciplines for the whole population
13	Summary of cross-tabulations by passage disciplines for each disciplinary group
14	Correlation coefficients between subtests for the whole population
15	Correlation coefficients between passages and subtotals for the whole population
16	Factor analysis for the whole population – careful global vs. quick global
17	Factor analysis for the whole population – careful global vs. careful local
18	Factor analysis for the whole population – quick local vs. careful local
19	Factor analysis for the whole population – passage totals (varimax rotation)
20	Factor analysis for the whole population – first two passages (varimax rotation)
21	Factor analysis for the whole population – 8 selected passages (varimax rotation)
22	Factor analysis for each disciplinary group – first two passages (varimax rotation)
23	ANOVA of the whole test by discipline and test of homogeneity of variances
24	ANOVA of the three subtests – by the whole population
25	ANOVA of the three subtests – by the three discipline groups
26	ANOVA of the three subtests – by the arts group
27	ANOVA of the three subtests – by the science group
28	ANOVA of the three subtests – by the life science group
29	ANOVA of global vs. local – by the whole population
30	ANOVA of quick vs. slow – by the whole population
31	ANOVA of the three passages in each section - by the three discipline groups
32	Questionnaire to students (main trial in October 1997)
33	Descriptives of the questionnaire data (variable order)
34	Frequency percentages of students' perceptions of the texts and tasks - summary data from the questionnaire survey
35	Effects of students' perceptions of the texts and tasks on their performance - summary data from the questionnaire survey
36	Effects of students' perceptions of the texts and tasks on their performance - original data from the questionnaire survey

Appendices - Chapter 5

Appendix 5.2 1
Descriptive statistics of Item01 to Item60 (variable order)

Variable	Mean	Std Dev	Min	Max	Valid N	Label
Number of valid observations (listwise) =					1068	
ITEM01	.68	.47	.00	1.00	1068	
ITEM02	.66	.47	.00	1.00	1068	
ITEM03	.24	.43	.00	1.00	1068	
ITEM04	.60	.49	.00	1.00	1068	
ITEM05	.46	.50	.00	1.00	1068	
ITEM06	.83	.38	.00	1.00	1068	
ITEM07	.77	.42	.00	1.00	1068	
ITEM08	.69	.46	.00	1.00	1068	
ITEM09	.54	.50	.00	1.00	1068	
ITEM10	.38	.49	.00	1.00	1068	
ITEM11	.63	.48	.00	1.00	1068	
ITEM12	.72	.45	.00	1.00	1068	
ITEM13	.12	.32	.00	1.00	1068	
ITEM14	.12	.32	.00	1.00	1068	
ITEM15	.35	.48	.00	1.00	1068	
ITEM16	.53	.50	.00	1.00	1068	
ITEM17	.36	.48	.00	1.00	1068	
ITEM18	.19	.39	.00	1.00	1068	
ITEM19	.73	.44	.00	1.00	1068	
ITEM20	.32	.47	.00	1.00	1068	
ITEM21	.39	.49	.00	1.00	1068	
ITEM22	.22	.42	.00	1.00	1068	
ITEM23	.50	.50	.00	1.00	1068	
ITEM24	.43	.50	.00	1.00	1068	
ITEM25	.34	.47	.00	1.00	1068	
ITEM26	.53	.50	.00	1.00	1068	
ITEM27	.40	.49	.00	1.00	1068	
ITEM28	.14	.35	.00	1.00	1068	
ITEM29	.24	.43	.00	1.00	1068	
ITEM30	.21	.41	.00	1.00	1068	
ITEM31	.75	.43	.00	1.00	1068	
ITEM32	.64	.48	.00	1.00	1068	
ITEM33	.28	.45	.00	1.00	1068	
ITEM34	.74	.44	.00	1.00	1068	
ITEM35	.35	.48	.00	1.00	1068	
ITEM36	.46	.50	.00	1.00	1068	
ITEM37	.56	.50	.00	1.00	1068	
ITEM38	.64	.48	.00	1.00	1068	
ITEM39	.20	.40	.00	1.00	1068	
ITEM40	.51	.50	.00	1.00	1068	
ITEM41	.40	.49	.00	1.00	1068	
ITEM42	.14	.35	.00	1.00	1068	
ITEM43	.09	.28	.00	1.00	1068	
ITEM44	.14	.34	.00	1.00	1068	
ITEM45	.12	.32	.00	1.00	1068	
ITEM46	.48	.50	.00	1.00	1068	
ITEM47	.47	.50	.00	1.00	1068	
ITEM48	.22	.42	.00	1.00	1068	
ITEM49	.27	.44	.00	1.00	1068	
ITEM50	.16	.37	.00	1.00	1068	
ITEM51	.46	.50	.00	1.00	1068	
ITEM52	.07	.26	.00	1.00	1068	
ITEM53	.51	.50	.00	1.00	1068	
ITEM54	.39	.49	.00	1.00	1068	
ITEM55	.33	.47	.00	1.00	1068	
ITEM56	.37	.48	.00	1.00	1068	
ITEM57	.70	.46	.00	1.00	1068	
ITEM58	.14	.34	.00	1.00	1068	
ITEM59	.51	.50	.00	1.00	1068	
ITEM60	.46	.50	.00	1.00	1068	

Appendix 5.2.2
Reliability analysis - scale (alpha)

Statistics for	Mean	Variance	Std Dev	No. of Variables
SCALE	24.8708	75.3816	8.6823	60

Item-total Statistics

	Scale Mean if Item Deleted	Scale Variance if Item Deleted	Corrected Item-Total Correlation	Alpha if Item Deleted
ITEM01	24.1901	73.2600	.2385	.8526
ITEM02	24.2097	73.2756	.2321	.8527
ITEM03	24.6264	73.3345	.2529	.8523
ITEM04	24.2753	71.9729	.3802	.8500
ITEM05	24.4157	71.8532	.3884	.8498
ITEM06	24.0421	74.3984	.1293	.8541
ITEM07	24.1021	73.1976	.2779	.8519
ITEM08	24.1835	72.5998	.3247	.8510
ITEM09	24.3333	73.1371	.2339	.8527
ITEM10	24.4878	72.7655	.2868	.8517
ITEM11	24.2388	72.9486	.2670	.8521
ITEM12	24.1554	72.9936	.2831	.8518
ITEM13	24.7556	73.8962	.2520	.8524
ITEM14	24.7537	73.9983	.2313	.8526
ITEM15	24.5159	72.9735	.2664	.8521
ITEM16	24.3380	72.7469	.2802	.8519
ITEM17	24.5103	72.9268	.2711	.8520
ITEM18	24.6826	73.1878	.3050	.8515
ITEM19	24.1376	73.3428	.2432	.8525
ITEM20	24.5478	73.4626	.2120	.8530
ITEM21	24.4803	72.2304	.3388	.8507
ITEM22	24.6470	73.8950	.1831	.8534
ITEM23	24.3680	72.5833	.2989	.8515
ITEM24	24.4419	72.1606	.3537	.8505
ITEM25	24.5346	72.7233	.3021	.8514
ITEM26	24.3455	72.3482	.3276	.8509
ITEM27	24.4757	72.9882	.2578	.8523
ITEM28	24.7294	73.9464	.2191	.8528
ITEM29	24.6292	72.9121	.3126	.8513
ITEM30	24.6629	73.3015	.2755	.8519
ITEM31	24.1236	73.3568	.2465	.8524
ITEM32	24.2294	72.5218	.3218	.8511
ITEM33	24.5936	72.5207	.3488	.8507
ITEM34	24.1320	72.9394	.2996	.8515
ITEM35	24.5197	73.8825	.1548	.8541
ITEM36	24.4157	73.2347	.2227	.8529
ITEM37	24.3062	72.1208	.3578	.8504
ITEM38	24.2313	72.1442	.3206	.8512
ITEM39	24.3558	72.2182	.3428	.8507
ITEM40				
ITEM41	24.4682	71.8612	.3943	.8497
ITEM42	24.7266	73.6234	.2710	.8521
ITEM43	24.7856	74.0505	.2607	.8524
ITEM44	24.7350	73.5933	.2842	.8519
ITEM45	24.7509	74.0204	.2246	.8527
ITEM46	24.3933	73.1048	.2372	.8527
ITEM47	24.3998	71.7716	.3972	.8496
ITEM48	24.6489	73.8794	.1860	.8533
ITEM49	24.6039	73.6902	.1968	.8532
ITEM50	24.7097	74.1631	.1710	.8535
ITEM51	24.4082	71.8576	.3873	.8498
ITEM52	24.7968	74.7394	.1267	.8538
ITEM53	24.3586	73.5030	.1899	.8536
ITEM54	24.4841	73.1385	.2407	.8526
ITEM55	24.5412	73.1857	.2454	.8525
ITEM56	24.5047	72.7469	.2922	.8516
ITEM57	24.1695	72.4914	.3438	.8507
ITEM58	24.7341	74.5871	.1139	.8541
ITEM59	24.3577	72.3143	.3313	.8509
ITEM60	24.4092	72.4782	.3126	.8512

Reliability Coefficients
No. of Cases = 1068.0
No. of Items = 60
Alpha = .8540

Appendices - Chapter 5

Appendix 5.2.3
Number of non-responses for each item in the main trial in October 1997

\multicolumn{2}{c}{Section 1}	\multicolumn{2}{c}{Section 2}	\multicolumn{2}{c}{Section 3}	\multicolumn{2}{c}{Section 4}	\multicolumn{2}{c}{Section 5}
Item No	No. of non-responses	Item No	No. of non-responses	Item No	No. of non-responses	Item No	No. of non-responses	Item No	No. of non-responses
1	15	16	4	19	24	31	20	46	7
2	29	17	64	20	35	32	52	47	7
3	11	18	148	21	61	33	61	48	6
4	8			22	70	34	99	49	9
5	5			23	116	35	430	50	10
6	6			24	181	36	115	51	6
7	48			25	301	37	283	52	7
8	10			26	222	38	255	53	10
9	6			27	288	39	452	54	13
10	14			28	419	40	420	55	13
11	103			29	615	41	503	56	7
12	130			30	609	42	769	57	9
13	74					43	846	58	9
14	79					44	872	59	20
15	66					45	883	60	24

Appendix 5.2.4
Reliability analysis - scale (alpha) of sections

Section 1 - careful reading (global)

Statistics for	Mean	Variance	Std Dev	No. of Variables
SCALE	7.7762	7.5890	2.7548	15

Item-total Statistics

	Scale Mean if Item Deleted	Scale Variance if Item Deleted	Corrected Item-Total Correlation	Alpha if Item Deleted
ITEM01	7.0955	6.8025	.2339	.6352
ITEM02	7.1152	6.7224	.2616	.6310
ITEM03	7.5318	6.8434	.2493	.6327
ITEM04	7.1807	6.3581	.3997	.6083
ITEM05	7.3212	6.4713	.3431	.6177
ITEM06	6.9476	7.1538	.1454	.6455
ITEM07	7.0075	6.8865	.2369	.6344
ITEM08	7.0890	6.6228	.3146	.6228
ITEM09	7.2388	6.6562	.2658	.6306
ITEM10	7.3933	6.5968	.3025	.6245
ITEM11	7.1442	6.7402	.2459	.6336
ITEM12	7.0609	6.8014	.2480	.6330
ITEM13	7.6610	7.1596	.1916	.6399
ITEM14	7.6592	7.1583	.1902	.6400
ITEM15	7.4213	6.6920	.2697	.6298

Reliability Coefficients
No. of Cases = 1068.0
No. of Items = 15
Alpha = .6468

Section 2 and 3 - skimming and search reading

Statistics for	Mean	Variance	Std Dev	No. of Variables
SCALE	5.5309	8.1424	2.8535	15

Item-total Statistics

	Scale Mean if Item Deleted	Scale Variance if Item Deleted	Corrected Item-Total Correlation	Alpha if Item Deleted
ITEM16	4.9981	7.2259	.2487	.6465
ITEM17	5.1704	7.1949	.2781	.6419
ITEM18	5.3427	7.3370	.3080	.6389
ITEM19	4.7978	7.4024	.2260	.6490
ITEM20	5.2079	7.4001	.2057	.6523
ITEM21	5.1404	7.1311	.2966	.6392
ITEM22	5.3071	7.6244	.1494	.6584
ITEM23	5.0281	7.0901	.3011	.6385
ITEM24	5.1021	7.0777	.3111	.6369
ITEM25	5.1948	7.1373	.3096	.6373
ITEM26	5.0056	7.0890	.3022	.6383
ITEM27	5.1358	7.1952	.2698	.6432
ITEM28	5.3895	7.5895	.2246	.6490
ITEM29	5.2893	7.1918	.3341	.6346
ITEM30	5.3230	7.3023	.3078	.6386

Reliability Coefficients
No. of Cases = 1068.0
No. of Items = 15
Alpha = .6587

Appendices - Chapter 5

Section 4 - scanning

Statistics for	Mean	Variance	Std Dev	No. of Variables
SCALE	5.0215	8.0098	2.8302	15

Item-total Statistics

	Scale Mean if Item Deleted	Scale Variance if Item Deleted	Corrected Item-Total Correlation	Alpha if Item Deleted
ITEM31	5.2743	7.3239	.2111	.6865
ITEM32	5.3801	6.9519	.3271	.6720
ITEM33	5.7444	7.0995	.2974	.6759
ITEM34	5.2828	7.2527	.2382	.6833
ITEM35	5.6704	7.2952	.1886	.6908
ITEM36	5.5665	7.1643	.2240	.6867
ITEM37	5.4569	6.7395	.3977	.6618
ITEM38	5.3820	6.7480	.4131	.6599
ITEM39	5.8174	7.1841	.3068	.6750
ITEM40	5.5066	6.8369	.3530	.6683
ITEM41	5.6189	6.7403	.4038	.6610
ITEM42	5.8773	7.3430	.2853	.6779
ITEM43	5.9363	7.4749	.2992	.6784
ITEM44	5.8858	7.3328	.3015	.6765
ITEM45	5.9017	7.4852	.2357	.6829

Reliability Coefficients
No. of Cases = 1068.0   No. of Items = 15
Alpha = .6910

Section 5 - careful reading (local)

Statistics for	Mean	Variance	Std Dev	No. of Variables
SCALE	5.5421	7.9523	2.8200	15

Item-total Statistics

	Scale Mean if Item Deleted	Scale Variance if Item Deleted	Corrected Item-Total Correlation	Alpha if Item Deleted
ITEM46	5.0646	7.2095	.1837	.6530
ITEM47	5.0712	6.6922	.3912	.6201
ITEM48	5.3202	7.3350	.1974	.6489
ITEM49	5.2753	7.3712	.1603	.6544
ITEM50	5.3811	7.4507	.1825	.6501
ITEM51	5.0796	6.7425	.3710	.6235
ITEM52	5.4682	7.6625	.1526	.6526
ITEM53	5.0300	7.0019	.2646	.6404
ITEM54	5.1554	6.9618	.2929	.6360
ITEM55	5.2125	6.9717	.3058	.6341
ITEM56	5.1760	6.9531	.3017	.6346
ITEM57	4.8408	6.8781	.3600	.6263
ITEM58	5.4054	7.5571	.1466	.6537
ITEM59	5.0290	6.8098	.3419	.6281
ITEM60	5.0805	6.8707	.3185	.6319

Reliability Coefficients
No. of Cases = 1068.0   No. of Items = 15
Alpha = .6554

Appendix 5.2.5
Reliability analysis on whole, 8 passages [Arts, Science and LMS], 8 passages [Arts & Science], and alternatives I & II.

i] WHOLE - 60 items

	60 items	careful items 1–15	skim/sch items 16–30	scan items 31–45	lexi items 46–60
Alpha	.8540	.6468	.6587	.6910	.6554

ii] 8 passages [3 Arts, 2 Science and 3 LMS]

	40 items	careful pass 1 & 2	skim/sch pass 5 & 6	scan pass 8 & 9	lexi pass 10 & 11
Alpha	.8037	.6003	.6204	.6644	.5547

iii] 8 passages [4 Arts and 4 Science]

	40 items	careful pass 1 & 3	skim/sch pass 4 & 6	scan pass 7 & 9	lexi pass 10 & 11
Alpha	.7879	.5667	.5619	.5970	.5547

iv] Alternative I: passages 2, 3, 4, 5, 7, 8, 11 & 12

	40 items	careful pass 2 & 3	skim/sch pass 4 & 5	scan pass 7 & 8	lexi pass 11 & 12
Alpha	.8020	.5298	.5863	.6411	.6144

v] Alternative II: passages 2, 3, 4, 5, 7, 8, 10 & 12

	40 items	careful pass 2 & 3	skim/sch pass 4 & 5	scan pass 7 & 8	lexi pass 10 & 12
Alpha	.7962	.5298	.5863	.6411	.5607

Appendices - Chapter 5

Appendix 5.2.6
Subject discipline of passages

Passage 1	TOTCARE 1	Arts
Passage 2	TOTCARE 2	Life
Passage 3	TOTCARE 3	Science
Passage 4	TOTSKCH 1	Arts
Passage 5	TOTSKCH 2	Life
Passage 6	TOTSKCH 3	Science
Passage 7	TOTSCAN 1	Science
Passage 8	TOTSCAN 2	Life
Passage 9	TOTSCAN 3	Arts
Passage 10	TOTILEX 1	Arts
Passage 11	TOTILEX 2	Science
Passage 12	TOTILEX 3	Life

Appendix 5.2.7
Descriptive statistics of subtotals and the total for the whole population

Number of valid observations (listwise) = 1068.00

Variable	Mean	Std Dev	Minimum	Maximum	Valid N Label
TOTCARE1	2.64	1.37	.00	5.00	1068
TOTCARE2	3.21	1.21	.00	5.00	1068
TOTCARE3	1.93	1.15	.00	5.00	1068
TOTSCH1	1.67	1.07	.00	4.00	1068
TOTSCH2	1.79	1.27	.00	4.00	1068
TOTSCH3	.99	1.11	.00	4.00	1068
TOTSKCH1	2.20	1.24	.00	5.00	1068
TOTSKCH2	2.15	1.45	.00	5.00	1068
TOTSKCH3	1.17	1.28	.00	5.00	1068
TOTSCAN1	2.76	1.28	.00	5.00	1068
TOTSCAN2	2.38	1.48	.00	5.00	1068
TOTSCAN3	.89	1.22	.00	5.00	1068
TOTLEXI1	1.60	1.19	.00	5.00	1068
TOTLEXI2	1.76	1.29	.00	5.00	1068
TOTLEXI3	2.18	1.36	.00	5.00	1068
TOTCARE	7.78	2.75	.00	15.00	1068
TOTSKIM	1.08	.97	.00	3.00	1068
TOTSKSCH	5.53	2.85	.00	15.00	1068
TOTSCAN	6.02	2.83	.00	15.00	1068
TOTLEXI	5.54	2.82	.00	13.00	1068
TOTQUICK	11.55	4.91	.00	29.00	1068
TOTSLOW	13.32	4.70	.00	27.00	1068
TOTGLOB	13.31	4.87	2.00	28.00	1068
TOTLOCAL	11.56	4.79	.00	25.00	1068
TOT1TART	7.33	3.27	.00	18.00	1068
TOT2SCIE	7.63	3.17	.00	18.00	1068
TOT3LIFE	9.92	3.68	.00	19.00	1068
WTOTAL	24.87	8.68	3.00	52.00	1068

Appendices - Chapter 5

Appendix 5.2.8
Descriptive statistics of each passage by three discipline groups

For discipline = 1 (arts students)
Number of valid observations (listwise) = 207.00

Variable	Mean	Std Dev	Minimum	Maximum	Valid N	Label
TOTCARE1	2.83	1.32	.00	5.00	207	
TOTCARE2	3.26	1.17	.00	5.00	207	
TOTCARE3	2.19	1.08	.00	4.00	207	
TOTSKCH1	2.51	1.23	.00	5.00	207	
TOTSKCH2	2.23	1.43	.00	5.00	207	
TOTSKCH3	1.30	1.33	.00	5.00	207	
TOTSCAN1	2.95	1.19	.00	5.00	207	
TOTSCAN2	2.56	1.48	.00	5.00	207	
TOTSCAN3	1.00	1.25	.00	5.00	207	
TOTLEXI1	1.68	1.18	.00	5.00	207	
TOTLEXI2	1.71	1.24	.00	5.00	207	
TOTLEXI3	2.48	1.35	.00	5.00	207	

For discipline = 2 (science students)
Number of valid observations (listwise) = 446.00

Variable	Mean	Std Dev	Minimum	Maximum	Valid N	Label
TOTCARE1	2.73	1.32	.00	5.00	446	
TOTCARE2	3.13	1.21	.00	5.00	446	
TOTCARE3	1.96	1.16	.00	5.00	446	
TOTSKCH1	2.13	1.23	.00	5.00	446	
TOTSKCH2	2.06	1.45	.00	5.00	446	
TOTSKCH3	1.16	1.26	.00	5.00	446	
TOTSCAN1	2.75	1.33	.00	5.00	446	
TOTSCAN2	2.32	1.53	.00	5.00	446	
TOTSCAN3	.92	1.19	.00	5.00	446	
TOTLEXI1	1.58	1.17	.00	5.00	446	
TOTLEXI2	1.70	1.26	.00	5.00	446	
TOTLEXI3	2.04	1.32	.00	5.00	446	

For discipline = 3 (life and medical science students)
Number of valid observations (listwise) = 415.00

Variable	Mean	Std Dev	Minimum	Maximum	Valid N	Label
TOTCARE1	2.45	1.44	.00	5.00	415	
TOTCARE2	3.26	1.23	.00	5.00	415	
TOTCARE3	1.79	1.15	.00	5.00	415	
TOTSKCH1	2.13	1.23	.00	5.00	415	
TOTSKCH2	2.22	1.45	.00	5.00	415	
TOTSKCH3	1.13	1.27	.00	.00	415	
TOTSCAN1	2.66	1.26	.00	5.00	415	
TOTSCAN2	2.35	1.43	.00	5.00	415	
TOTSCAN3	.79	1.22	.00	5.00	415	
TOTLEXI1	1.58	1.22	.00	5.00	415	
TOTLEXI2	1.86	1.34	.00	5.00	415	
TOTLEXI3	2.17	1.39	.00	5.00	415	

Appendix 5.2.9
Descriptive statistics of subtotals and the total by three discipline groups

Discipline = 1 (arts/humanities/business/management)

Number of valid observations (listwise) = 207.00

Variable	Mean	Std Dev	Minimum	Maximum	Valid N	Label
TOT1TART	8.02	3.29	.00	17.00	207	
TOT2SCIE	8.15	2.97	1.00	17.00	207	
TOT3LIFE	10.53	3.60	1.00	18.00	207	
WTOTAL	26.71	8.32	9.00	52.00	207	

Discipline = 2 (science and technology)

Number of valid observations (listwise) = 446.00

Variable	Mean	Std Dev	Minimum	Maximum	Valid N	Label
TOT1TART	7.35	3.04	1.00	17.00	446	
TOT2SCIE	7.57	3.19	.00	18.00	446	
TOT3LIFE	9.56	3.57	1.00	19.00	446	
WTOTAL	24.48	8.34	5.00	50.00	446	

Discipline = 3 (life and medical science)

Number of valid observations (listwise) = 415.00

Variable	Mean	Std Dev	Minimum	Maximum	Valid N	Label
TOT1TART	6.95	3.45	.00	18.00	415	
TOT2SCIE	7.43	3.23	.00	16.00	415	
TOT3LIFE	10.00	3.79	.00	18.00	415	
WTOTAL	24.38	9.11	3.00	48.00	415	

Appendices - Chapter 5

Appendix 5.2.10
Histogram of the total score for the whole population

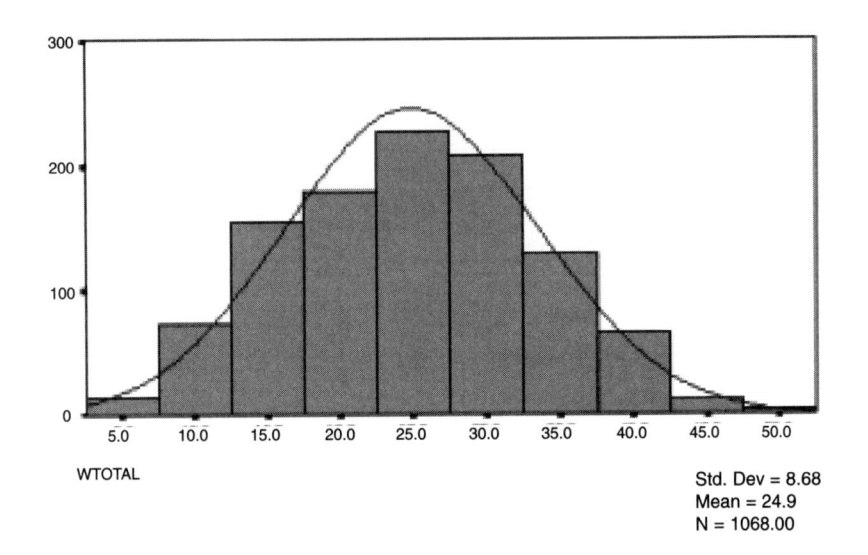

WTOTAL

Std. Dev = 8.68
Mean = 24.9
N = 1068.00

Appendices - Chapter 5

Appendix 5.2.11
Summary of cross-tabulations by subtotals for the whole population

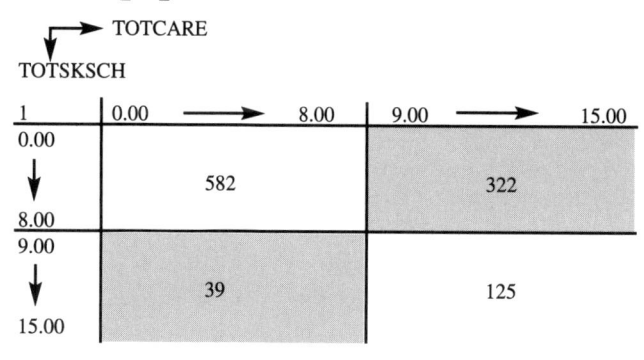

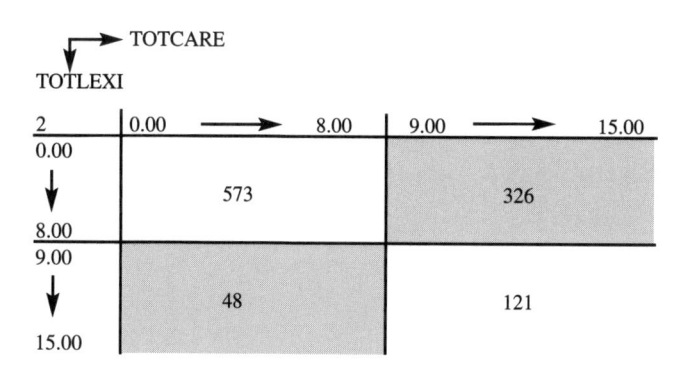

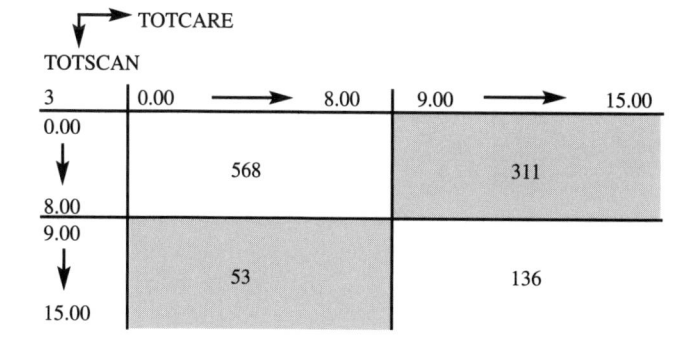

TOTSKSCH ↓ → TOTCARE

1	0.00 → 8.00	9.00 → 15.00
0.00 ↓ 8.00	582	322
9.00 ↓ 15.00	39	125

TOTLEXI ↓ → TOTCARE

2	0.00 → 8.00	9.00 → 15.00
0.00 ↓ 8.00	573	326
9.00 ↓ 15.00	48	121

TOTSCAN ↓ → TOTCARE

3	0.00 → 8.00	9.00 → 15.00
0.00 ↓ 8.00	568	311
9.00 ↓ 15.00	53	136

Appendices - Chapter 5

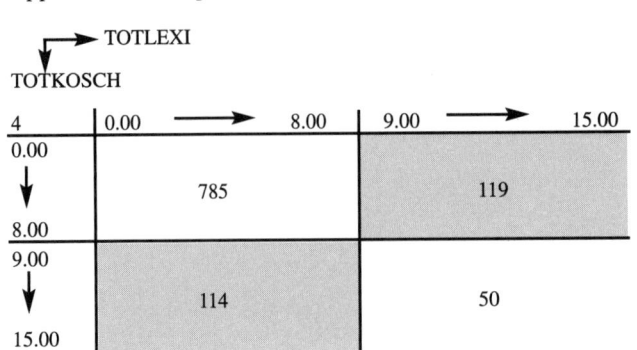

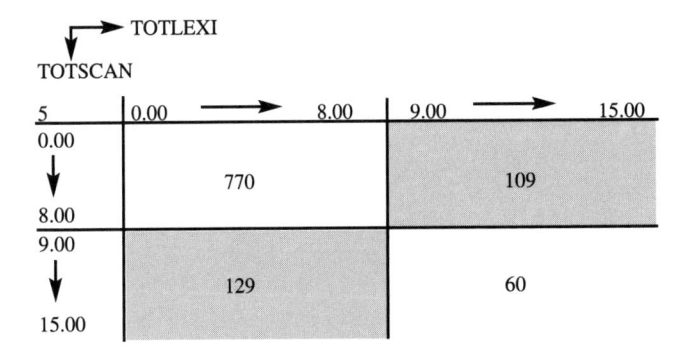

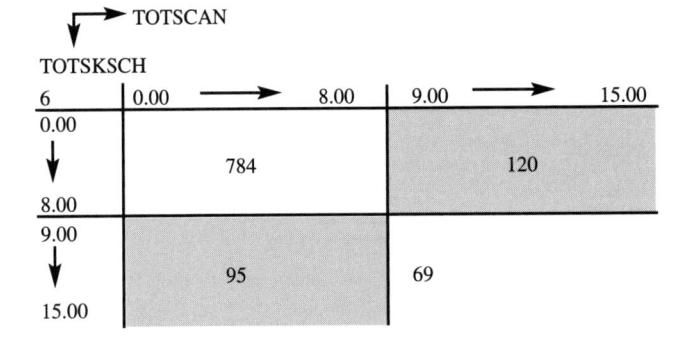

TOTKOSCH → TOTLEXI

4	0.00 → 8.00	9.00 → 15.00
0.00 ↓ 8.00	785	119
9.00 ↓ 15.00	114	50

TOTSCAN → TOTLEXI

5	0.00 → 8.00	9.00 → 15.00
0.00 ↓ 8.00	770	109
9.00 ↓ 15.00	129	60

TOTSKSCH → TOTSCAN

6	0.00 → 8.00	9.00 → 15.00
0.00 ↓ 8.00	784	120
9.00 ↓ 15.00	95	69

Appendices - Chapter 5

```
         ┌──► TOTGLOBAL
TOTLOCAL
```

7	0.00 ──► 8.00	9.00 ──► 15.00
0.00 ↓ 8.00	627	221
9.00 ↓ 15.00	70	150

```
         ┌──► TOTSLOW
TOTQUICK
```

8	0.00 ──► 8.00	9.00 ──► 15.00
0.00 ↓ 8.00	626	208
9.00 ↓ 15.00	83	151

Appendices - Chapter 5

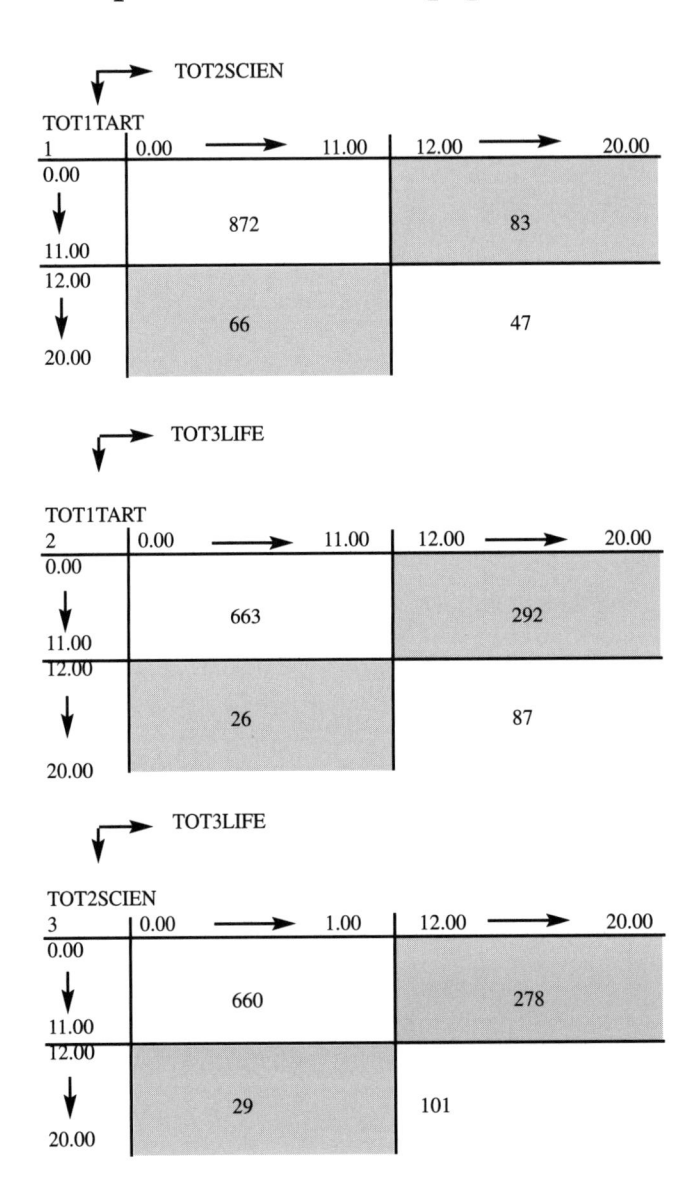

Appendix 5.2.12
Summary of cross-tabulations by passage disciplines for the whole population

	TOT2SCIEN 0.00 → 11.00	12.00 → 20.00
TOT1TART 1 0.00 ↓ 11.00	872	83
12.00 ↓ 20.00	66	47

	TOT3LIFE 0.00 → 11.00	12.00 → 20.00
TOT1TART 2 0.00 ↓ 11.00	663	292
12.00 ↓ 20.00	26	87

	TOT3LIFE 0.00 → 1.00	12.00 → 20.00
TOT2SCIEN 3 0.00 ↓ 11.00	660	278
12.00 ↓ 20.00	29	101

Appendices - Chapter 5

Appendix 5.2.13
Summary of cross-tabulations by passage disciplines for each disciplinary group

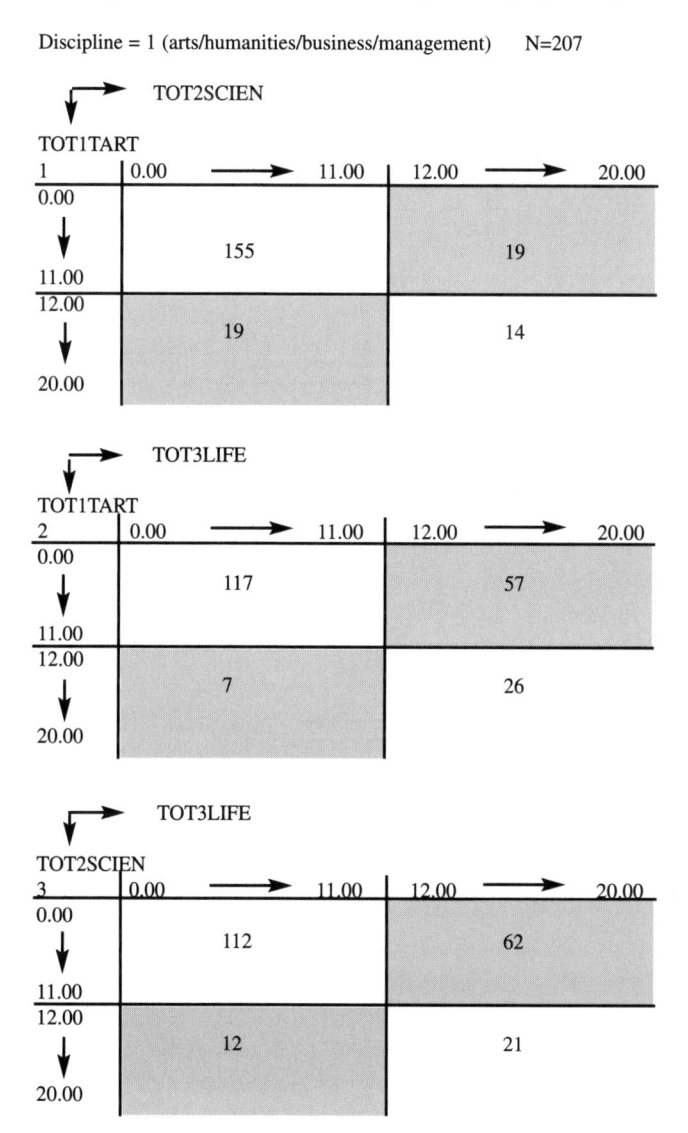

Discipline = 1 (arts/humanities/business/management)   N=207

	TOT2SCIEN 0.00 → 11.00	TOT2SCIEN 12.00 → 20.00
TOT1TART 0.00 → 11.00	155	19
TOT1TART 12.00 → 20.00	19	14

	TOT3LIFE 0.00 → 11.00	TOT3LIFE 12.00 → 20.00
TOT1TART 0.00 → 11.00	117	57
TOT1TART 12.00 → 20.00	7	26

	TOT3LIFE 0.00 → 11.00	TOT3LIFE 12.00 → 20.00
TOT2SCIEN 0.00 → 11.00	112	62
TOT2SCIEN 12.00 → 20.00	12	21

Appendices - Chapter 5

Discipline = 2 (science and technology)   N=446

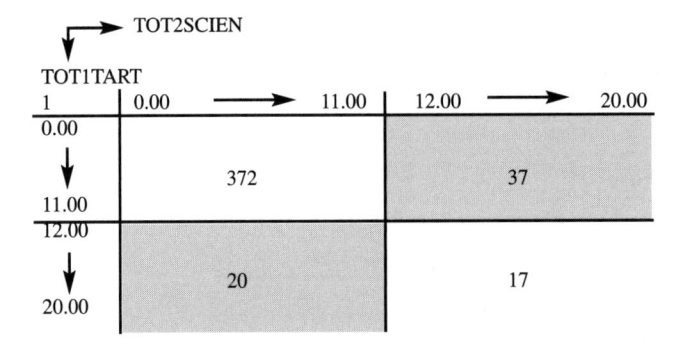

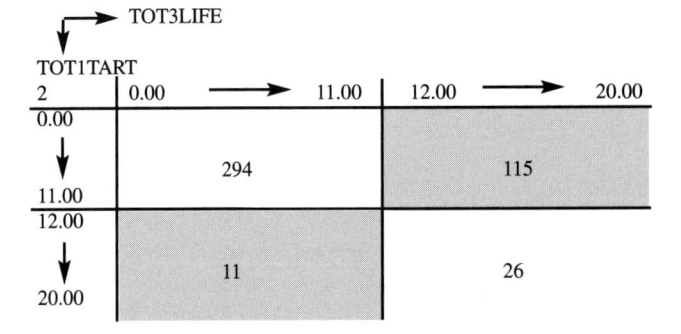

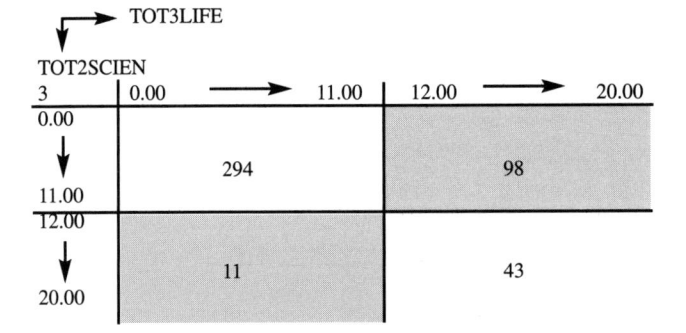

	TOT2SCIEN	
TOT1TART 1	0.00 → 11.00	12.00 → 20.00
0.00 ↓ 11.00	372	37
12.00 ↓ 20.00	20	17

	TOT3LIFE	
TOT1TART 2	0.00 → 11.00	12.00 → 20.00
0.00 ↓ 11.00	294	115
12.00 ↓ 20.00	11	26

	TOT3LIFE	
TOT2SCIEN 3	0.00 → 11.00	12.00 → 20.00
0.00 ↓ 11.00	294	98
12.00 ↓ 20.00	11	43

Appendices - Chapter 5

Discipline = 3 (life science/biology/medical science)   N=415

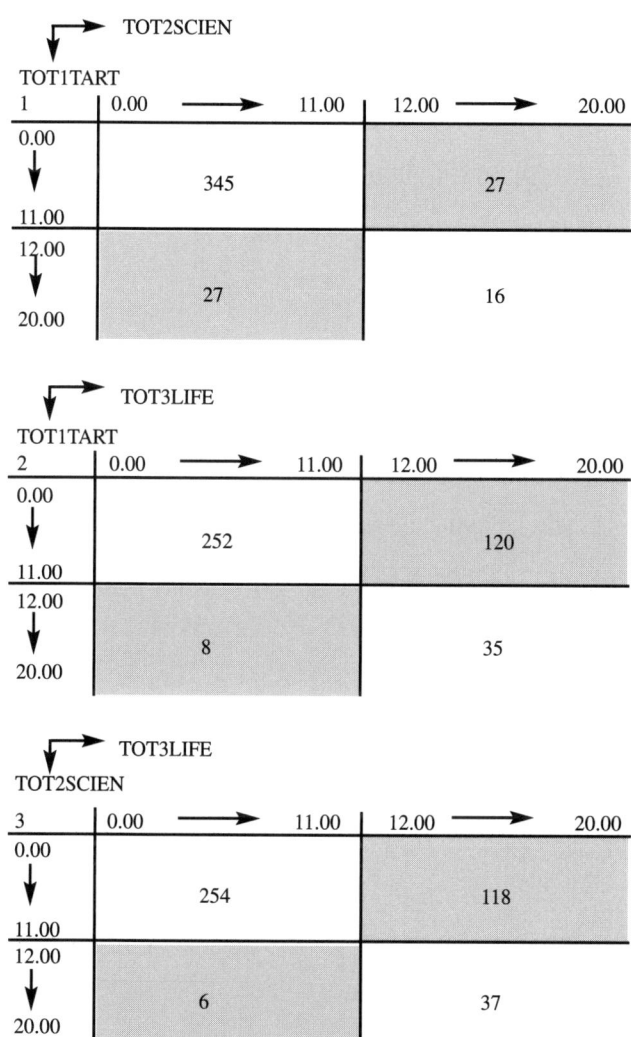

```
        ↱──→ TOT2SCIEN
TOT1TART
  1    | 0.00  ───→  11.00 | 12.00  ───→  20.00
```

TOT1TART	0.00 → 11.00	12.00 → 20.00
0.00 ↓ 11.00	345	27
12.00 ↓ 20.00	27	16

```
        ↱──→ TOT3LIFE
TOT1TART
  2    | 0.00  ───→  11.00 | 12.00  ───→  20.00
```

TOT1TART	0.00 → 11.00	12.00 → 20.00
0.00 ↓ 11.00	252	120
12.00 ↓ 20.00	8	35

```
        ↱──→ TOT3LIFE
TOT2SCIEN
  3    | 0.00  ───→  11.00 | 12.00  ───→  20.00
```

TOT2SCIEN	0.00 → 11.00	12.00 → 20.00
0.00 ↓ 11.00	254	118
12.00 ↓ 20.00	6	37

Appendices - Chapter 5

Appendix 5.2.14
Correlation coefficients of subtests for the whole population

	TOTCARE	TOTSKSCH	TOTSCAN	TOTLEXI	TOTQUICK	TOTSLOW	TOTGLOB	WTOTAL
TOTCARE	1.0000							
TOTSKSCH	.5062	1.0000						
TOTSCAN	.4799	.4947	1.0000					
TOTLEXI	.4188	.4208	.4371	1.0000				
TOTQUICK	.5704	.8657	.8633	.4961	1.0000			
TOTSLOW	.8382	.5497	.5441	.8463	.6326	1.0000		
TOTGLOB	.8628	.8728	.5616	.4837	.8304	.7967	1.0000	
WTOTAL	.7761	.7872	.7828	.7385	.9081	.8988	.9008	1.0000

Appendix 5.2.15

Correlation coefficients between passages and subtotals for the whole population

15 Correlation coefficients between passages and subtotals for the whole population

	TOTCARE	TOTCARE 1	TOTCARE 2	TOTCARE 3	TOTILEX	TOTILEX 1	TOTILEX 2	TOTILEX 3	TOTSCAN	TOTSCAN 1	TOTSCAN 2	TOTSCAN 3	TOTSKSCH	TOTSKSCH 1	TOTSKSCH 2	TOTSKSCH 3
TOTCARE	1.000															
TOTCARE 1	.774	1.000														
TOTCARE 2	.757	.388	1.000													
TOTCARE 3	.673	.250	.298	1.000												
TOTILEX	.416	.364	.290	.263	1.000											
TOTILEX 1	.327	.264	.231	.224	.701	1.000										
TOTILEX 2	.291	.286	.195	.151	.750	.319	1.000									
TOTILEX 3	.307	.253	.214	.206	.750	.276	.330	1.000								
TOTSCAN	.480	.363	.332	.367	.437	.331	.296	.337	1.000							
TOTSCAN 1	.382	.303	.295	.244	.343	.270	.235	.253	.713	1.000						
TOTSCAN 2	.358	.272	.229	.290	.329	.253	.226	.246	.777	.347	1.000					
TOTSCAN 3	.279	.194	.183	.244	.256	.177	.166	.218	.630	.182	.226	1.000				
TOTSKSCH	.506	.359	.366	.398	.421	.327	.250	.349	.495	.326	.372	.355	1.000			
TOTSKSCH 1	.373	.300	.273	.247	.322	.265	.191	.256	.345	.259	.277	.192	.709	1.000		
TOTSKSCH 2	.411	.280	.316	.318	.342	.250	.209	.293	.361	.264	.268	.236	.764	.331	1.000	
TOTSKSCH 3	.303	.195	.196	.288	.239	.191	.137	.199	.362	.179	.258	.338	.680	.240	.252	1.000

Appendices - Chapter 5

Appendices - Chapter 5

Appendix 5.2.16
Factor analysis for the whole population careful global vs. quick global

Analysis number 1 Listwise deletion of cases with missing values Extraction 1 for analysis 1, Principal Components Analysis (PC)

Factor	Eigenvalue *	Pct of Var	Cum Pct
1	3.93784	13.1	13.1
2	1.71645	5.71	8.8
3	1.35670	4.52	3.4

Factor Matrix:

	Factor 1	Factor 2	Factor 3
ITEM01	.27335	.21249	.22989
ITEM02	.30196	.23074	.21132
ITEM03	.31091	.18701	.28167
ITEM04	.47656	.31692	.27443
ITEM05	.47380	.13231	.29355
ITEM06	.17324	.19443	-.06412
ITEM07	.34510	.07168	-.07908
ITEM08	.41624	.11075	.25523
ITEM09	.33765	.24971	.08560
ITEM10	.38361	.10681	.19787
ITEM11	.35075	-.06692	-.16116
ITEM12	.37178	-.07514	-.25665
ITEM13	.34236	-.14708	-.06464
ITEM14	.29094	.00165	-.05116
ITEM15	.36477	.06820	.03942
ITEM16	.32797	.04885	-.03378
ITEM17	.37623	.10060	-.17241
ITEM18	.40742	-.30159	.00216
ITEM19	.32855	.16141	.15923
ITEM20	.27230	.08141	.15082
ITEM21	.43138	.00723	-.11300
ITEM22	.22642	.04385	.12106
ITEM23	.39308	.17182	-.43095
ITEM24	.44232	.12506	-.33999
ITEM25	.40490	.06296	-.41475
ITEM26	.40527	-.00100	-.33962
ITEM27	.35069	-.21268	-.10680
ITEM28	.31726	-.32192	.21471
ITEM29	.41028	-.68883	.14507
ITEM30	.37300	-.69941	.15022

Appendices - Chapter 5

Appendix 5.2.17
Factor analysis for the whole population - careful global vs. careful local

Analysis number 1 Listwise deletion of cases with missing values Extraction 1 for analysis 1, Principal Components Analysis (PC)

Factor *	Eigenvalue	Pct of Var	Cum Pct
1	3.71835	12.4	12.4
2	1.57811	5.3	17.7
3	1.30144	4.3	22.0

Factor Matrix:

	Factor 1	Factor 2	Factor 3
ITEM01	.32136	.09343	.32745
ITEM02	.31980	.22214	.29486
ITEM03	.35574	.18524	.22844
ITEM04	.48987	.29691	.14585
ITEM05	.49593	.14230	.12059
ITEM06	.18220	.14107	.05044
ITEM07	.31912	.10227	.01669
ITEM08	.40099	.24609	.03202
ITEM09	.32339	.32880	-.04784
ITEM10	.37193	.31967	-.01263
ITEM11	.30567	.25697	-.36541
ITEM12	.29160	.30142	-.26552
ITEM13	.23439	.26303	-.12488
ITEM14	.29247	.06674	-.33048
ITEM15	.33631	.19946	-.16174
ITEM46	.30306	-.01600	-.06960
ITEM47	.50288	-.15917	-.02317
ITEM48	.25979	-.03751	.13939
ITEM49	.25588	.06520	.24275
ITEM50	.21991	-.16949	.18880
ITEM51	.49349	-.16901	.17505
ITEM52	.18914	-.13914	.28099
ITEM53	.31434	-.31907	.24159
ITEM54	.35455	-.31656	.13968
ITEM55	.36759	-.32352	.15182
ITEM56	.41224	-.25751	-.18967
ITEM57	.45893	-.27382	-.22770
ITEM58	.16031	-.27934	-.02457
ITEM59	.42380	-.32139	-.38410
ITEM60	.42269	-.26191	-.30351

Appendices - Chapter 5

Appendix 5.2.18
Factor analysis for the whole population - quick local vs. careful local

Analysis number 1 Listwise deletion of cases with missing values Extraction 1 for analysis 1, Principal Components Analysis (PC)

Factor	Eigenvalue	Pct of Var	Cum Pct
1	4.03350	13.4	13.4
2	2.00214	6.7	20.1
3	1.59335	5.3	25.4

Factor Matrix:

	Factor 1	Factor 2	Factor 3
ITEM31	.29775	.16479	-.07464
ITEM32	.39656	.20173	-.21235
ITEM33	.42147	.14335	-.10199
ITEM34	.34292	.20772	-.05343
ITEM35	.21014	.07343	-.27927
ITEM36	.26399	.20770	-.26517
ITEM37	.46121	.22974	-.43915
ITEM38	.48838	.18140	-.42679
ITEM39	.41669	-.02126	-.21550
ITEM40	.43252	.04671	-.35684
ITEM41	.49326	-.31521	-.20747
ITEM42	.36464	-.54069	-.09116
ITEM43	.37674	-.52555	-.06234
ITEM44	.39836	-.67577	.05922
ITEM45	.33465	-.65378	.10498
ITEM46	.27613	.07542	.06711
ITEM47	.48763	.13934	.19051
ITEM48	.23109	.14307	.10281
ITEM49	.25265	.07243	.00778
ITEM50	.23314	.00835	.12331
ITEM51	.48143	.12624	.18010
ITEM52	.18408	-.01919	.16135
ITEM53	.28245	.13901	.34263
ITEM54	.35373	.11972	.25130
ITEM55	.31143	.17796	.36545
ITEM56	.37219	.13329	.25017
ITEM57	.43363	.10394	.29344
ITEM58	.17615	-.04325	.23912
ITEM59	.44415	.12569	.24997

Appendix 5.2.19
Factor analysis for the whole population - passage totals (varimax rotation)

Analysis number 1 Listwise deletion of cases with missing values Extraction 1 for analysis 1, Principal Components Analysis (PC) Initial Statistics:

Variable	Communality	Factor	Eigenvalue	Pct of Var	Cum Pct
TOTCARE1	1.00000	1	3.75357	31.3	31.3
TOTCARE2	1.00000	2	1.08715	9.1	40.3
TOTCARE3	1.00000	3	.95868	8.0	48.3
TOTSKCH1	1.00000	4	.82375	6.9	55.2
TOTSKCH2	1.00000	5	.78677	6.6	61.7
TOTSKCH3	1.00000	6	.73662	6.1	67.9
TOTSCAN1	1.00000	7	.73293	6.1	74.0
TOTSCAN2	1.00000	8	.67365	5.6	79.6
TOTSCAN3	1.00000	9	.64002	5.3	84.9
TOTLEXI1	1.00000	10	.62589	5.2	90.2
TOTLEXI2	1.00000	11	.60413	5.0	95.2
TOTLEXI3	1.00000	12	.57684	4.8	100.0

PC extracted 4 factors.

Factor Matrix:

	Factor 1	Factor 2	Factor 3	Factor 4
TOTCARE1	.60479	-.20908	-.28000	.15766
TOTCARE2	.57716	-.04865	-.48066	.24819
TOTCARE3	.56220	.32888	-.18709	-.03061
TOTSKCH1	.57788	.01690	-.16243	.13160
TOTSKCH2	.60972	.10742	-.13351	.26801
TOTSKCH3	.50441	.54433	.24196	.00980
TOTSCAN1	.57745	-.17463	-.17466	-.49690
TOTSCAN2	.58604	.05473	.00174	-.59035
TOTSCAN3	.48155	.46673	.37652	.08373
TOTLEXI1	.55353	-.29573	.21600	-.04041
TOTLEXI2	.50327	-.48059	.39916	.08901
TOTLEXI3	.55682	-.23459	.36501	.18742

Appendices - Chapter 5

Final Statistics:

Variable	Communality	Factor	Eigenvalue	Pct of Var	Cum Pct
TOTCARE1	.51274	1	3.75357	31.3	31.3
TOTCARE2	.62812	2	1.08715	9.1	40.3
TOTCARE3	.46017	3	.95868	8.0	48.3
TOTSKCH1	.37793	4	.82375	6.9	55.2
TOTSKCH2	.47295				
TOTSKCH3	.60936				
TOTSCAN1	.64136				
TOTSCAN2	.69495				
TOTSCAN3	.59850				
TOTLEXI1	.44214				
TOTLEXI2	.65150				
TOTLEXI3	.53344				

VARIMAX rotation 1 for extraction 1 in analysis 1 - Kaiser Normalization.

VARIMAX converged in 6 iterations.

Rotated Factor Matrix:

	Factor 1	Factor 2	Factor 3	Factor 4
TOTCARE1	.63323	.27929	-.01238	.18330
TOTCARE2	.78164	.06362	.02408	.11194
TOTCARE3	.45075	-.04469	.42112	.27867
TOTSKCH1	.52220	.19578	.20315	.16014
TOTSKCH2	.57891	.19831	.31092	.04261
TOTSKCH3	.14528	.06335	.75241	.13465
TOTSCAN1	.26668	.19174	-.00020	.73040
TOTSCAN2	.11039	.14692	.25339	.77264
TOTSCAN3	.07666	.19381	.74376	.04345
TOTLEXI1	.19440	.57126	.09333	.26324
TOTLEXI2	.10354	.79266	.01265	.11090
TOTLEXI3	.19457	.66666	.22333	.03553

Factor Transformation Matrix:

	Factor 1	Factor 2	Factor 3	Factor 4
Factor 1	.62319	.48567	.43121	.43568
Factor 2	-.02734	-.60558	.79223	-.06992
Factor 3	-.65452	.60448	.42547	-.15871
Factor 4	.42719	.17889	.07354	-.88323

Appendix 5.2.20
Factor analysis for the whole population - first two passages (varimax rotation)

Analysis number 1 Listwise deletion of cases with missing values Extraction 1 for analysis 1, Principal Components Analysis (PC) Initial Statistics:

Variable	Communality	Factor	Eigenvalue	Pct of Var	Cum Pct
TOTCARE1	1.00000	1	2.90512	36.3	36.3
TOTCARE2	1.00000	2	.90808	11.4	47.7
TOTSKCH1	1.00000	3	.82361	10.3	58.0
TOTSKCH2	1.00000	4	.79015	9.9	67.8
TOTSCAN1	1.00000	5	.68251	8.5	76.4
TOTSCAN2	1.00000	6	.68093	8.5	84.9
TOTLEXI1	1.00000	7	.63109	7.9	92.8
TOTLEXI2	1.00000	8	.57851	7.2	100.0

PC extracted 4 factors.

Factor Matrix:

	Factor 1	Factor 2	Factor 3	Factor 4
TOTCARE1	.65431	-.10050	-.34394	-.29016
TOTCARE2	.61397	-.36303	-.37971	-.27792
TOTSKCH1	.60270	-.26211	.08574	.48090
TOTSKCH2	.60771	-.29857	-.02198	.39200
TOTSCAN1	.62198	.00533	.36401	-.38448
TOTSCAN2	.59502	.03662	.59691	-.14396
TOTLEXI1	.58497	.45275	-.04939	.27424
TOTLEXI2	.53327	.63403	-.24911	-.00600

Appendices - Chapter 5

Final Statistics:

Variable	Communality	Factor	Eigenvalue	Pct of Var	Cum Pct
TOTCARE1	.64070	1	2.90512	36.3	36.3
TOTCARE2	.73017	2	.90808	11.4	47.7
TOTSKCH1	.67056	3	.82361	10.3	58.0
TOTSKCH2	.61261	4	.79015	9.9	67.8
TOTSCAN1	.66722				
TOTSCAN2	.73243				
TOTLEXI1	.62482				
TOTLEXI2	.74847				

VARIMAX rotation 1 for extraction 1 in analysis 1 - Kaiser Normalization.
VARIMAX converged in 6 iterations.

Rotated Factor Matrix:

	Factor 1	Factor 2	Factor 3	Factor 4
TOTCARE1	.72703	.13579	.17502	.25112
TOTCARE2	.81472	.23076	.11198	.02463
TOTSKCH1	.11897	.78478	.16049	.12152
TOTSKCH2	.24244	.7278	.11488	.10456
TOTSCAN1	.30422	.06140	.74402	.13166
TOTSCAN2	.02158	.23206	.81318	.12980
TOTLEXI1	.03651	.31284	.16053	.70700
TOTLEXI2	.20215	-.01396	.10234	.83483

Factor Transformation Matrix:

	Factor 1	Factor 2	Factor 3	Factor 4
Factor 1	.52534	.51552	.49737	.45922
Factor 2	-.35821	-.41714	.04042	.83429
Factor 3	-.58654	.07996	.76654	-.24899
Factor 4	-.50167	.74420	-.40424	.17628

Appendix 5.2.21
Factor analysis for the whole population - 8 selected passages (varimax rotation)

Analysis number 1 Listwise deletion of cases with missing values Extraction 1 for analysis 1, Principal Components Analysis (PC)

Initial Statistics:

Variable	Communality	Factor	Eigenvalue	Pct of Var	Cum Pct
TOTCARE1	1.00000	1	2.69208	33.7	33.7
TOTCARE2	1.00000	2	1.03000	12.9	46.5
TOTSKCH2	1.00000	3	.88785	11.1	57.6
TOTSKCH3	1.00000	4	.75175	9.4	67.0
TOTSCAN2	1.00000	5	.72464	9.1	76.1
TOTSCAN3	1.00000	6	.68205	8.5	84.6
TOTLEXI1	1.00000	7	.64532	8.1	92.7
TOTLEXI2	1.00000	8	.58631	7.3	100.0

PC extracted 4 factors.

Factor Matrix:

	Factor 1	Factor 2	Factor 3	Factor 4
TOTCARE1	.63870	-.29677	-.28662	.12039
TOTCARE2	.60196	-.20656	-.55138	.13085
TOTSKCH2	.61716	.04774	-.25224	-.10869
TOTSKCH3	.53949	.58377	.06041	.02794
TOTSCAN2	.59273	.08092	.12203	-.71937
TOTSCAN3	.52444	.56213	.13058	.36551
TOTLEXI1	.57873	-.27785	.40916	.00599
TOTLEXI2	.53719	-.39554	.48483	.23752

Appendices - Chapter 5

Final Statistics:

Variable	Communality	Factor	Eigenvalue	Pct of Var	Cum Pct
TOTCARE1	.59265	1	2.69208	33.7	33.7
TOTCARE2	.72616	2	1.03000	12.9	46.5
TOTSKCH2	.45860	3	.88785	11.1	57.6
TOTSKCH3	.63627	4	.75175	9.4	67.0
TOTSCAN2	.89027				
TOTSCAN3	.74167				
TOTLEXI1	.57958				
TOTLEXI2	.73649				

VARIMAX rotation 1 for extraction 1 in analysis 1 - Kaiser Normalization.
VARIMAX converged in 5 iterations.

Rotated Factor Matrix:

	Factor 1	Factor 2	Factor 3	Factor 4
TOTCARE1	.70554	.06053	.29231	.07584
TOTCARE2	.84572	.08371	.05184	.03486
TOTSKCH2	.53129	.25923	.08363	.31959
TOTSKCH3	.12039	.74327	.02590	.26202
TOTSCAN2	.15085	.12663	.17147	.90668
TOTSCAN3	.11688	.83807	.15371	-.04496
TOTLEXI1	.15103	.10482	.70159	.23140
TOTLEXI2	.14047	.07570	.84323	-.00073

Factor Transformation Matrix:

	Factor 1	Factor 2	Factor 3	Factor 4
Factor 1	.61890	.47024	.49208	.39203
Factor 2	-.29908	.80903	-.49178	.11903
Factor 3	-.71149	.13570	.68140	.10516
Factor 4	.14591	.32546	.22737	-.90614

Appendices - Chapter 5

Appendix 5.2.22
Factor analysis for each disciplinary group - first two passages (varimax rotation)

Discipline = 1 (arts/humanities/business/management group)

Analysis number 1 Listwise deletion of cases with missing values Extraction 1 for analysis 1, Principal Components Analysis (PC)

Initial Statistics:

Variable	Communality	Factor	Eigenvalue	Pct of Va	Cum Pct
TOTCARE1	1.00000	1	2.96746	37.1	37.1
TOTCARE2	1.00000	2	.98499	12.3	49.4
TOTSKCH1	1.00000	3	.88702	11.1	60.5
TOTSKCH2	1.00000	4	.77920	9.7	70.2
TOTSCAN1	1.00000	5	.68396	8.5	78.8
TOTSCAN2	1.00000	6	.65579	8.2	87.0
TOTLEXI1	1.00000	7	.55470	6.9	93.9
TOTLEXI2	1.00000	8	.48688	6.1	100.0

PC extracted 4 factors.

Factor Matrix:

	Factor 1	Factor 2	Factor 3	Factor 4
TOTCARE1	.73274	.02460	-.34876	.00106
TOTCARE2	.61023	-.03980	-.61156	.23973
TOTSKCH1	.60626	-.34548	.07268	.28014
TOTSKCH2	.60106	-.10324	.42432	.34859
TOTSCAN1	.42785	.78386	.21001	.02375
TOTSCAN2	.64909	.26463	.14425	.06157
TOTLEXI1	.59418	-.40962	.35914	-.29878
TOTLEXI2	.60987	.02294	-.11026	-.65430

Appendices - Chapter 5

Final Statistics:

Variable	Communality	Factor	Eigenvalue	Pct of Var	Cum Pct
TOTCARE1	.65914	1	2.96746	37.1	37.1
TOTCARE2	.80544	2	.98499	12.3	49.4
TOTSKCH1	.57067	3	.88702	11.1	60.5
TOTSKCH2	.67349	4	.77920	9.7	0.2
TOTSCAN1	.84217				
TOTSCAN2	.51595				
TOTLEXI1	.73908				
TOTLEXI2	.81273				

VARIMAX rotation 1 for extraction 1 in analysis 1 - Kaiser Normalization.
VARIMAX converged in 7 iterations.

Rotated Factor Matrix:

	Factor 1	Factor 2	Factor 3	Factor 4
TOTCARE1	.21596	.68222	.21751	.31586
TOTCARE2	.13083	.88467	.05734	.04885
TOTSKCH1	.65646	.35901	-.03306	.09869
TOTSKCH2	.76852	.08818	.27366	.01459
TOTSCAN1	.02318	.05530	.91395	.05714
TOTSCAN2	.35855	.25394	.52798	.21010
TOTLEXI1	.59111	-.01940	-.05109	.62184
TOTLEXI2	.00124	.25932	.19453	.84121

Factor Transformation Matrix:

	Factor 1	Factor 2	Factor 3	Factor 4
Factor 1	.57039	.55452	.39119	.46275
Factor 2	-.44170	-.02753	.88099	-.16731
Factor 3	.54928	-.79228	.26053	.05211
Factor 4	.42172	.25308	.05431	-.86900

Appendices - Chapter 5

Discipline = 2 (science and technology group)

Analysis number 1 Listwise deletion of cases with missing values Extraction 1 for analysis 1, Principal Components Analysis (PC)

Initial Statistics:

Variable	Communality	Factor	Eigenvalue	Pct of Var	Cum Pct
TOTCARE1	1.00000	1	2.69301	33.7	33.7
TOTCARE2	1.00000	2	.98558	12.3	46.0
TOTSKCH1	1.00000	3	.88037	11.0	57.0
TOTSKCH2	1.00000	4	.83135	10.4	67.4
TOTSCAN1	1.00000	5	.74958	9.4	76.7
TOTSCAN2	1.00000	6	.69750	8.7	85.5
TOTLEXI1	1.00000	7	.60352	7.5	93.0
TOTLEXI2	1.00000	8	.55910	7.0	100.0

PC extracted 4 factors.

Factor Matrix:

	Factor 1	Factor 2	Factor 3	Factor 4
TOTCARE1	.62058	-.08811	-.04049	.36919
TOTCARE2	.53540	-.54968	.20454	.39763
TOTSKCH1	.56353	-.13300	.26220	-.55163
TOTSKCH2	.60713	-.16422	.42429	-.22280
TOTSCAN1	.64217	-.07243	-.51174	.11093
TOTSCAN2	.59447	-.02169	-.53173	-.36019
TOTLEXI1	.55485	.45452	.12651	.18042
TOTLEXI2	.51129	.64707	.16584	.09173

Appendices - Chapter 5

Final Statistics:

Variable	Communality	Factor	Eigenvalue	Pct of Var	Cum Pct
TOTCARE1	.53083	1	2.69301	33.7	33.7
TOTCARE2	.78874	2	.98558	12.3	46.0
TOTSKCH1	.70830	3	.88037	11.0	57.0
TOTSKCH2	.62524	4	.83135	10.4	67.4
TOTSCAN1	.69182				
TOTSCAN2	.76633				
TOTLEXI1	.56301				
TOTLEXI2	.71604				

VARIMAX rotation 1 for extraction 1 in analysis 1 - Kaiser Normalization.
VARIMAX converged in 6 iterations.

Rotated Factor Matrix:

	Factor 1	Factor 2	Factor 3	Factor 4
TOTCARE1	.31791	.27868	.59080	.05527
TOTCARE2	-.04012	.04637	.85779	.22176
TOTSKCH1	.08721	.21045	.02714	.80973
TOTSKCH2	.19810	.02739	.30892	.69986
TOTSCAN1	.18084	.73417	.34654	-.00437
TOTSCAN2	.07752	.82983	-.01909	.26710
TOTLEXI1	.71161	.12674	.16571	.11440
TOTLEXI2	.83189	.08348	-.01264	.12989

Factor Transformation Matrix:

	Factor 1	Factor 2	Factor 3	Factor 4
Factor 1	.49299	.52386	.49217	.49020
Factor 2	.80853	-.04270	-.54329	-.22202
Factor 3	.20453	-.82019	.16062	.50956
Factor 4	.24780	-.22589	.66092	-.67138

Appendices - Chapter 5

Discipline = 3 (biology/medical/life science group)

Analysis number 1 Listwise deletion of cases with missing values Extraction 1 for analysis 1, Principal Components Analysis (PC)

Initial Statistics:

Variable	Communality	Factor	Eigenvalue	Pct of Var	Cum Pct
TOTCARE1	1.00000	1	3.12206	39.0	39.0
TOTCARE2	1.00000	2	.92892	11.6	50.6
TOTSKCH1	1.00000	3	.82557	10.3	61.0
TOTSKCH2	1.00000	4	.69259	8.7	69.6
TOTSCAN1	1.00000	5	.67261	8.4	78.0
TOTSCAN2	1.00000	6	.64302	8.0	86.1
TOTLEXI1	1.00000	7	.60445	7.6	93.6
TOTLEXI2	1.00000	8	.51078	6.4	100.0

PC extracted 4 factors.

Factor Matrix:

	Factor 1	Factor 2	Factor 3	Factor 4
TOTCARE1	.65686	-.07601	-.49100	.30878
TOTCARE2	.69006	-.15426	-.35112	.13432
TOTSKCH1	.63160	-.34635	.15719	-.00159
TOTSKCH2	.61277	-.44532	.06961	-.30175
TOTSCAN1	.67928	.01194	.14491	-.28890
TOTSCAN2	.56788	.09223	.59830	.52444
TOTLEXI1	.60984	.40445	.13633	-.35974
TOTLEXI2	.53310	.63941	-.18469	.01539

Appendices - Chapter 5

Final Statistics:

Variable	Communality	Factor	Eigenvalue	Pct of Var	Cum Pct
TOTCARE1	.77366	1	3.12206	39.0	39.0
TOTCARE2	.64131	2	.92892	11.6	50.6
TOTSKCH1	.54359	3	.82557	10.3	61.0
TOTSKCH2	.66969	4	.69259	8.7	69.6
TOTSCAN1	.56602				
TOTSCAN2	.96399				
TOTLEXI1	.68349				
TOTLEXI2	.72739				

VARIMAX rotation 1 for extraction 1 in analysis 1 - Kaiser Normalization.
VARIMAX converged in 7 iterations.

Rotated Factor Matrix:

	Factor 1	Factor 2	Factor 3	Factor 4
TOTCARE1	.16596	.84585	.14892	.09201
TOTCARE2	.35065	.69596	.16826	.07542
TOTSKCH1	.62087	.26904	.04194	.28976
TOTSKCH2	.79161	.19689	.06246	.01932
TOTSCAN1	.57050	.13029	.45234	.13769
TOTSCAN2	.17670	.10951	.17007	.94438
TOTLEXI1	.32701	.01981	.75325	.09368
TOTLEXI2	-.11806	.34545	.76147	.11946

Factor Transformation Matrix:

	Factor 1	Factor 2	Factor 3	Factor 4
Factor 1	.59338	.53598	.49578	.33887
Factor 2	-.59681	-.12053	.78911	.08120
Factor 3	.24573	-.70301	.00980	.66731
Factor 4	-.48097	.45164	-.36251	.65823

Appendices - Chapter 5

Appendix 5.2.23
ANOVA of the whole test by discipline and test of homogeneity of variances

		Sum of squares	df	Mean square	F	Sig.
WTOTAL	Between Groups	866.264	2	433.132	5.798	.003
	Within Groups	79565.905	1065	74.710		
	Total	80432.169	1067			

WTOTAL = the total score of the test

Post Hoc Tests

(I) A00DISCI	(J) A00DISCI	Mean Difference (I–J)	STD. Error	Sig.	95% Confidence interval Lower Bound	95% Confidence interval Upper Bound
1	2	2.2277*	.727	.007	.4847	3.9707
	3	2.3270*	.735	.005	.5635	4.0905
2	1	-2.2277*	.727	.007	-3.9707	-.4847
	3	9.927E-02	.590	1.000	-1.3143	1.5128
3	1	-2.3270*	.735	.005	-4.0905	-.5635
	2	-9.93E-02	.590	1.000	-1.5128	1.3143

A00DISCI 1 = the arts/humanities/business/management group
A00DISCI 2 = the science/technology group
A00DISCI 3 = the biology/medical/life science group

	Levene statistic	df1	df2	Sig.
WTOTAL	2.509	2	1065	.082

Appendices - Chapter 5

Appendix 5.2.24
ANOVA of three subtests - by the whole population

		Sum of squares	df	Mean square	F	Sig.
SUB 123	Between Groups	4281.865	2	2140.933	187.100	.000
	Within Groups	36628.191	3201	11.443		
	Total	40910.056	3203			

sub123 = the total of the three subtests (arts, science, life science)

Post Hoc Tests

(I) facnumb	(J) facnumb	Mean Difference (I–J)	STD. Error	Sig.	95% Confidence interval Lower Bound	95% Confidence interval Upper Bound
1.00	2.00	-.3034	.146	.115	-.6540	4.725E-02
	3.00	-2.5899*	.146	.000	-2.9405	-2.2393
2.00	1.00	.3034*	.146	.115	-4.73E-02	.6540
	3.00	-2.2865*	.146	.000	-2.6371	-1.9359
3.00	1.00	2.5899*	.146	.000	-2.2393	2.9405
	2.00	2.2865*	.146	.000	-1.9359	2.6371

facnumb 1 = subtest of arts
facnumb 2 = subtest of science
facnumb 3 = subtest of life science

Appendices - Chapter 5

Appendix 5.2.25
ANOVA of the three subtests - by the three discipline groups

	Sum of squares	df	Mean square	F	Sig.
TOT1TART Between Groups	160.057	2	80.027	7.558	.001
Within Groups	11276.550	1065		10.588	
Total	11436.607	1067			
TOT2SCIE Between Groups	74.977	2	37.489	3.740	.024
Within Groups	10676.191	1065		10.025	
Total	10751.169	1067			
TOT2SCIE Between Groups	74.977	2	37.489	3.740	.024
Within Groups	10676.191	1065		10.025	
Total	10751.169	1067			

Post Hoc Tests

Depwndant (I) Variable	A00DISCI	(J) A00DISCI	Mean Difference (I–J)	STD. Error	Sig	95% Confidence interval Lower Bound	Upper Bound
TOT1TART	1	2	.6721*	.274	.043	1.595E-02	1.3283
		3	1.0748*	.277	.000	.4109	1.7387
	2	1	-.6721*	.274	.043	-1.3283	-1.60E-02
		3	.4026	.222	.210	-.1295	.9348
	3	1	-1.0748*	.277	.000	-1.7387	-.4109
		2	-.4026	.222	.210	-.9348	.1295
TOT2SCIE	1	2	.5851	.266	.085	-5.34E-02	.2236
		3	.7233*	.269	.022	7.727E-02	1.3693
	2	1	-.5851	.266	.085	-1.2236	5.339E-02
		3	.1382	.216	1.000	-.3796	.6560
	3	1	-.7233*	.269	.022	-1.3693	-7.73E-02
		2	-.1382	.216	1.00	-.6560	.3796
TOT3LIFE	1	2	.9705*	.308	.005	.2315	1.7095
		3	.5290	.312	.270	-.2187	1.2767
	2	1	-.9705*	.308	.005	-1.7095	-.2315
		3	-.4415	.250	.233	-1.0408	.1578
	3	1	-.5290	.312	.270	-1.2767	.2187
		2	.4415	.250	.233	-.1578	1.0408

TOT1TART= total of the arts subtest
TOT2SCIE = total of the science subtest
TOT3LIFE = total of the life science subtest

A00DISCI 1 = the arts/humanities/business/management group
A00DISCI 2 = the science/technology group
A00DISCI 3 = the biology/medical/life science group

Appendices - Chapter 5

Appendix 5.2.26
ANOVA of the three subtests - by the arts group

		Sum of squares	df	Mean square	F	Sig.
SUB 123	Between Groups	821.472	2	410.736	37.809	.000
	Within Groups	6713.536	618	10.863		
	Total	7535.008	620			

sub123 = the total of the three subtests (arts, science, life science) of the arts group

Post Hoc Tests

(I) facnumb	(J) facnumb	Mean Difference (I–J)	STD. Error	Sig.	95% Confidence interval Lower Bound	Upper Bound
1.00	2.00	-.1304	.324	1.000	-.9081	.6473
	3.00	-2.5024*	.324	.000	-3.2801	-1.7247
2.00	1.00	.1304	.324	1.000	.6473	.9081
	3.00	-2.3720*	.324	.000	-3.1497	-1.5943
3.00	1.00	2.5024*	.324	.000	1.7247	3.2801
	2.00	2.3720*	.324	.000	1.5943	3.1497

facnumb 1 = the subtest of arts
facnumb 2 = the subtest of science
facnumb 3 = the subtest of life science

Appendices - Chapter 5

Appendix 5.2.27
ANOVA of the three subtests - by the science group

		Sum of squares	df	Mean square	F	Sig.
SUB 123	Between Groups	1315.915	2	657.957	61.214	.000
	Within Groups	14349.177	1335	10.748		
	Total	15665.092	1337			

sub123 = the total of the three subtests (arts, science, life science) of the science group

Post Hoc Tests

(I) facnumb	(J) facnumb	Mean Difference (I−J)	STD. Error	Sig.	95% Confidence interval Lower Bound	95% Confidence interval Upper Bound
1.00	2.00	-.2175	.220	.966	-.7437	.3088
	3.00	-2.2040*	.220	.000	-2.7303	-1.6778
2.00	1.00	.2175	.220	.966	.3088	.7437
	3.00	-1.9865*	.220	.000	-2.5128	-1.4603
3.00	1.00	2.2040*	.220	.000	1.6778	2.7303
	2.00	1.9865*	.220	.000	1.4603	2.5128

facnumb 1 = the subtest of arts
facnumb 2 = the subtest of science
facnumb 3 = the subtest of life science

Appendices - Chapter 5

Appendix 5.2.28
ANOVA of the three subtests - by the life science group

		Sum of squares	df	Mean square	F	Sig.
SUB 123	Between Groups	2228.474	2	1114.237	91.088	.000
	Within Groups	15192.728	1242	12.232		
	Total	17421.202	1244			

sub123 = the total of the three subtests (arts, science, life science) of the life science group

Post Hoc Tests

(I) facnumb	(J) facnumb	Mean Difference (I−J)	STD. Error	Sig.	95% Confidence interval Lower Bound	95% Confidence interval Upper Bound
1.00	2.00	-.4819	.243	.142	-1.0640	.1001
	3.00	-3.0482*	.243	.000	-3.6302	-2.4661
2.00	1.00	.4819	.243	.142	.1001	1.0640
	3.00	-2.5663*	.243	.000	-3.1483	-1.9842
3.00	1.00	3.0482*	.243	.000	2.4661	3.6302
	2.00	2.5663*	.243	.000	1.9842	3.1483

facnumb 1 = the subtest of arts
facnumb 2 = the subtest of science
facnumb 3 = the subtest of life science

Appendices - Chapter 5

Appendix 5.2.29
ANOVA of global vs. local - by the whole population

	Sum of squares	df	Mean square	F	Sig.
GLOLOC12 Between Groups	433.132	2	216.566	9.068	.000
Within Groups	50943.952	2133	23.884		
Total	51377.084	2135			

GLOLOC12 = the total of the global items (Sections 1, 2, 3) and local items (Sections 4, 5)

Post Hoc Tests

(I) A00DISCI	(J) A00DISCI	Mean Difference (I–J)	STD. Error	Sig.	95% Confidence interval Lower Bound	95% Confidence interval Upper Bound
1.00	2.00	1.1138*	.291	.000	.4176	1.8102
	3.00	1.1635*	.294	.000	.4590	1.8680
2.00	1.00	-1.1139*	.291	1.000	-1.8102	-.4176
	3.00	4.963E-02	.236	.000	-.5151	.6143
3.00	1.00	-1.1635*	.294	.000	-1.8680	-.4590
	2.00	-4.96E-02	.236	1.000	-.6143	.5151

A00DISCI 1 = the arts/humanities/business/management group
A00DISCI 2 = the science/technology group
A00DISCI 3 = the biology/medical/life science group

Appendices - Chapter 5

Appendix 5.2.30
ANOVA of quick vs. slow - by the whole population

	Sum of squares	df	Mean square	F	Sig.
QKSLW12 Between Groups	433.132	2	216.566	9.144	.000
Within Groups	50517.952	2133	23.884		
Total	50951.084	2135			

QKSLW12 = the total of the expeditious items (Sections 2, 3, 4) and careful items (Sections 1, 5)

Post Hoc Tests

(I) A00DISCI	(J) A00DISCI	Mean Difference (I–J)	STD. Error	Sig.	95% Confidence interval Lower Bound	95% Confidence interval Upper Bound
1.00	2.00	1.1138*	.289	.000	.4205	1.8073
	3.00	1.1635*	.293	.000	.4619	1.8651
2.00	1.00	-1.1139*	.289	.000	-1.8073	-.4205
	3.00	4.963E-02	.235	1.000	-.5127	.6120
3.00	1.00	-1.1635*	.293	.000	-1.8651	-.4619
	2.00	-4.96E-02	.235	1.000	-.6120	.5127

A00DISCI 1 = the arts/humanities/business/management group
A00DISCI 2 = the science/technology group
A00DISCI 3 = the biology/medical/life science group

Appendices - Chapter 5

Appendix 5.2.31
ANOVA of the three passages in each section - by the three discipline groups

Section 1 - careful reading (global)

		Sum of squares	df	Mean square	F	Sig.
TOTCARE1	Between Groups	26.144	2	13.072	6.993	.001
	Within Groups	1990.897	1065	1.869		
	Total	2017.041	1067			
TOTCARE2	Between Groups	3.809	2	1.905	1.302	.273
	Within Groups	1558.284	1065	1.463		
	Total	1562.093	1067			
TOTCARE3	Between Groups	22.743	2	11.372	8.721	.000
	Within Groups	1388.669	1065	1.304		
	Total	1411.412	1067			

TOTCARE1 = first passage in Section 1; TOTCARE2 = second passage in Section 1;
TOTCARE3 = third passage in Section 1

Post Hoc Tests

Depwndant Variable	(I) A00DISCI	(J) A00DISCI	Mean Difference (I-J)	STD. Error	Sig	95% Confidence interval Lower Bound	95% Confidence interval Upper Bound
TOTCARE1	1	2	9.963E02	.115	1.000	-.1761	.3753
		3	.3803*	.116	.003	.1013	.6593
	2	1	-9.96E-20	.115	1.000	-.3753	.1761
		3	.2807	.093	.008	5.708E-20	.5043
	3	1	-.3803*	.116	.003	-.6593	-.1013
		2	-.2807*	.093	.008	-.5043	-5.71E-20
TOTCARE2	1	2	.1215	.102	.698	-.1224	.3654
		3	6.170E-04	.103	1.000	-.2462	.2474
	2	1	-.1215	.102	.698	-.3654	.1224
		3	-.1209	.083	.429	-.3187	7.693E-02
	3	1	-6.17E-04*	.103	1.000	-.2474	.2462
		2	.1209	.083	.429	-7.69E-02	.3187
TOTCARE3	1	2	.2332*	.096	.046	2.980E-03	.4635
		3	.4029	.097	.000	.1699	.6358
	2	1	-.2332*	.096	.046	-.4635	-2.98E-03
		3	-.1696	.078	.089	-1.71E-02	.3564
	3	1	-.4029*	.097	.000	-.6358	-.1699
		2	.1696	.078	.089	-.3564	1.713E-02

A00DISCI 1 = the arts/humanities/business/management group
A00DISCI 2 = the science/technology group
A00DISCI 3 = the biology/medical/life science group

Appendices - Chapter 5

Section 2 and 3 - skimming and search reading

	Sum of squares	df	Mean square	F	Sig.
TOTSKCH1 Between Groups	24.510	2	12.255	8.125	.000
Within Groups	1606.399	1065	1.508		
Total	1630.909	1067			
TOTSKCH2 Between Groups	6.981	2	3.490	1.664	.190
Within Groups	2233.836	1065	2.097		
Total	2240.816	1067			
TOTSKCH3 Between Groups	4.316	2	2.158	1.323	.267
Within Groups	1737	1065	1.631		
Total	1741.607	1067			

TOTSKCH1 = first passage in Sections 2 and 3;
TOTSKCH2 = second passage in Sections 2 and 3;   TOTSKCH3 = third passage in Sections 2 and 3

Post Hoc Tests

Depwndant (I) Variable	A00DISCI	(J) A00DISCI	Mean Difference (I–J)	STD. Error	Sig	95% Confidence interval Lower Bound	Upper Bound
TOTSKCH1	1	2	.3865*	.103	.001	.1389	.6342
		3	.3795*	.105	.001	.1290	.6301
	2	1	-.3865*	.103	.001	-.6342	-.1389
		3	-6.97E-03	.084	1.000	-.2078	.1939
	3	1	-.3795*	.105	.001	-.6301	-.1290
		2	6.970E-03	.084	1.000	-.1939	.2078
TOTSKCH2	1	2	.1736	.122	.463	-.1185	.4656
		3	1.502E-02	.123	1.000	-.2805	.3105
	2	1	-.1736	.122	.463	-.4656	.1185
		3	.1586	.099	.326	-.3954	7.828E-02
	3	1	-1.50E-02	.123	1.000	-.3105	.2805
		2	-.1586	.099	.326	-7.83E-02	.3954
TOTSKCH3	1	2	.1381	.107	.597	.1195	.3956
		3	.1742	.109	.328	-8.64E-02	.4348
	2	1	-.1381	.107	.597	-.3956	.1195
		3	3.613E-02	.087	1.000	-.1727	.2450
	3	1	-.1742	.109	.328	-.4348	8.637E-02
		2	-3.61E-02	.087	1.000	-.2450	.1727

A00DISCI 1 = the arts/humanities/business/management group
A00DISCI 2 = the science/technology group   A00DISCI 3 = the biology/medical/life science group

Appendices - Chapter 5

Section 4 - scanning

	Sum of squares	df	Mean square	F	Sig.
TOTSCAN1 Between Groups	11.735	2	5.868	3.593	.028
Within Groups	1639.481	1065	1.633		
Total	1751.216	1067			
TOTSCAN2 Between Groups	8.346	2	4.173	1.907	.149
Within Groups	2330.830	1065	2.189		
Total	2339.176	1067			
TOTSCAN3 Between Groups	4.316	2	3.545	2.403	.091
Within Groups	1571.427	1065	1.476		
Total	1578.517	1067			

TOTSCAN1 = first passage in Section 4;
TOTSCAN2 = second passage in Section 4;   TOTSCAN3 = third passage in Section 4

Post Hoc Tests

Depwndant Variable	(I) A00DISCI	(J) A00DISCI	Mean Difference (I–J)	STD. Error	Sig	95% Confidence interval Lower Bound	95% Confidence interval Upper Bound
TOTSCAN1	1	2	.1983	.107	.196	-5.94E-02	.4560
		3	.2914	.109	.022	3.070E-02	.5522
	2	1	-.1983	.107	.196	-.4560	5.939E-02
		3	9.312E-03	.087	.857	-.1159	.3021
	3	1	-.2914*	.109	.022	-.5522	-3.07E02
		2	-9.31E-02	.087	.857	-.3021	-.1159
TOTSCAN2	1	2	.2372	.124	.171	-6.12E-02	.5355
		3	.2013	.126	.330	-.1005	.5032
	2	1	-.2372	.124	.171	-.5355	6.116E-02
		3	3.58E-02	.101	1.000	-.2778	.2061
	3	1	-.2013*	.126	.330	-.5032	.1005
		2	3.583E-02	.101	1.000	-.2061	.2778
TOTSCAN3	1	2	8.331E-02	.102	1.000	-.1616	.3283
		3	.2121	.103	.121	-.1699	.4599
	2	1	-8.33E-02	.102	1.000	-.3283	.1616
		3	-.1288	.083	.361	-6.99E-02	.3274
	3	1	-.2121	.103	.121	-.4599	3.578E-02
		2	.1288	.083	.361	-.3274	6.990E-02

A00DISCI 1 = the arts/humanities/business/management group
A00DISCI 2 = the science/technology group   A00DISCI 3 = the biology/medical/life science group

Appendices - Chapter 5

Section 5 - careful reading (local)

		Sum of squares	df	Mean square	F	Sig.
TOTLEXI1	Between Groups	1.762	2	.881	.621	.538
	Within Groups	1510.915	1065	1.419		
	Total	1512.677	1067			
TOTLEXI2	Between Groups	6.193	2	3.096	1.872	.154
	Within Groups	1761.817	1065	1.654		
	Total	1768.010	1067			
TOTLEXI3	Between Groups	27.195	2	13.597	7.435	.001
	Within Groups	1947.647	1065	1.829		
	Total	1974.842	1067			

TOTILEX1 = first passage in Section 5;
TOTILEX2 = second passage in Section 5;   TOTILEX3 = third passage in Section 5

Post Hoc Tests

Depwndant (I) Variable	(I) A00DISCI	(J) A00DISCI	Mean Difference (I–J)	STD. Error	Sig	95% Confidence interval Lower Bound	Upper Bound
TOTLEXI1	1	2	.1027	.100	.917	-.1375	.3429
		3	.1028	.101	.931	-.1402	.3459
	2	1	-.1027	.100	.917	-.3429	.1375
		3	1.621E-04	.081	1.000	-.1946	.1950
	3	1	-.1028	.101	.931	-.3459	.1402
		2	-1.62E-04	.081	1.000	-.1950	.1946
TOTLEXI2	1	2	1.542E-02	.108	1.000	-.2439	.2748
		3	-.1453	.109	.554	-.4077	.1172
	2	1	-1.54E-02	.108	1.000	-.2748	.2439
		3	-.1607	.088	.202	-.3710	4.965E-02
	3	1	.1453	.109	.554	-.1172	.4077
		2	.1607	.088	.202	-4.97E-02	.3710
TOTLEXI3	1	2	.4382*	.114	.000	-.1655	.7110
		3	.3120*	.115	.020	3.609E-02	.5879
	2	1	-.4382*	.114	.000	-.7110	-.1655
		3	-.1262	.092	.514	-.3474	9.491E-02
	3	1	-.3120*	.115	.020	-.5879	-3.61E-02
		2	.1262	.092	.514	-9.49E-02	.3474

A00DISCI 1 = the arts/humanities/business/management group
A00DISCI 2 = the science/technology group   A00DISCI 3 = the biology/medical/life science group

Appendices - Chapter 5

Appendix 5.2.32
Questionnaire to students (Main trial in October 1997)

Name _____
University _____
Disciplinary area _____
Registration No. _____

Date of passing CET-4 _____
CET-4 score _____
Date of passing CET-6 _____
CET-6 score _____

I   About the Passages

Passages	A - language difficulty			B - topic familiarity			C - disciplinary area				D - subject specificity			E - text interestingness			
	not diff	not very diff	quite diff	very diff	not fam	not very fam	quite fam	very fam	arts business mngmt	science tech	biology medical life sci	not spec	not very spec	quite spec	very spec	not int	not very int	quite int	very int
1 A billion consumers																			
2 Cancer-stranglers																			
3 Mindless machine																			
4 Japanese women ...																			
5 Sugaring the pill																			
6 Tomorrow's bitter ...																			
7 Tricks of nature																			
8 Themes in the study ...																			
9 Successful advertising...																			
10 Andropov ...																			
11 Quark ...																			
12 Elephants ...																			

Appendices - Chapter 5

II About the test formats

Formats	F - your familiarity with the test format			
	not familiar	not very familiar	quite familiar	very familiar
1 short-answer questions				
2 true/false judgement				
3 table/flow chart completion				
4 sentence completion				
5 banked cloze				

G - your opinion of the format suitability for testing EAP reading			
not suitable	not very suitable	quite suitable	very suitable

III Comments on each section

Sections	H - time sufficiency for each section			
	not sufficient	not very sufficient	quite sufficient	very sufficient
1 careful global reading				
2 skimming				
3 search reading				
4 scanning				
5 careful local reading				

I - difficulty of each section			
not difficult	not very difficult	quite difficult	very difficult

Appendices - Chapter 5

IV Comments on the test paper

	J - general comments			
	not suitable	not very suitable	quite suitable	very suitable
length of the test				
test paper layout				
rubrics in the test				

V Frequency of use in real life and training received for each skill/strategy

Skills/Strategies	K - frequency of use in real life				M - training received			
	not frequent	not very frequent	quite frequent	very frequent	very little	not much	quite a lot	a lot
Section 1 careful reading at the global level								
Section 2 skimming								
Section 3 search reading								
Section 4 scanning								
Section 5 careful reading at the local level								

Appendices - Chapter 5

Appendix 5.2.33
Descriptive of the questionnaire data (variable order)

Number of valid observations (listwise) = 603.00

Variable	Mean	Std Dev	Minimum	Maximum	Valid N	Label
A01DIFF	2.30	.80	1.00	4.00	1065	
A02DIFF	2.37	.87	1.00	4.00	1058	
A03DIFF	2.51	.81	1.00	4.00	1050	
A04DIFF	1.86	.82	1.00	4.00	1053	
A05DIFF	2.85	.81	1.00	4.00	1051	
A06DIFF	2.55	.82	1.00	4.00	1048	
A07DIFF	2.71	.81	1.00	4.00	1051	
A08DIFF	2.88	.77	1.00	4.00	1038	
A09DIFF	2.23	.88	1.00	4.00	1027	
A10DIFF	2.78	.86	1.00	4.00	1049	
A11DIFF	2.73	.84	1.00	4.00	1044	
A12DIFF	2.04	.86	1.00	4.00	1053	
B01FAM	2.35	.77	1.00	4.00	1060	
B02FAM	2.24	.91	1.00	4.00	1059	
B03FAM	2.31	.80	1.00	4.00	1040	
B04FAM	2.69	.75	1.00	4.00	1042	
B05FAM	1.84	.81	1.00	4.00	1046	
B06FAM	1.97	.77	1.00	4.00	1044	
B07FAM	1.83	.72	1.00	4.00	1021	
B09FAM	2.45	.83	1.00	4.00	1013	
B10FAM	1.77	.76	1.00	4.00	1026	
B11FAM	1.88	.77	1.00	4.00	1013	
B12FAM	2.42	.80	1.00	4.00	1020	
C01DISP	1.08	.32	1.00	3.00	1055	
C02DISP	2.95	.24	1.00	3.00	1060	
C03DISP	1.97	.33	1.00	3.00	1046	
C04DISP	1.10	.37	1.00	3.00	1037	
C05DISP	2.88	.41	1.00	4.00	1056	
C06DISP	2.02	.72	1.00	4.00	1031	
C07DISP	2.13	.57	1.00	4.00	1032	
C08DISP	2.14	.85	1.00	4.00	1015	
C09DISP	1.14	.42	1.00	4.00	1011	
C10DISP	1.26	.52	1.00	4.00	1007	
C11DISP	1.97	.45	1.00	4.00	1018	
C12DISP	2.05	.82	1.00	4.00	1058	
D02SPEC	2.78	.84	1.00	4.00	1052	
D03SEPC	2.24	.80	1.00	4.00	1038	
D04SPEC	1.53	.72	1.00	4.00	1043	
D05SPEC	2.76	.91	1.00	4.00	1039	
D06SPEC	2.13	.82	1.00	4.00	1036	
D07SPEC	2.32	.88	1.00	4.00	1027	
D08SPEC	2.41	.87	1.00	4.00	1009	
D09SPEC	1.95	.82	1.00	4.00	1005	
D10SPEC	2.01	.93	1.00	4.00	1025	
D11SPEC	2.55	.95	1.00	4.00	1010	
D12SPEC	1.82	.79	1.00	4.00	1028	

Appendices - Chapter 5

Descriptive of the questionnaire data (variable order) – continued

E01INT	2.50	.78	1.00	4.00	1064
E02INT	2.62	.90	1.00	4.00	1058
E03INT	2.60	.85	1.00	4.00	1053
E04INT	2.63	.85	1.00	4.00	1051
E05INT	2.30	.93	1.00	4.00	1054
E06INT	2.33	.84	1.00	4.00	1043
E07INT	2.19	.84	1.00	4.00	1042
E08INT	2.25	.84	1.00	4.00	1032
E09INT	2.64	.86	1.00	4.00	1028
E10INT	2.13	.89	1.00	4.00	1040
E11INT	2.23	.91	1.00	4.00	1036
E12INT	2.66	.84	1.00	4.00	1055
F1FRFAM	2.43	.81	1.00	4.00	1061
F2FRFAM	2.63	.88	1.00	4.00	1058
F3FRFAM	1.79	.74	1.00	4.00	1060
F4FRFAM	2.64	.83	1.00	4.00	1052
F5FRFAM	3.27	.79	1.00	4.00	1059
G1FRSUIT	2.81	.80	1.00	4.00	1059
G2FRSUIT	2.96	.77	1.00	4.00	1055
G3FRSUIT	2.66	.84	1.00	4.00	1054
G4FRSUIT	2.56	.83	1.00	4.00	1048
G5FRSUIT	2.55	.97	1.00	4.00	1055
H1TMSUF	2.43	.92	1.00	4.00	1062
H2TMSUF	1.75	.75	1.00	4.00	1059
H3TMSUF	1.58	.70	1.00	4.00	1058
H4TMSUF	1.53	.70	1.00	4.00	1058
H5TMSUF	3.09	.87	1.00	4.00	1058
I1SECDIF	2.41	.79	1.00	4.00	1058
I2SECDIF	2.81	.78	1.00	4.00	1053
I3SECDIF	2.86	.81	1.00	4.00	1055
I4SECDIF	2.80	.89	1.00	4.00	1050
I5SECDIF	2.39	.89	1.00	4.00	1051
J1TMSUF	2.06	.79	1.00	4.00	1036
J2LAYOUT	2.49	.85	1.00	4.00	1032
J3DIRECT	2.57	.86	1.00	4.00	1035
K1APFREQ	2.87	.88	1.00	4.00	1029
K2APFREQ	2.41	.84	1.00	4.00	1027
K3APFREQ	2.13	.88	1.00	4.00	1026
K4APFREQ	2.08	.92	1.00	4.00	1028
K5APFREQ	2.50	.99	1.00	4.00	1027
M1TRAIN	.88	.90	1.00	4.00	1031
M2TRAIN	1.97	.80	1.00	4.00	1032
M3TRAIN	1.58	.67	1.00	4.00	1031
M4TRAIN	1.57	.69	1.00	4.00	1031
M5TRAIN	2.52	1.01	1.00	4.00	1033

Appendices - Chapter 5

Appendix 5.2.34
Frequency percentages of students' perceptions of the texts and tasks – summary data from the questionnaire survey

Value Label: 1 not difficult   2 not very difficult   3 quite difficult   4 very difficult

Value Label	Passage No.											
	1	2	3	4	5	6	7	8	9	10	11	12
1	15.4	17.3	10.6	37.0	5.9	9.9	7.0	4.0	20.8	8.2	7.6	28.7
2	45.6	36.5	36.3	42.6	23.3	35.2	29.6	23.1	40.5	24.5	28.7	43.0
3	32.4	36.9	41.8	15.2	49.1	42.0	46.3	50.7	27.0	46.0	44.3	21.1
4	6.4	8.3	9.6	3.8	20.1	11.0	15.4	19.3	7.9	19.5	17.1	5.9
missing	0.3	0.9	1.7	1.4	1.6	1.9	1.6	2.8	3.8	1.8	2.2	1.4

Frequency percentages of students' perception of: B – topic familiarity
Value Label: 1 not familiar   2 not very familiar   3 quite familiar   4 very familiar

Value Label	Passage No.											
	1	2	3	4	5	6	7	8	9	10	11	12
1	14.0	24.4	17.1	7.4	38.4	28.7	33.7	29.2	14.6	39.3	33.1	12.4
2	40.4	34.5	37.0	25.0	39.1	45.1	47.1	43.0	29.7	40.8	41.1	36.5
3	41.0	32.5	39.4	55.9	17.9	22.2	14.9	21.3	44.1	14.2	19.3	40.4
4	3.8	7.8	3.8	9.3	2.5	1.8	1.2	2.1	6.5	1.7	1.4	6.2
missing	0.7	0.8	2.6	2.4	2.1	2.2	3.1	4.4	5.1	3.9	5.1	4.5

Frequency percentages of students' perception of: C — disciplinary area
Value Label: 1 arts/business/management   2 science/technology   3 biology/medical/life science

Value Label	Passage No.											
	1	2	3	4	5	6	7	8	9	10	11	12
1	92.8	0.5	6.7	90.4	2.9	24.0	9.7	28.0	83.6	73.8	11.0	30.0
2	4.5	4.3	87.0	4.0	6.3	46.7	64.6	26.1	8.7	16.8	76.7	30.9
3	1.5	94.5	4.2	2.6	89.2	25.6	22.0	40.6	2.2	3.7	7.5	34.8
missing	1.2	0.7	2.1	2.9	1.6	3.8	3.7	5.3	5.5	5.8	4.9	4.3

Frequency percentages of students' perception of: D – subject specificity
Value Label: 1 not specific   2 not very specific   3 quite specific   4 very specific

Value Label	Passage No.											
	1	2	3	4	5	6	7	8	9	10	11	12
1	31.7	10.7	17.3	57.6	12.6	22.7	19.4	16.7	30.8	34.6	15.5	38.2
2	47.9	15.7	44.1	28.9	16.7	43.6	34.5	30.7	40.2	32.1	26.8	40.3
3	17.9	56.3	30.9	10.2	49.0	26.2	34.9	39.2	19.9	23.1	36.5	15.2
4	1.5	15.8	4.9	0.9	19.0	4.5	7.4	7.9	3.2	6.2	15.7	2.6
missing	0.9	1.5	2.8	2.3	2.7	3.0	3.8	5.5	5.9	4.0	5.4	3.7

Frequency percentages of students' perception of: E – text interestingness
Value Label: 1 not interesting   2 not very interesting   3 quite interesting   4 very interesting

Value Label	Passage No.											
	1	2	3	4	5	6	7	8	9	10	11	12
1	12.0	13.0	11.1	11.5	22.4	17.1	21.2	18.9	11.0	26.6	23.5	10.6
2	31.8	27.2	30.0	26.0	33.8	38.1	41.9	40.8	26.0	37.6	35.9	25.2
3	49.9	43.4	45.1	48.4	33.0	36.0	29.2	30.8	45.8	26.9	29.8	50.1
4	5.9	15.5	12.4	12.5	9.6	6.5	5.3	6.1	13.4	6.3	7.9	12.9
missing	0.4	0.9	1.4	1.6	1.3	2.3	2.4	3.4	3.7	2.6	3.0	1.2

Appendices - Chapter 5

Frequency percentages of students' perception of: F – test formats
Value Label: 1 not familiar   2 not very familiar   3 quite familiar   4 very familiar

Value Label	Test Formats				
	1 short answer questions	2 true/false judgement	3 table/flow-chart completion	4 sentence completion	5 banked cloze
1	13.4	11.0	38.5	9.8	4.2
2	36.3	29.9	44.4	28.2	8.3
3	42.7	42.4	15.2	48.0	42.6
4	6.9	15.7	1.2	12.5	44.0
missing	0.7	0.9	0.7	1.5	0.8

Frequency percentages of students' perception of: G – format suitability for testing EAP reading
Value Label: 1 not suitable   2 not very suitable   3 quite suitable   4 very suitable

Value Label	Test Formats				
	1 short answer questions	2 true/false judgement	3 table/flow-chart completion	4 sentence completion	5 banked cloze
1	8.1	4.9	9.8	11.2	16.9
2	18.4	17.3	27.7	31.6	27.2
3	56.3	53.9	47.7	44.5	37.8
4	16.3	22.7	13.5	10.8	16.9
missing	0.8	1.2	1.3	1.9	1.2

Frequency percentages of students' perception of: H – time sufficiency of each section
Value Label: 1 not sufficient   2 not very sufficient   3 quite sufficient   4 very sufficient

Value Label	Sections				
	1 careful global	2 skimming	3 search reading	4 scanning	5 careful local
1	18.8	42.4	52.9	57.9	7.4
2	30.1	40.4	35.6	30.9	11.0
3	39.8	15.3	9.9	9.6	45.8
4	10.7	1.1	0.7	0.7	34.8
missing	0.6	0.8	0.9	0.9	0.9

Frequency percentages of students' perception of: I – section difficulty
Value Label: 1 not difficult   2 not very difficult   3 quite difficult   4 very difficult

Value Label	Sections				
	1 careful global	2 skimming	3 search reading	4 scanning	5 careful local
1	11.0	4.2	5.9	8.6	16.1
2	44.2	28.1	22.7	24.8	39.0
3	36.0	48.3	49.2	42.2	31.9
4	7.9	18.0	21.1	22.7	11.3
missing	0.9	1.4	1.2	1.7	1.6

Appendices - Chapter 5

Frequency percentages of students' perception of: J - general comments on the test
Value Label: 1 not suitable   2 not very suitable 3 quite suitable   4 very suitable

Value Label	Test Conditions		
	length of the test	test paper layout	rubrics in the test
1	26.2	15.4	13.2
2	40.5	26.3	26.5
3	28.7	47.3	46.4
4	1.5	7.7	10.8
missing	3.0	3.4	3.1

Frequency percentages of students' perception of: K - Frequency of use in real life
Value Label: 1 not frequent   2 not very frequent 3 quite frequent   4 very frequent

Value Label	Skill/Strategy				
	careful global	skimming	search reading	scanning	careful local
1	8.9	15.5	26.5	30.8	19.1
2	18.1	32.0	36.5	33.5	26.1
3	46.1	42.2	27.4	25.4	35.1
4	23.3	6.4	5.6	6.6	15.8
missing	3.7	3.8	3.9	3.7	3.8

Frequency percentages of students' perception of: M - training received
Value Label: 1 very little   2 not much   3 quite a lot   4 a lot

Value Label	Skill/Strategy				
	careful global	skimming	search reading	scanning	careful local
1	11.5	30.7	50.0	52.0	21.6
2	10.8	40.4	37.9	35.0	19.0
3	52.2	23.7	8.0	8.8	40.5
4	22.1	1.9	0.7	0.7	15.5
missing	3.5	3.4	3.5	3.5	3.3

Appendix 5.2.35
Effects of students' perceptions of the texts and tasks on their performance – summary data from the questionnaire survey

Mean scores of students by students' perception of: A – language difficulty
Value Label: 1 not difficult   2 not very difficult   3 quite difficult   4 very difficult

Value Label	Passage No. 1	2	3	4	5	6	7	8	9	10	11	12
1	3.14	3.55	2.27	2.36	2.59	1.53	3.07	2.63	2.76	2.10	2.30	2.48
2	2.76	3.35	2.18	2.20	2.54	1.33	3.09	2.55	2.94	1.71	1.80	2.18
3	2.35	3.04	1.76	1.97	2.13	1.05	2.66	2.41	2.61	1.55	1.71	1.97
4	1.97	2.61	1.47	1.63	1.67	0.89	2.30	2.06	2.37	1.37	1.57	1.65

Mean scores of students by students' perception of: B – topic familiarity
Value Label: 1 not familiar   2 not very familiar   3 quite familiar   4 very familiar

Value Label	Passage No. 1	2	3	4	5	6	7	8	9	10	11	12
1	2.28	3.08	1.47	1.84	2.00	1.02	2.57	2.20	2.56	1.48	1.72	1.90
2	2.53	3.19	1.81	2.02	2.27	1.19	2.86	2.48	2.71	1.67	1.78	2.11
3	2.81	3.19	2.23	2.28	2.16	1.31	2.84	2.41	2.86	1.70	1.81	2.29
4	3.29	3.77	2.41	2.56	3.00	1.79	3.08	2.86	2.86	2.11	2.20	2.39

Mean scores of students by students' perception of: E – text interestingness
Value Label: 1 not interesting   2 not very interesting 3 quite interesting   4 very interesting

Value Label	Passage No. 1	2	3	4	5	6	7	8	9	10	11	12
1	2.08	2.83	1.49	2.17	1.91	0.89	2.59	2.26	2.67	1.57	1.69	1.89
2	2.53	3.14	1.81	2.10	2.02	1.10	2.79	2.29	2.71	1.52	1.60	2.05
3	2.78	3.24	2.09	2.29	2.30	1.35	2.80	2.52	2.81	1.66	1.94	2.28
4	3.13	3.57	2.13	2.14	2.72	1.55	2.96	2.77	2.86	1.96	2.17	2.30

Mean scores of sections by students' perception of: H – time sufficiency
Value Label: 1 not sufficient   2 not very sufficient   3 quite sufficient   4 very sufficient

Value Label	Section 1 careful global	2 skimming	3 search reading	4 scanning	5 careful local
1	6.67	0.93	3.93	5.46	4.11
2	7.29	1.10	4.92	6.62	4.92
3	8.35	1.39	5.24	7.42	5.41
4	9.04	1.83	7.57	8.14	6.23

Appendices - Chapter 5

Mean scores of sections by students' perception of: I – section difficulty
Value Label: 1 not difficult   2 not very difficult   3 quite difficult   4 very difficult

Value Label	Section 1 careful global	2 skimming	3 search reading	4 scanning	5 careful local
1	8.59	0.98	5.10	7.46	6.45
2	8.37	1.22	4.94	7.10	5.68
3	7.11	1.06	4.37	5.70	5.33
4	6.45	0.97	3.93	5.00	4.35

Mean scores of sections by students' perception of: K – frequency of use in real life
Value Label: 1 not frequent   2 not very frequent   3 quite frequen t   4 very frequent

Value Label	Skill/Strategy careful global	skimming	search reading	scanning	careful local
1	7.12	1.01	4.23	5.65	5.12
2	7.61	1.07	4.45	6.12	5.28
3	7.78	1.15	4.67	6.24	5.82
4	8.24	0.94*	4.75	6.46	5.87

Mean scores of sections by students' perception of: M – training received
Value Label: 1 very little   2 not much   3 quite a lot   4 a lot

Value Label	Skill/Strategy careful global	skimming	search reading	scanning	careful local
1	6.94	1.00	4.26	5.74	5.03
2	7.45	1.08	4.56	6.26	5.41
3	7.83	1.20	5.14	6.94	5.78
4	8.36	1.15	5.00	5.13**	5.84

*   There are only 3 items in the section, and 68 cases for this cell.
** There are only 8 cases for this cell compared to 94 for cell 3.

Appendices - Chapter 5

Appendix 5.2.36
Effects of students' perceptions of the texts and tasks on their performance – original data from the questionnaire survey

Summaries of   TOTCARE1
By levels of   A01DIFF

Variable	Value Label	Mean	Std Dev	Cases
For Entire Population		2.6366	1.3753	1065
A01DIFF	1.00	3.1402	1.3101	164
A01DIFF	2.00	2.7618	1.3134	487
A01DIFF	3.00	2.3526	1.3631	346
A01DIFF	4.00	1.9706	1.4759	68

Total Cases = 1068
Missing Cases = 3 or 3 Pct

Summaries of   TOTCARE2
By levels of   A02DIFF

Variable	Value Label	Mean	Std Dev	Cases
For Entire Population		3.2070	1.2108	1058
A02DIFF	1.00	3.5514	1.1510	185
A02DIFF	2.00	3.3462	1.1807	390
A02DIFF	3.00	3.0431	1.2067	394
A02DIFF	4.00	2.6067	1.1640	89

Total Cases = 1068
Missing Cases = 10 or 9 Pct

Summaries of   TOTCARE3
By levels of   A03DIFF

Variable	Value Label	Mean	Std Dev	Cases
For Entire Population		1.9381	1.1474	1050
A03DIFF	1.00	2.2743	1.1971	113
A03DIFF	2.00	2.1753	1.0974	388
A03DIFF	3.00	1.7556	1.1242	446
A03DIFF	4.00	1.4660	1.0830	103

Total Cases = 1068
Missing Cases = 18 or 1.7 Pct

Summaries of   TOTSKCH1
By levels of   A04DIFF

Variable	Value Label	Mean	Std Dev	Cases
For Entire Population		2.2042	1.2406	1053
A04DIFF	1.00	2.3646	1.2273	395
A04DIFF	2.00	2.2000	1.2477	455
A04DIFF	3.00	1.9691	1.2026	162
A04DIFF	4.00	1.6341	1.1566	41

Total Cases = 1068
Missing Cases = 15 or 1.4 Pct

Summaries of   TOTSKCH2
By levels of   A05DIFF

Variable	Value Label	Mean	Std Dev	Cases
For Entire Population		2.1589	1.4562	1051
A05DIFF	1.00	2.5873	1.5412	63
A05DIFF	2.00	2.5422	1.3967	249
A05DIFF	3.00	2.1260	1.4207	524
A05DIFF	4.00	1.6698	1.4332	215

Total Cases = 1068
Missing Cases = 17 or 1.6 Pct

Appendices - Chapter 5

```
Summaries of          TOTLEXI2
By levels of          A11DIFF
Variable    Value Label      Mean      Std Dev    Cases
For Entire Population        1.7586    1.2883     1044
A11DIFF    1.00              2.2963    1.1559       81
A11DIFF    2.00              1.8046    1.2989      307
A11DIFF    3.00              1.7104    1.2850      473
A11DIFF    4.00              1.5683    1.2772      183
Total Cases = 1068
Missing Cases = 24 or 2.2 Pct

Summaries of          TOTLEXI3
By levels of          A12DIFF
Variable    Value Label      Mean      Std Dev    Cases
For Entire Population        2.1899    1.3587     1053
A12DIFF    1.00              2.4771    1.3794      306
A12DIFF    2.00              2.1808    1.2983      459
A12DIFF    3.00              1.9689    1.3476      225
A12DIFF    4.00              1.6508    1.4386       63
Total Cases = 1068
Missing Cases = 15 or 1.4 Pct

Summaries of          TOTCARE1
By levels of          B01FAM
Variable    Value Label      Mean      Std Dev    Cases
For Entire Population        2.6377    1.3732     1060
B01FAM    1.00               2.2752    1.4652      149
B01FAM    2.00               2.5301    1.3739      432
B01FAM    3.00               2.8059    1.3157      438
B01FAM    4.00               3.2927    1.1671       41
Total Cases = 1068
Missing Cases = 8 or 7 Pct

Summaries of          TOTCARE2
By levels of          B02FAM
Variable    Value Label      Mean      Std Dev    Cases
For Entire Population        3.2059    1.2093     1059
B02FAM    1.00               3.0766    1.1840      261
B02FAM    2.00               3.1875    1.2131      368
B02FAM    3.00               3.1873    1.2174      347
B02FAM    4.00               3.7711    1.0968       83
Total Cases = 1068
Missing Cases = 9 or 8 Pct

Summaries of          TOTCARE3
By levels of          B03FAM
Variable    Value Label      Mean      Std Dev    Cases
For Entire Population  1.9452 1.1432    1040
B03FAM    1.00               1.4699    1.0419      183
B03FAM    2.00               1.8101    1.1497      395
B03FAM    3.00               2.2328    1.0946      421
B03FAM    4.00               2.4146    1.0482       41
Total Cases = 1068
Missing Cases = 28 or 2.6 Pct
```

Appendices - Chapter 5

```
Summaries of         TOTSKCH1
By levels of         B04FAM
Variable    Value Label      Mean      Std Dev    Cases
For Entire Population        2.2044    1.2364     1042
B04FAM    1.00               1.8354    1.2550       79
B04FAM    2.00               2.0187    1.1998      267
B04FAM    3.00               2.2781    1.2246      597
B04FAM    4.00               2.5556    1.2635       99
Total Cases = 1068
Missing Cases = 26 or 2.4 Pct

Summaries of         TOTSKCH2
By levels of         B05FAM
Variable    Value Label      Mean      Std Dev    Cases
For Entire Population        2.1587    1.4508     1046
B05FAM    1.00               1.9951    1.4297      410
B05FAM    2.00               2.2656    1.4605      418
B05FAM    3.00               2.1571    1.4497      191
B05FAM    4.00               3.0000    1.2403       27
Total Cases = 1068
Missing Cases = 22 or 2.1 Pct

Summaries of         TOTSKCH3
By levels of         B06FAM
Variable    Value Label      Mean      Std Dev    Cases
For Entire Population        1.1782    1.2755     1044
B06FAM    1.00               1.0229    1.2104      306
B06FAM    2.00               1.1888    1.2927      482
B06FAM    3.00               1.3080    1.2798      237
B06FAM    4.00               1.7895    1.5121       19
Total Cases = 1068
Missing Cases = 24 or 2.2 Pct

Summaries of         TOTSCAN1
By levels of         B07FAM
Variable    Value Label      Mean      Std Dev    Cases
For Entire Population        2.7594    1.2796     1035
B07FAM    1.00               2.5694    1.3250      360
B07FAM    2.00               2.8608    1.2720      503
B07FAM    3.00               2.8428    1.1667      159
B07FAM    4.00               3.0769    1.1152       13
Total Cases = 1068
Missing Cases = 33 or 3.1 Pct

Summaries of         TOTSCAN2
By levels of         B08FAM
Variable    Value Label      Mean      Std Dev    Cases
For Entire Population        2.3888    1.4762     1021
B08FAM    1.00               2.1987    1.4848      312
B08FAM    2.00               2.4837    1.4707      459
B08FAM    3.00               2.4123    1.4560      228
B08FAM    4.00               2.8636    1.4572       22
Total Cases = 1068
Missing Cases = 47 or 4.4 Pct
```

Appendices - Chapter 5

```
Summaries of          TOTSCAN1
By levels of          B09FAM
Variable    Value Label          Mean      Std Dev   Cases
For Entire Population            2.7670    1.2835    1013
B09FAM      1.00                 2.5641    1.4105    156
B09FAM      2.00                 2.7129    1.3059    317
B09FAM      3.00                 2.8577    1.2077    471
B09FAM      4.00                 2.8551    1.3425    69
  Total Cases = 1068
Missing Cases = 55 or 5.1 Pct

Summaries of          TOTLEXI1
By levels of          B10FAM
Variable    Value Label          Mean      Std Dev   Cases
For Entire Population            1.6043    1.1932    1026
B10FAM      1.00                 1.4786    1.1548    420
B10FAM      2.00                 1.6720    1.1862    436
B10FAM      3.00                 1.6974    1.2504    152
B10FAM      4.00                 2.1111    1.4907    18
  Total Cases = 1068
Missing Cases = 42 or 3.9 Pct

Summaries of          TOTLEXI2
By levels of          B11FAM
Variable    Value Label          Mean      Std Dev   Cases
For Entire Population            1.7700    1.2905    1013
B11FAM      1.00                 1.7167    1.2987    353
B11FAM      2.00                 1.7790    1.3012    439
B11FAM      3.00                 1.8107    1.2680    206
B11FAM      4.00                 2.2000    1.0823    15
Total Cases = 1068
Missing Cases = 55 or 5.1 Pct

Summaries of          TOTLEXI3
By levels of          B12FAM
Variable    Value Label          Mean      Std Dev   Cases
For Entire Population            2.1775    1.3615    1020
B12FAM      1.00    1.9015       1.3696    132
B12FAM      2.00    2.1103       1.3417    390
B12FAM      3.00    2.2894       1.3339    432
B12FAM      4.00    2.3939       1.5480    66
Total Cases = 1068
Missing Cases = 48 or 4.5 Pct

Summaries of          TOTCARE1
By levels of          E01INT
Variable    Value Label          Mean      Std Dev   Cases
For Entire Population            2.6353    1.3766    1064
E01INT      1.00                 2.0781    1.4396    128
E01INT      2.00                 2.5294    1.4045    340
E01INT      3.00                 2.7786    1.3306    533
E01INT      4.00                 3.1270    1.0700    63
Total Cases = 1068
Missing Cases = 4 or 4 Pct
```

Appendices - Chapter 5

```
Summaries of          TOTCARE2
By levels of          E02INT
Variable    Value  Label      Mean      Std Dev    Cases
For Entire Population         3.2108    1.2039     1058
E02INT      1.00              2.8345    1.2831      139
E02INT      2.00              3.1414    1.1928      290
E02INT      3.00              3.2376    1.1713      463
E02INT      4.00              3.5723    1.1458      166
  Total Cases = 1068
  Missing Cases = 10 or 9 Pct

Summaries of          TOTCARE3
By levels of          E03INT
Variable    Value  Label      Mean      Std Dev    Cases
For Entire Population         1.9430    1.1447     1053
E03INT      1.00              1.4874    1.1414      119
E03INT      2.00              1.8094    1.1105      320
E03INT      3.00              2.0934    1.1213      482
E03INT      4.00              2.1288    1.1748      132
  Total Cases = 1068
  Missing Cases = 15 or 1.4 Pct

Summaries of          TOTSKCH1
By levels of          E04INT
Variable    Value  Label      Mean      Std Dev    Cases
For Entire Population         2.2065    1.2368     1051
E04INT      1.00              2.1707    1.1922      123
E04INT      2.00              2.0971    1.2694      278
E04INT      3.00              2.2921    1.2270      517
E04INT      4.00              2.1353    1.2357      133
  Total Cases = 1068
  Missing Cases = 17 or 1.6 Pct

Summaries of          TOTSKCH2
By levels of          E05INT
Variable    Value  Label      Mean      Std Dev    Cases
For Entire Population         2.1575    1.4500     1054
E05INT      1.00              1.9121    1.4453      239
E05INT      2.00              2.0249    1.4460      361
E05INT      3.00              2.2983    1.4319      352
E05INT      4.00              2.7157    1.3525      102
  Total Cases = 1068
  Missing Cases = 14 or 1.3 Pct

Summaries of          TOTSKCH3
By levels of          E06INT
Variable    Value  Label      Mean      Std Dev    Cases
For Entire Population         1.1831    1.2788     1043
E06INT      1.00               .8852    1.1781      183
E06INT      2.00              1.1007    1.2165      407
E06INT      3.00              1.3464    1.3314      384
E06INT      4.00              1.5507    1.3989       69
  Total Cases = 1068
  Missing Cases = 25 or 2.3 Pct
```

Appendices - Chapter 5

```
Summaries of          TOTSCAN1
By levels of          E07INT
Variable    Value Label       Mean      Std Dev    Cases
For Entire Population         2.7610    1.2800     1042
E07INT      1.00              2.5929    1.3442     226
E07INT      2.00              2.7897    1.2690     447
E07INT      3.00              2.8045    1.2385     312
E07INT      4.00              2.9649    1.2951      57
Total Cases = 1068
Missing Cases = 26 or 2.4 Pct

Summaries of          TOTSCAN2
By levels of          E08INT
Variable    Value Label       Mean      Std Dev    Cases
For Entire Population         2.3866    1.4703     1032
E08INT      1.00              2.2624    1.4881     202
E08INT      2.00              2.2867    1.4818     436
E08INT      3.00              2.5198    1.4484     329
E08INT      4.00              2.7692    1.3552      65
Total Cases = 1068
Missing Cases = 36 or 3.4 Pct

Summaries of          TOTSCAN1
By levels of          E09INT
Variable    Value Label       Mean      Std Dev    Cases
For Entire Population         2.7724    1.2800     1028
E09INT      1.00              2.6695    1.4206     118
E09INT      2.00              2.7050    1.2457     278
E09INT      3.00              2.8098    1.2686     489
E09INT      4.00              2.8601    1.2649     143
Total Cases = 1068
Missing Cases = 40 or 3.7 Pct

Summaries of          TOTLEXI1
By levels of          E10INT
Variable    Value Label       Mean      Std Dev    Cases
For Entire Population         1.6000    1.1925     1040
E10INT      1.00              1.5669    1.2606     284
E10INT      2.00              1.5249    1.0989     402
E10INT      3.00              1.6551    1.1986     287
E10INT      4.00              1.9552    1.3533      67
Total Cases = 1068
Missing Cases = 28 or 2.6 Pct

Summaries of          TOTLEXI2
By levels of          E11INT
Variable    Value Label       Mean      Std Dev    Cases
For Entire Population         1.7722    1.2915     1036
E11INT      1.00              1.6932     .3136     251
E11INT      2.00              1.5953    1.2346     383
E11INT      3.00              1.9434    1.3160     318
E11INT      4.00              2.1667    1.2402      84
Total Cases = 1068
Missing Cases = 32 or 3.0 Pct
```

Appendices - Chapter 5

```
Summaries of         TOTLEXI3
By levels of         E12INT
Variable    Value Label        Mean       Std Dev    Cases
For Entire Population          2.1848     1.3633     1055
E12INT      1.00               1.8938     1.3520     113
E12INT      2.00               2.0483     1.3304     269
E12INT      3.00               2.2841     1.3469     535
E12INT      4.00               2.3043     1.4530     138
Total Cases = 1068
Missing Cases = 13 or 1.2 Pct

Summaries of         TOTCARE
By levels of         H1TMSUF
Variable    Value Label        Mean       Std Dev    Cases
For Entire Population          7.7825     2.7457     1062
H1TMSUF     1.00               6.6667     2.5521     201
H1TMSUF     2.00               7.2888     2.6192     322
H1TMSUF     3.00               8.3459     2.6724     425
H1TMSUF     4.00               9.0439     2.6951     114
Total Cases = 1068
Missing Cases = 6 or 6 Pct

Summaries of         TOTSKIM
By levels of         H2TMSUF
Variable    Value Label        Mean       Std Dev    Cases
For Entire Population          1.0803     .9655      1059
H2TMSUF     1.00                .9338     .8925      453
H2TMSUF     2.00               1.0951     .9730      431
H2TMSUF     3.00               1.3926    1.0449      163
H2TMSUF     4.00               1.8333     .9374       12
Total Cases = 1068
Missing Cases = 9 or 8 Pct

Summaries of         TOTSCH
By levels of         H3TMSUF
Variable    Value Label        Mean       Std Dev    Cases
For Entire Population          4.4433     2.3966     1058
H3TMSUF     1.00               3.9327     2.2335     565
H3TMSUF     2.00               4.9237     2.4119     380
H3TMSUF     3.00               5.2358     2.4902     106
H3TMSUF     4.00               7.5714     2.2991       7
Total Cases = 1068
Missing Cases = 10 or 9 Pct

Summaries of         TOTSCAN
By levels of         H4TMSUF
Variable    Value Label        Mean       Std Dev    Cases
For Entire Population          6.0274     2.8278     1058
H4TMSUF     1.00               5.4579     2.6489     618
H4TMSUF     2.00               6.6152     2.7390     330
H4TMSUF     3.00               7.4175     3.2253     103
H4TMSUF     4.00               8.1429     2.8536       7
Total Cases = 1068
Missing Cases = 10 or 9 Pct
```

Appendices - Chapter 5

```
Summaries of           TOTLEXI
By levels of           H5TMSUF
Variable    Value Label         Mean        Std Dev     Cases
For Entire Population           5.5463      2.8194      1058
H5TMSUF  1.00                   4.1139      3.5805        79
H5TMSUF  2.00                   4.9153      2.8542       118
H5TMSUF  3.00                   5.4070      2.6364       489
H5TMSUF  4.00                   6.2339      2.6790       372
Total Cases = 1068
Missing Cases = 10 or 9 Pct


Summaries of           TOTCARE
By levels of           I1SECDIF
Variable    Value Label         Mean        Std Dev     Cases
For Entire Population           7.7854      2.7391      1058
I1SECDIF  1.00                  8.5932      3.0220       118
I1SECDIF  2.00                  8.3729      2.5540       472
I1SECDIF  3.00                  7.1068      2.6347       384
I1SECDIF  4.00                  6.4524      2.6086        84
Total Cases = 1068
Missing Cases = 10 or 9 Pct


Summaries of           TOTSKIM
By levels of I2SECDIF
Variable    Value Label         Mean        Std Dev     Cases
For Entire Population           1.0845       .9679      1053
I2SECDIF  1.00                   .9778       .9883        45
I2SECDIF  2.00                  1.2167      1.0328       300
I2SECDIF  3.00                  1.0601       .9504       516
I2SECDIF  4.00                   .9688       .8856       192
Total Cases = 1068
Missing Cases = 15 or 1.4 Pct


Summaries of           TOTSCH
By levels of           I3SECDIF
Variable    Value Label         Mean        Std Dev     Cases
For Entire Population           4.4521      2.3985      1055
I3SECDIF  1.00                  5.0952      2.5382        63
I3SECDIF  2.00                  4.9421      2.5484       242
I3SECDIF  3.00                  4.3733      2.3488       525
I3SECDIF  4.00                  3.9289      2.1742       225
Total Cases = 1068
Missing Cases = 13 or 1.2 Pct


Summaries of           TOTSCAN
By levels of           I4SECDIF
Variable    Value Label         Mean        Std Dev     Cases
For Entire Population           6.0438      2.8183      1050
I4SECDIF  1.00                  7.4565      2.6329        92
I4SECDIF  2.00                  7.1019      2.8420       265
I4SECDIF  3.00                  5.6962      2.6747       451
I4SECDIF  4.00                  4.9959      2.5352       242
Total Cases = 1068
Missing Cases = 18 or 1.7 Pct
```

Appendices - Chapter 5

```
Summaries of          TOTLEXI
By levels of          I5SECDIF
Variable    Value Label         Mean      Std Dev    Cases
For Entire Population           5.5385    2.8192     1051
I5SECDIF    1.00                6.4535    2.5895      172
I5SECDIF    2.00                5.6811    2.7720      417
I5SECDIF    3.00                5.3255    2.6540      341
I5SECDIF    4.00                4.3471    3.2499      121
Total Cases = 1068
Missing Cases = 17 or 1.6 Pct

Summaries of          TOTCARE
By levels of          K1APFREQ
Variable    Value Label         Mean      Std Dev    Cases
For Entire Population           7.7998    2.7313     1029
K1APFREQ    1.00                7.1158    2.7009       95
K1APFREQ    2.00                7.6062    2.7081      193
K1APFREQ    3.00                7.7846    2.7780      492
K1APFREQ    4.00                8.2410    2.6070      249
Total Cases = 1068
Missing Cases = 39 or 3.7 Pct

Summaries of          TOTSKIM
By levels of          K2APFREQ
Variable    Value Label         Mean      Std Dev    Cases
For Entire Population           1.0847    .9701      1027
K2APFREQ    1.00                1.0060    .9178       166
K2APFREQ    2.00                1.0673    .9618       342
K2APFREQ    3.00                1.1486    .9922       451
K2APFREQ    4.00                 .9412    .9756        68
Total Cases = 1068
Missing Cases = 41 or 3.8 Pct

Summaries of          TOTSCH
By levels of          K3APFREQ
Variable    Value Label         Mean      Std Dev    Cases
For Entire Population           4.4688    2.4145     1026
K3APFREQ    1.00                4.2261    2.3622      283
K3APFREQ    2.00                4.4538    2.4551      390
K3APFREQ    3.00                4.6655    2.3577      293
K3APFREQ    4.00                4.7500    2.6078       60
Total Cases = 1068
Missing Cases = 42 or 3.9 Pct

Summaries of          TOTSCAN
By levels of          K4APFREQ
Variable    Value Label         Mean      Std Dev    Cases
For Entire Population           6.0263    2.8302     1028
K4APFREQ    1.00                5.6535    2.7064      329
K4APFREQ    2.00                6.1201    2.9656      358
K4APFREQ    3.00                6.2435    2.7928      271
K4APFREQ    4.00                6.4571    2.7010       70
Total Cases = 1068
Missing Cases = 40 or 3.7 Pct
```

Appendices - Chapter 5

Summaries of TOTLEXI
By levels of   K5APFREQ
Variable	Value Label	Mean	Std Dev	Cases
For Entire Population		5.5443	2.8292	1027
K5APFREQ	1.00	5.1225	3.0722	204
K5APFREQ	2.00	5.2832	2.6987	279
K5APFREQ	3.00	5.8213	2.7591	375
K5APFREQ	4.00	5.8698	2.8064	169

Total Cases = 1068
Missing Cases = 41 or 3.8 Pct

Summaries of TOTCARE
By levels of   M1TRAIN
Variable	Value Label	Mean	Std Dev	Cases
For Entire Population		7.8021	2.7298	1031
M1TRAIN	1.00	6.9431	2.5100	123
M1TRAIN	2.00	7.4522	2.8875	115
M1TRAIN	3.00	7.8259	2.6614	557
M1TRAIN	4.00	8.3644	2.7972	236

Total Cases = 1068
Missing Cases = 37 or 3.5 Pct

Summaries of TOTSKIM
By levels of   M2TRAIN
Variable	Value Label	Mean	Std Dev	Cases
For Entire Population		1.0853	.9702	1032
M2TRAIN	1.00	1.0030	.9336	328
M2TRAIN	2.00	1.0766	1.0029	431
M2TRAIN	3.00	1.2016	.9527	253
M2TRAIN	4.00	1.1500	.9881	20

Total Cases = 1068
Missing Cases = 36 or 3.4 Pct

Summaries of TOTSCH
By levels of   M3TRAIN
Variable	Value Label	Mean	Std Dev	Cases
For Entire Population		4.4559	2.4163	1031
M3TRAIN	1.00	4.2584	2.3198	534
M3TRAIN	2.00	4.5630	2.4764	405
M3TRAIN	3.00	5.1412	2.5735	85
M3TRAIN	4.00	5.0000	2.7080	7

Total Cases = 1068
Missing Cases = 37 or 3.5 Pct

Appendices - Chapter 5

```
Summaries of          TOTSCAN
By levels of          M4TRAIN
Variable    Value Label        Mean      Std Dev   Cases
For Entire Population          6.0310    2.8252    1031
M4TRAIN  1.00                  5.7369    2.7572     555
M4TRAIN  2.00                  6.2594    2.7680     374
M4TRAIN  3.00                  6.9362    3.1786      94
M4TRAIN  4.00                  5.1250    2.9490       8
Total Cases = 1068
Missing Cases = 37 or 3.5 Pct


Summaries of          TOTLEXI
By levels of          M5TRAIN
Variable    Value Label        Mean      Std Dev   Cases
For Entire Population          5.5518    2.8253    1033
M5TRAIN  1.00                  5.0346    2.9457     231
M5TRAIN  2.00                  5.4138    2.6507     203
M5TRAIN  3.00                  5.7806    2.7463     433
M5TRAIN  4.00                  5.8434    2.9766     166
Total Cases = 1068
Missing Cases = 35 or 3.3 Pct
```

Appendix 6.1
Expert judgement/Student retrospection questionnaire

What skill/strategy do you think is being tested in each section?

* Please double tick (√√) for the primary focus of the skill/strategy tested.
* Please tick (√) for the secondary focus of the skill/strategy tested if you think there is one.

Section 1 primary	secondary	Section 2 primary	secondary	Section 3 primary	secondary	Section 4 primary	secondary	Section 5 primary	secondary

reading carefully for main ideas

reading quickly to get the overall idea of a text

reading quickly to search for information on main ideas

reading quickly to find specific information: words/numbers/symbols

carefully working out meaning of words from context

others
(please specify)

Appendices - Chapter 6

Appendix 6.1
Expert judgement/Student retrospection questionnaire

What skill/strategy do you think is being tested in each section?

* Please double tick (✓✓) for the primary focus of the skill/strategy tested.
* Please tick (✓) for the secondary focus of the skill/strategy tested if you think there is one.

	Section 1 primary	Section 1 secondary	Section 2 primary	Section 2 secondary	Section 3 primary	Section 3 secondary	Section 4 primary	Section 4 secondary	Section 5 primary	Section 5 secondary
reading carefully for main ideas										
reading quickly to get the overall idea of a text										
reading quickly to search for inform-ation on main ideas										
reading quickly to find specific infor-mation: words/numbers/symbols										
carefully working out meaning of words from context										
others (please specify)										

[Source: Reading in a Second Language, Urquhart A. H. and Weir C. J. (1998). Longman]

Appendix 6.2.1
Student perception of skills/strategies being tested in each section

1 – Total of Shanghai Jiao Tong University students (N=27)

	Section 1 primary	Section 1 secondary	Section 2 primary	Section 2 secondary	Section 3 primary	Section 3 secondary	Section 4 primary	Section 4 secondary	Section 5 primary	Section 5 secondary
reading carefully for main ideas	18 67%	5	1	2	1	3	3	4	2	9
reading quickly to get the overall idea of a text	3	7	22 82%	6	2	11	2	9	4	3
reading quickly to search for inform-ation on main ideas	6	6	5	11	18 67%	5	6	9	1	6
reading quickly to find specific infor-mation: words/numbers/ symbols	5	6	2	3	10	6	21 78%	9	1	5
carefully working out meaning of words from context	2	8	0	2	2	1	2	1	22 82%	2
others (please specify)	0	0	0	0	0	0	0	0	0	1

Appendices - Chapter 6

Appendix 6.2.2
Total of Shanghai Medical University students (N=24)

2 – Total of Shanghai Medical University students (N=24)

	Section 1 primary	Section 1 secondary	Section 2 primary	Section 2 secondary	Section 3 primary	Section 3 secondary	Section 4 primary	Section 4 secondary	Section 5 primary	Section 5 secondary
reading carefully for main ideas	12 50%	2	2	1	4	2	0	0	6	5
reading quickly to get the overall idea of a text	3	4	15 63%	4	4	5	3	3	5	1
reading quickly to search for inform-ation on main ideas	5	5	2	10	5 21%	7	5	8	2	1
reading quickly to find specific infor-mation: words/numbers/symbols	4	6	5	3	8	7	15 63%	6	2	7
carefully working out meaning of words from context	0	4	0	1	2	2	1	4	9 38%	6
others (please specify)	0	1	0	0	1	0	0	1	0	1

Appendices - Chapter 6

Appendix 6.2.3
Total of East China Normal University students (N=18)

3 – Total of East China Normal University students (N=18)

	Section 1 primary	Section 1 secondary	Section 2 primary	Section 2 secondary	Section 3 primary	Section 3 secondary	Section 4 primary	Section 4 secondary	Section 5 primary	Section 5 secondary
reading carefully for main ideas	8 44%	4	3	1	1	0	1	0	5	3
reading quickly to get the overall idea of a text	8	6	11 61%	5	1	2	3	6	2	4
reading quickly to search for inform-ation on main ideas	2	4	3	6	8 44%	5	6	2	3	1
reading quickly to find specific infor-mation: words/numbers/ symbols	1	2	1	4	8	4	9 50%	4	1	2
carefully working out meaning of words from context	0	1	0	0	2	4	0	2	6 33%	6
others (please specify)	0	0	0	0	0	0	0	0	0	0

Appendices - Chapter 6

Appendix 6.3.1
Tables for introspection data transcript

Table 1: Student No.　　Total:　　(A/H subtest)　Subject:

Section		Item	
1 careful global passage 1		1 ( )	
		2 ( )	
		3 ( )	
		4 ( )	
		5 ( )	
2 skim passage 4		16 ( )	
3 search reading passage 4		19 ( )	
		20 ( )	
		21 ( )	
		22 ( )	
4 scan passage 9		41 ( )	
		42 ( )	
		43 ( )	
		44 ( )	
		45 ( )	
5 careful local passage 10		46 ( )	
		47 ( )	
		48 ( )	
		49 ( )	
		50 ( )	

Appendices - Chapter 6

Table 2   Student No.   **Discipline:**   **Total Score:**

Typical Example(s):

General Comment(s):

Background Knowledge	Language Competence	Skills/Strategies Using

Appendices - Chapter 6

Appendix 6.3.2
Examples of students' introspection records

Student No. H18   Total: 18 (ST test)   Subject: Teaching Chinese to Foreign Learners

Section	text-processing performance
1 careful global passage 3	- Very smooth reading, word by word, sentence by sentence. - No translation, no re-reading, very few pauses. - Seems no unknown words in reading the text. - Read passages without reading questions first. - Seems to have understood the passage quite well after first reading. - Total 6 minutes for the first reading of the text.
2 skim passage 6	- Read most of the passage very quickly, more carefully than expected, very smooth reading. - Paid more attention to the first and the last several paragraphs in the passage and the first several sentences in each paragraph. - More like speeded up careful reading - Total 4 minutes 40 minutes for text reading.
3 search reading passage 6	- Read questions before the text. - Read the text selectively, only those parts relevant to the questions. - Took her quite long time to locate relevant part of the text for each question because she was trying hard to locate the same words in the question as those in the text. - Typical search reading.
4 scan passage 7	- Reading questions before the text. - Making full use of the words in questions to locate the right place in the passage and got the answers very quickly. - Texts were read more selectively than in search reading. - Very confident in answering all the questions in the section. Much more confident than the search reading section.
5 careful local passage 11	Usually chose a word after completing the whole paragraph (instead of finishing the whole text) in which the word was deleted. - When finished all the five items, went back to read the whole text to further confirm her choices. Item 54: According to the context, probably 'existence' is also a possible answer or a very strong distractor. Besides it was not used in other items. Markers of the item reported the strong distraction of this choice. (key: characteristics)

Item	task-completion performance
11 (✔)	Located the answer in para. 6 using the topic '5th generation computer'. Read the paragraph carefully, trying hard to squeeze it into 8 words.
12 (✔)	Quickly went to the last paragraph and got the answer.
13 (✔)	Found the right place and read it. But hesitating between two sentences in the paragraph for the supporting sentence.
14 (X)	Took her quite long time to locate the relevant paragraph. Made correct judgement but chose the wrong (or inappropriate??) supporting sentence.
15 (✔)	Seems very easy to her. So EXMI or IPROP for her?
18 (✔)	Report: difficult to summarise the whole text in just one sentence. Finally she provided a very long phrase but since it covers the major points it was marked correct.
27 (✔)	Read paras. 2 and 3 and got the answer easily.
28 (✔)	Took her quite some time to locate the relevant paragraph. See typical example 2.
29 (✔)	Seems lack confidence for her answers of Nos. 29 and 30 because she couldn't locate the phrase 'new problem' in the question anywhere in the text. But this is what we meant by 'search reading' - looking for information with a pre-determined topic in mind!
30 (✔)	
31 (✔)	Matching words - biological material.
32 (✔)	Matching words - nacre, pearl.
33 (✔)	Matching words - wood, load-bearing.
34 (✔)	Matching words - synthetic nacre.
35 (✔)	Matching words - turbine blades.
51 (✔)	Found the item very easy. See typical example 4.
52 (✔)	Hesitated for a long time between 'demonstration' and the key 'equivalent'. Finally after reading the text again and again, abandoned the distractor.
53 (✔)	Took quite long to make the decision. She didn't seem to doubt her choice of 'existence'.
54 (X)	This was indeed a strong distractor.
55 (✔)	Not very easy for her. But after reading the paragraph several times, got the answer.

283

Appendices - Chapter 6

Student No. H12 Total: 17 (AH test) Subject: Teaching Chinese to foreign learners

Section	text-processing performance
1 careful global passage 1	- Very fluent reading, fast, word by word. - No unknown words at all. - Finished the first reading of the text in 5 minutes. - Read questions and went back to the passage for answers. - Finished 5 items in 5 minutes. So total 10 minutes for the section. Didn't do anything for the time left. - Seemed very confident of her answers but actually 2 were wrong. - Report: difficult to report while reading. - Report to have been trained to read fast for GRE test.
2 skim passage 4	- Aware of the strategy: reading the first one or two sentences in each paragraph. - Then proceeded to read more carefully, actually almost everything. - Spent 4 minutes finished the text and 2 minutes on the sentence.
3 search reading passage 4	- Didn't re-read the text carefully. Read the first one or two sentences of the text again. - When the relevant paragraphs were located (using the topic of the question), read the located paragraph carefully. - Finished the 4 items in only 4 minutes.
4 scan passage 9	- Read paras. 1, 2, and 3 quite carefully but quickly. - Paras. 4, 5 and 6 were also read carefully but some sentences with examples were skipped. - In reading paras. 7, 8, 9 and 10, she seemed to stop whenever she felt she had known what the paragraph was about. - Finished the reading in 3 minutes. - Read the questions and located the answers using subtitles.
5 careful local passage 10	- Read the text carefully in 3.5 minutes without trying to fill in the blanks. - Used the part of speech of words. - Finished the items in 5 minutes.

Item	task-completion performance
1 (X)	Located the answer in the right paragraph, but didn't read it carefully.
2 (✓)	Not reported.
3 (X)	Correct judgement but supported with a wrong sentence. But seemed to have understood this part of the text (Quite careless and too confident.)
4 (✓)	Without finding the supporting sentence, judged true/false first from the comprehension of the text and then went back to the text for the sentence.
5 (✓)	
16 (✓)	Writing the summarising sentence quickly using her own words instead of copying a long phrase or a sentence structure from the text.
19 (✓)	Answered the question (pay) using her memory from skimming.
20 (X)	Re-read first one or two sentences in paras. 3, 4 and 5. Since the answer of this item was in the middle part of the paragraph, she failed to locate it.
21 (✓)	Got the answer from the second sentence in para. 5.
22 (✓)	Located the last paragraph quickly using the topic of divorce. Re-read the paragraph carefully and answered the item correctly.
41 (✓)	Used her memory from the first reading, answered the item correctly but went back to para.2 to confirm.
42 (✓)	Located under the subtitles making decisions and looked for the word media.
43 (✓)	Located the relevant paragraphs quickly using subtitles. Then matched some words in the questions with those in the text and arrived at the answers.
44 (✓)	
45 (✓)	
46 (✓)	At first, denounced was chosen. When she finished Q47, she returned to this item and changed it into approved. So some global reading involved?
47 (✓)	Read the sentence and got the answer very easily.
48 (✓)	Read the sentence and got the answer very easily.
49 (✓)	Hesitated between sensitivity and evidence. After reading the paragraph more carefully, rejected sensitivity.
50 (✓)	Tried compelled, revealed, concealed and decided on compelled after reading the sentence several times.

Appendices - Chapter 6

Student No. J20   Total: 17 (ST test)   Subject: Computer Science

Section	text-processing performance
1 careful global passage 3	- Read questions before reading the text. - Spent about 6 minutes for the first reading of the text carefully, few reports provided during the reading. - No translation. - Smooth reading.
2 skim passage 6	- Not skimming but reading the text word by word quickly for about 5 minutes.
3 search reading passage 6	- Read questions first. - Continued to read the text in a careful manner. - When got to the relevant paragraphs, stopped to answer the questions. So it's a combination of careful reading and search reading. - Since he can read quite quickly there is time left for him to complete the items.
4 scan passage 7	- Read questions first. - Carefully but quickly read the passage for about 4 minutes then started to answer questions. - A combination of speeded up careful reading and scanning. - Aware of making use of key words, but only when the answers were confirmed through further careful reading, did he feel confident about the answers.
5 careful local passage 11	- Read all the words in the bank first. - Carefully read the text for 5 minutes during which no answer was arrived at. - Carefully read the text again and arrived at the answers for Nos. 51, 54 and 55. - Carefully read the text again, arrived at the answers for Nos. 53 and lastly 52. - Seemed to be reading both globally and locally for arriving at the answers.

Item	task-completion performance
11 (X)	Re-read paras. 3, 4, 5, 6, 7 and couldn't locate the relevant part of the text.
12 (✓)	Without going back to the text, got the answer. Then confirmed it when reading the last sentence of the text for item 15.
13 (✓)	Spent a long time reading paras. 3, 4, 5 again. Got the answer from paras. 4.
14 (✓)	Located para. 8 and got the answer.
15 (X)	From para. 10 got the wrong answer. He didn't go on with paras. 11 where the transition of discourse was indicated by the discourse marker: however.
18 (✓)	Provided a good summarising sentence based on the careful reading instead of skimming.
27 (✓)	Started with paras. 1, 2 and 3. Got the answer from para. 3.
28 (✓)	Read quickly but couldn't find the answer until he got to the last several paragraphs. After reading paras. 10, 11, and 12 got the answer.
29 (✓)	Continued to read the text and located the answer from paras. 13 and 14 using phrases: 'gene banks' and 'the second problem'. Arrived at the answer.
30 (✓)	Located the answer in paras. 13, 14 and got the answer after reading the two paragraphs.
31 (✓)	Read paras. 1, 2 and 3. Found the answer from para. 3 through careful reading.
32 (✓)	Located the answer in para. 4 using words: nacre and toughness.
33 (✓)	Spent a long time because the last paragraph was located using the word 'wood'. But the answer is in para. 9. Finally got the answer.
34 (✓)	No report. But from the time he spent on the two items (very short), he must have been using scanning.
35 (✓)	
51 (✓)	Got the answer after the text was read carefully twice. Distractors were not reported.
52 (X)	Didn't seem to doubt his answer, which was arrived at after the text was read carefully three times.
53 (✓)	Report a noun is needed here. Got the answer after the text was read carefully three times. Distractors were not reported.
54 (✓)	Got the answer after the text was read carefully twice. Distractors were not reported.
55 (✓)	Got the answer after the text was read carefully twice. Distractors were not reported.

Appendices - Chapter 6

Student No. M22   Total: 17 (ML test)   Subject: Medical Science

Section	text-processing performance
1 careful global passage 2	- Word by word careful reading, very fluent. - Translate almost every sentence, very accurate and almost simultaneous translation. All the questions were also translated. - He was definitely thinking in Chinese because all the reports were done in Chinese. - Since this is a medical subtest, sometimes extra detailed information was added in his translation trying to make it clearer. - Seemed to know the topic very well. - Finished the text in 10 minutes and the questions in 12 minutes.
2 skim passage 5	- Read every other paragraph of the text (i.e., paras. 1, 3, 5 ...) - A lot of translation. - Careful word by word reading of those paragraphs. - Total 5 minutes for the text.
3 search reading passage 5	- Read questions first. - Didn't re-read the text, since it has been read quite carefully in the skimming section. - Used the key words in the questions to help locate the relevant parts of the text for the questions. - Translated everything into Chinese.
4 scan passage 8	- Read the questions first. - Carefully read the text, word by word, with a lot of translation. - Slow down at the places where he felt likely to be the question areas, read carefully and got the answers for Q36, 37, and 38. - Not enough time for Q39 and 40. - Not scanning, therefore, even though he is proficient, he failed the last two items.
5 careful local passage 12	- Carefully read the text first, word by word. - Tried to fill in the blanks in the first reading. And succeeded for Q57, 59. - Q58 seemed to have been caused by the confusion between the two words. - Spent a long time for Q56 and Q60. After he finished the whole text and the other items, he finally got the two items correct.

Item	task-completion performance
6 (✔)	Re-read para. 1 briefly and got the answer.
7 (✔)	Re-read paras. 2, 3, 4, 5 and 6 and got the answer finally.
8 (✔)	Without re-reading the text, arrived at the correct judgement and then looked for the supporting sentence.
9 (✔)	Not so sure as Q8. Re-read para. 6 and especially the last sentence several times before he made the correct judgement.
10 (✔)	Without re-reading the text, arrived at the correct judgement and then looked for the supporting sentence.
17 (✔)	A good summarising sentence was provided.
23 (✔)	Used the word 'polymer' to locate the answer in paras. 3, 4, and 5.
24 (✔)	Used the phrase 'biodegradable polymer' to locate the answer in para. 9.
25 (✔)	Used memory from skimming, went directly to the end of the text and located the answer in para. 12.
26 (✔)	The same as in Q25. Used memory and easily got the answer in para. 13.
36 (✔)	Answered these three questions through careful reading. When he arrived at para. 3, got the answer for Q36, para. 4 for Q37 and para. 5 for Q38.
37 (✔)	
38 (✔)	
39 (X)	Didn't have time to finish these two items.
40 (X)	
56 (✔)	Chose 'reduction' after reading para. 1. But when he finished the whole text, changed it to 'constrain'.
57 (✔)	Got the answer in the first reading of the text. Seemed to have used only the immediate context of the text.
58 (X)	Confused between 'variables' and 'varieties'. Seemed to have understood the text.
59 (✔)	Got the answer in the first reading of the text. Seemed to have used only the immediate context of the text.
60 (✔)	Linked para.1 and this concluding paragraph. First chose 'increase' but after more careful reading, changed to 'reduction'.

Appendices - Chapter 6

Student No. H2   Total: 12 (ML test)   Subject: Teaching Chinese to Foreign Learners

Section	text-processing performance
1 careful global passage 2	- Read the passage carefully, word by word. - Quite smooth, no translation, no re-reading. - Finished the passage in about 7 minutes. - Spent long time on three IPROP items. - Seemed to use the sequence of questions to locate answers. When he got the answer for Q6 in para.1 he started with para. 2 for Q7. When para.2 was used by him to answer Q7 (wrongly), he started with para. 3 for Q8.... - Located the relevant parts of the text for all the three IPROP items, read them again and again trying hard to make inferences but failed the last two.
2 skim passage 5	- Able to skim: Read the first two paragraphs and the last paragraph carefully, then first one or two sentences in each paragraph. - Return to the first paragraph, read it again.
3 search reading passage 5	- Didn't read the text from the beginning to the end. - Able to use the topic in the question to locate information and when got to the right place, often read the relevant part of the text at least twice to make sure the answer was correct. - Should FDA appear in its full forms instead of the abbreviation in para. 12? (Although the full form appeared in para. 7.)
4 scan passage 8	- Didn't read the whole text. Read the question and located the answers in the text by matching words in the text. Very typical scanning. - Failed the first one because the sentence structure in the question was different from that in the text and he failed to understand the sentence structure.
5 careful local passage 12	- Read the text carefully first, word by word with some translation. - Tried to fill in the blanks in the first reading. - Made use of part of speech of words. - The text was not understood (from his translation). - Some words and distractors seem unknown. - Guessing in most cases.

Item	task-completion performance
6 (✔)	Read para. 1, didn't get the answer. Went on to read para. 2 and then returned to para. 1, read more carefully and got the answer.
7 (X)	Didn't read paras. 2 and 3 carefully enough. Simply matched the word 'show' with 'demonstration' in the question and got the wrong answer from para.2.
8 (✔)	Read paras. 3, 4 and 5. Located the answer in para. 5 and read the paragraph very carefully twice and made the correct inference.
9 (X)	Started with para. 6 to look for the answer. Read para. 6 and 7 several times. Actually located the place but failed to understand it and make inference.
10 (X)	Started with para. 8 to look for the answer. Read it again. But failed to answer the question. The key in fact is in this paragraph. But he could not get it.
17 (✔)	Summarised the text after skimming the text for 4 minutes. After he got the summarising sentence, went back to the text and started to read it more carefully in order to confirm the answer.
23 (✔)	Used the topic of limitation of polymer and located the answer quickly in para. 23, because he equated 'drawback' with 'limitation'.
24 (✔)	Looked for paragraphs about 'biodegradable polymer', found in paras. 8 and 9. Read them carefully. Equated 'crumble suddenly into chunks' with 'break into large pieces' and got the answer.
25 (X)	Found it hard to locate the answer because he failed to understand FDA represents the government.
26 (✔)	Located the answer quickly in the last paragraph using the topic 'save lives'.
36 (X)	Located the right place but failed to understand the grammatical structure of the sentence and put down the wrong phrase in the sentence.
37 (✔)	Matched the word 'fun' and confirmed the answer by reading the sentence carefully.
38 (✔)	Matched the phrase 'the emergent properties' and got the answer.
39 (✔)	Matched the word 'dilemma' and got to the right place. Then matched the word 'holism' and got the answer.
40 (✔)	Matched the word 'DNA', read the sentence and quickly got the answer.
56 (✔)	Got the answer in the first reading. Translated the word correctly into Chinese.
57 (X)	Eliminate a 'calculate' using the logic that 5% increase rate should enable us to calculate.
58 (X)	Failed to understand the context and didn't know the meaning of the distractor 'application'. Seemed to be guessing.
59 (X)	From his translation, he didn't understand the text except the first paragraph.
60 (✔)	Guessing. Tried to use collocation 'achieve a solution', which is actually a wrong collocation. Linked this last sentence with the first paragraph, which he seemed to have comprehended and got the answer.

Appendices - Chapter 6

Student No. M2   Total: 12 (ST test)   Subject: Medical Science

Section	text-processing performance
1 careful global passage 3	- Careful word by word reading, not very fast. - Long pauses between sentences, probably re-reading or translating. - From the translation, he didn't seem to have undersood the text very well. - Finished the first reading in 8 minutes. 12 minutes spent on 5 items. - Had particular difficulty with making inferences.
2 skim passage 6	- Read the first three paragraphs quite carefully. - Then skipped several paragraphs. Read the last paragraph carefully. - A lot of translation and even the answer was at first in Chinese.
3 search reading passage 6	- Didn't re-read the text. Read the questions and used the topics to locate the information in the text. - Worked everything out in Chinese. - Didn't understand Questions 29 and 30 very well and confused between the two problems talked about in the text.
4 scan passage 7	- Didn't read the text first. Read the questions and looked for the answers in the text. - Able to match words in the questions with those in the text and thus successfully located relevant information for all the five questions.
5 careful local passage 11	- Read the text first carefully. Tried to fill in the blanks in the first reading. But unable to get any of them. - A lot of translation. - Text comprehended quite well. - Not know the exact meaning or the exact usage of some keys and thus failed Q51 and 52. - Expected distractors seemed to have distracted him indeed.

Item	task-completion performance
11 (✓)	Used the topic of the 5th generation computer, correctly located the answer in para. 6, read it carefully and got the answer.
12 (X)	Didn't read the question carefully enough. Located the answer in para. 6 by using the topic of competition.
13 (X)	Couldn't locate the answer in relevant part of the text. Seemed not to have understood the text.
14 (X)	Couldn't locate the answer in relevant part of the text. Read here and there for a long time.
15 (X)	Couldn't locate the answer in relevant part of the text.
18 (✓)	Got the gist of the passage. But at first summarised in Chinese instead of English, later translated it into English, which is not as clear as the Chinese version.
27 (✓)	Used the topic of potato and read the first several paragraphs. Got the answer quickly from para. 3.
28 (✓)	Looked for the cause and used the topic of crop varieties decrease.
29 (X)	Looked for problem and found it in para. 14. But this is not the problem in this question. So he was searching for information but didn't understand the question very well.
30 (X)	Didn't distinguish the new problem in this question with the problem in Q29.
31 (✓)	Matched the words 'biological materials' and located the answer in para. 3.
32 (✓)	Matched words 'nacre, mother of pearl' and located the answer in para. 4.
33 (✓)	Matched the words 'wood' and read para. 8 and 9. Arrived at the answer from para. 9.
34 (✓)	Looked for a number (because it's a temperature). Matched the words 'withstand' and 'temperature'.
35 (✓)	Matched words 'turbine blades' and got the answer.
51 (X)	The context had been understood (from his translation). But he failed to distinguish the two synonyms 'consist' and 'constitute'.
52 (X)	Didn't know the word 'equivalent'. Tried this word and rejected it.
53 (✓)	Got the answer easily and seemed confident of his choice.
54 (✓)	Tried 'characteristics' and 'demonstrations', the only two plural nouns. Since 'demonstrations' has been used and from the context, confidently decided the correct answer.
55 (✓)	Tried 'mechanism' and 'existence'. Read the paragraph again and got the answer.

Appendices - Chapter 6

Student No. J25   Total: 11 (ST test)   Subject: Computer science

Section	text-processing performance
1 careful global passage 3	- Didn't read the whole text continuously from beginning to the end. - Instead, read one question then went back to the text looking for the answer. Then the next question. - Matching words in the question with those in the text while looking for the answers. - Didn't understand the instruction properly because he answered Q11 and 12 with the first four words in the sentence (as required for Q13 to 15). But from the verbal report, it is clear that he had located the relevant parts of the text and understood them (from his translation). So Q11 and 12 were marked correct for the study.
2 skim passage 6	- Careful word by word reading. - Forgot to turn over the page when finished the first page of the text. Later found out and read them carefully. - Didn't read the instruction carefully enough, thought that the sentence should be less than 8 words. Very careless reader.
3 search reading passage 6	- Read questions first. - Didn't re-read the text. - Used memory from skimming to locate answers for Q27 and 28. - Carefully read the last two paragraphs for Q29 and 30. - No idea of search reading at all.
4 scan passage 7	- Read questions first. - Scanned the text by matching words in the questions with those in the text. - Read more than necessary for scanning, usually the whole relevant paragraphs before he could get to the answers. - Therefore, no time left for items 34 and 35.
5 careful local passage 11	- Read the text carefully first. - Tried to fill in each blank during the first reading. - Used part of speech in eliminating distractors and choosing words. - Quite a lot translation. - Showed quite a large degree of comprehension except the last paragraph.

Item	task-completion performance
11 (✔)	Match the words '5th generation computer' in para. 5 and 6, read these two paragraphs carefully.
12 (✔)	Found difficult to locate the relevant part of the text. First read paras. 7–11 (because Q11 was in para. 6) and then went back to paras. 1–5. Finally got the answer from the last paragraph.
13 (X)	Match the word 'expert' in para. 9 with the 'expert system' in the question. (Key in para. 4)
14 (X)	Match the word 'compile' in para. 9 with the same word in the question and could not answer it. (key in para. 8)
15 (✔)	Match the words 'unique human qualities' and got the answer from the last paragraph.
18 (X)	Tried to write the sentence in less than 8 words. Failed to get the discourse topic of the text although he knew that it was about crops.
27 (✔)	Used memory from skimming, went directly to para.1, failed to find the answer. Then he went to para. 3, read it carefully and got the answer.
28 (✔)	Used memory from skimming, went directly to para. 12 and got the answer.
29 (X)	
30 (X)	Read paras. 13 and 14 carefully.
31 (✔)	Read paras. 2 and 3, matched 'inconvenience' and got the answer.
32 (✔)	Matched the word 'mother of pearl' in para. 4 and read the paragraph quite carefully and finally got the key.
33 (✔)	Looked for the word 'wood'. Located it in para. 8 and read it carefully but failed to find the answer. Then went on to para. 9 and read carefully. Finally got the answer.
34 (X)	Didn't have time for Q34 and 35.
35 (X)	
51 (✔)	Completed in the first reading of the text. Used only the immediate context of the text.
52 (✔)	Found the word in the first reading and translated correctly into Chinese, suggesting his correct understanding of this part of the text.
53 (✔)	Couldn't find the answer from the sentence and read further 2 sentences in the paragraph before he found the answer.
54 (X)	Didn't seem to have understood the sentence and the last paragraph very well.
55 (X)	Hesitated between 'mechanism (key)' and its distractor 'characteristics'. But made a guess (reported) and a wrong one.

Appendices - Chapter 6

Student No. J16   Total: 11 (AH test)   Subject: Computer Science

Section	text-processing performance
1 careful global passage 1	- Read questions carefully for about 3 minutes. - Read the text carefully for 4 minutes. - Marking the relevant part of the text during the first reading (reported). - Focused on reading the marked parts of the text. - The speed of reading is average (somewhere between those 17s and 6s).
2 skim passage 4	- Very typical skimming: - Read the title carefully trying hard to understand the word 'apart' (0.5 minute). - Then read the first and the last paragraphs for 2 minutes. - Then quickly read the first one or two sentences of other paragraphs for about 2 minutes.
3 search reading passage 4	- Aware of the need to search read: - Didn't re-read the text carefully, instead searched for answers in para 2 and 3 for Q19, 20, and 21 using the topic of discrimination (translated into Chinese and reported).
4 scan passage 9	- Read questions carefully first. - Read the title and then subtitles carefully. - Looked for information using words in the questions. - Able to scan. But when the right place is located, a little more careful reading is necessary. Exclusively matching words in the question with those in the text may lead to wrong answer. See example Q45.
5 careful local passage 10	- Read the word bank first. - Read the text quickly from beginning to the end. - Returned to the sentences where words were deleted. Read just that sentence and tried with words in the bank. - Able to make use of the part of speech. - Many words in the bank were unknown: e.g., report: 'what is unanimity, don't know'; translated 'denounce' into announce. - Seemed to have no comprehension of the text.

Item	task-completion performance
1 (✔)	Read para. 2 carefully and answered the question in his own words.
2 (✔)	Read para. 3 carefully and answered the question in his own words. Found difficult to control the number of words under 10 in the answer.
3 (✔)	Spent a long time making judgement. Hesitating between sentences in para. 5.
4 (X)	Inferred correctly and made correct judgement but failed to locate the exact supporting sentence. (Used a neighbouring sentence of the key).
5 (X)	Had no time to finish the item. Did it in a hurry and made the wrong judgement.
16 (✔)	After reading the first and the last paragraph, he reported to have got the main idea of the text. But he continued to confirm his idea by reading the first one or two sentences of the remaining paragraphs. Spent about 1.5 minutes for the summarising sentence. Perfect timing for the section.
19 (✔)	From para. 2 easily got the answer for 'pay'.
20 (X)	Seemed unable to get the main idea from para. 3, which was correctly located. Used the first sentence as the answer.
21 (X)	Missed paras. 4 and 5. Searched only in paras. 2 and 3 and thus failed to get the answer.
22 (✔)	Used the idea of 'divorce' located the last paragraph and easily got the answer.
41 (✔)	Quickly located the answer in para. 2 using the subtitle and matching 'exercise control over'.
42 (✔)	Looked for information in the paragraph of 'make some decisions' and matched the word 'media'.
43 (X)	Report: should be in the 'make some decisions' section but didn't find it.
44 (✔)	Went directly to the paragraph of 'why advertise' and found the answer.
45 (X)	Simply match the word 'sell' and located the answer in the last sentence. But is it also correct??
46 (✔)	Aware that a verb is needed. Chose between 'denounce' and 'approve'. Since denounce is mistaken as announce, so decided on approve.
47 (✔)	Didn't know either 'reveal' or 'conceal', just made a guess but happened to be correct.
48 (X)	Aware that a noun is needed. But reported that he didn't know the word 'unanimity' so made a wrong guess.
49 (X)	The same as in Q48.
50 (X)	Not reported. Short of time and mostly likely a pure guess.

Appendices - Chapter 6

Student No. J3   Total: 6 (ML test)   Subject: Computer Science

Section	text-processing performance
1 careful global passage 2	- Word by word careful reading, extremely slow. - Long pauses after each sentence to try to understand what has just been read. - Spent 10 minutes for the first reading of the text. - Seemed to be able to locate the relevant paragraphs in answering the questions but failed to comprehend what has been read.
2 skim passage 5	- Tried to skim the text by reading every first or first and second sentences in each paragraph. - But she didn't seem to get much idea from the first reading (about 3 minutes). - Read the text in more detail for 2 minutes. - Aware of the skill but linguistically too poor to comprehend what she was reading.
3 search reading passage 5	- Read questions first. - Looking for relevant paragraphs for each question using key words. - Even when the relevant part of the text was located, she couldn't get the answer because she didn't read the located part carefully.
4 scan passage 8	- Read questions first. - Started with every 2 or 3 sentences of each paragraph. Got answers for Q.36 and 38, whose answers happen to be in the first and the second sentence of the paragraph. - Skipped reading rather than scanning.
5 careful local passage 12	- Read the text carefully for 3 times before starting with the items. - Showed no comprehension whatsoever of the text, e.g., 'humane' is translated as 'human', many key words were reported unknown, e.g., 'cull', 'habitat', 'constrain' etc. - Grammatically, her choices for No. 56 and No. 59 are both incorrect.

Item	task-completion performance
6 (X)	Read the text again from the beginning but could not locate the answer.
7 (X)	She actually paraphrased the 'the more powerful drug' with 'the stronger version' in para. 3. But she didn't comprehend the paragraph.
8 (X)	The judgement was correctly made but the supporting sentence was a completely irrelevant one. So most likely the answer was a guess.
9 (X)	Both supporting sentences were chosen correctly but with wrong judgements. So
10 (X)	she got to the right place but failed to understand what she was reading.
17 (X)	Unable to get some idea from what she read. And unable to summarise the text.
23 (✔)	Read paras. 3, 4, 5 and got the answer.
24 (X)	Matching the words 'biodegradable polymers' to locate the answer in paras. 8 and 9. But failed to get the answer.
25 (✔)	Tried to match the word 'government'. When reached the para. 12, equated FDA with government and got the answer.
26 (✔)	Matched the phrase 'save lives' and located the last paragraph.
36 (✔)	Got the answer when reading the first sentence of para. 3.
37 (X)	Since the answer was in the last sentence of para. 4 she failed to reach it, so didn't get the answer.
38 (✔)	Got the answer when reading the second sentence of para. 5.
39 (✔)	Spot the answer by chance.
40 (X)	Didn't get to the end of para. 8 so failed to answer the item.
56 (X)	Hesitated between 'increase' and 'reduction', both are grammatically incorrect choices.
57 (X)	
58 (X)	Unable to decide which to choose because the text was not comprehended at all. Pure guesses.
59 (X)	
60 (X)	

Appendices - Chapter 6

Student No. M1   Total: 6 (ST test)   Subject: Medical science

Section	text-processing performance
1 careful global passage 3	- While reading the passage, nothing was reported; silent reading. - In doing 11 and 12, read the located paragraphs again carefully and slowly. - Extremely slow reading, word by word. - Unable to make inferences because relevant paragraphs were located for Questions 13, 14, 15 but he failed to understand the text and failed to arrive at correct true/false judgements.
2 skim passage 6	- Read the passage from the very beginning, slowly, carefully, skipping only unknown words. - Translate quite often in reading. - Finished only less than half of the text within the time limit and had no time for the item. - Report 'loss of genes' indicating some comprehension.
3 search reading passage 6	- Continued with reading the text and finished all the text before starting with the items. - Didn't know how to locate relevant paragraphs for answer questions, randomly selecting some paragraphs. - Used memory from reading the text and background knowledge trying to answer Q.27 and 28 without going back to the text.
4 scan passage 7	- Read the questions before the text. - After the questions, read the text from the very beginning, word by word, skipping only unknown words. - Spent about 5 minutes for the text, and finished only paras. 1 to 5. - Aware of the time pressure started to scan or skipped reading for the last two items.
5 careful local passage 11	- Read the text carefully and stopped for each blank trying possible words in the bank. - Some translation: e.g., equivalent (translated wrongly into being equal), mechanism (correctly) - Comprehended the text to some degree after careful reading but confused by words in the bank since they are all new to him. So: for linguistically very poor students, this section is not testing inferring lexical meanings from the context because it could be the case that the context is understood but the key is an unknown word to him. - Able to use grammatical knowledge to decide whether a noun or a verb is needed for a blank.

Item	task-completion performance
11 (✓)	Located para. 6, read it several times and got the answer.
12 (✓)	Located para. 11, read it carefully and got the answer.
13 (X)	Located relevant paragraphs for all these three items. But failed to arrive at correct judgments.
14 (X)	No supporting sentences were provided for any of them.
15 (X)	
18 (X)	No time was left for completing the summarising sentence. Only a short phrase was provided but the meaning of the phrase is unclear and irrelevant.
27 (X)	For he didn't know how to locate the relevant paragraph, he used his memory from skimming and careful reading trying to answer the question in his own words.
28 (X)	
29 (✓)	Both the keys were in the last paragraph, so matching the word 'problem', he got the answers for both items from the last paragraph.
30 (✓)	
31 (X)	Went back to the text to read from the beginning came across the answer in para. 3 but didn't get it.
32 (X)	Went back to the text to continue from para. 3 and came across the answer in para. 4 but didn't get it.
33 (X)	Located the answer in para. 2 matching the word 'wood' (instead of load-bearing, which is the key word in the item because he didn't understand it.
34 (✓)	Matched the word 'nacre' to get to para. 6. Scanned for numbers and got the correct answer.
35 (X)	Unable to decide on a word to be matched, so read first sentences in paras. 7, 8 and 9. But failed to get the answer (which is at the end of para. 7).
51 (X)	Reported in Chinese that the word should be 'consisted of' or 'composed' but took 'create' as the word for this meaning. Report a verb is needed.
52 (X)	Translated 'equivalent' as 'being equal' and looked for a word meaning 'description'.
53 (X)	Report a noun is needed here. But from his translation, he didn't seem to have understood the context.
54 (✓)	Reported a noun is needed here. Translated 'characteristics' correctly into Chinese.
55 (X)	Translated 'mode' as the same as 'mechanism' (the key).

Appendices - Chapter 6

Student No.M14   Total: 6 (AH test)   Subject: Medical Science

Section	text-processing performance
1 careful global passage 1	- Read the text first word by word, slowly. - Long pauses between sentences. - Occasional translation. - First reading about 12 minutes. Report that the passage was not well understood, only got a rough idea after the first reading. - Read instructions after reading the text! - Translated every question into Chinese before looking for answers in the text. - Aware of the time pressure: only 5 minutes left the three IPROP items. - So did them in a hurry and no supporting sentences were provided for any of them.
2 skim passage 4	- Read paras.1 and 2 word by word, but faster than he did in the careful reading section. - Started to read first one or two sentences in the rest of the paragraphs. - Read the last paragraph carefully with quite a lot of translation. - Reading the text for about 5 minutes.
3 search reading passage 4	- Read questions before re-reading the text. - Didn't understand the question Q22 (from his translation). - Aware of the strategy but did not know how to search because no words or phrases could be matched. - Looking for the word discrimination. And arrived at Sexual discrimination as one answer but later changed his mind. - Report very difficult to locate the answers. - Searched randomly in every paragraph.
4 scan passage 9	- Read questions carefully first, translated all of them into Chinese. - First and second paragraphs were read word by word with some translation. - Tried to scan from Q42, but didn't know how. Instead, he jumped here and there. And in fact read quite carefully for answering Q42. - No time left for the other three items.
5 careful local passage 10	- Read the word bank first. - Didn't read the text continuously from the beginning to the end. - Directly went to sentences with blanks. If failed to understand the sentence, went on to read the whole paragraph. - Made use of part of speech of words. - No comprehension of the whole text at all (from his translation).

Item	task-completion performance
1 (X)	Read paras. 1 and 2 for the answer. Translated para. 2 a lot. Spent about 4 minutes. Didn't understand para. 2 from his translation.
2 (✓)	Match the phrase 'middle class' and located in para. 3. Got the answer after reading it more carefully. About 1 minute.
3 (X)	Match the word 'problem' and located it in the last paragraph (wrongly).
4 (X)	Read the last paragraph carefully again but failed to understand it (from his translation). Report that he was not sure about the answer.
5 (X)	No time left for this item. Guessed it wrongly.
16 (X)	Seemed to summarise only the idea from the title and first paragraph. Nothing from the rest of the text was summarised into the sentence. Used his background knowledge that the low status of women in Japan was caused by the Japanese tradition.
19 (✓)	Happened to find the answer in para. 2.
20 (X)	Searched randomly in every paragraph but failed to comprehend what was read.
21 (X)	
22 (X)	No time was left for the item.
41 (✓)	While reading para. 2 carefully, got the answer.
42 (✓)	Read paras. 4, 5, 6 7 and 8. He didn't match the words in the questions. Tried to with the answer 'TV' using his background knowledge.
43 (X)	No time was left for the three items because too much time had been spent on carefully reading the text for the first two items.
44 (X)	
45 (X)	
46 (✓)	Reading only this sentence and got the answer.
47 (✓)	Tried to answer the question by reading only the sentence but failed, went back to read carefully the whole para. 4 and got the answer.
48 (X)	Tried to answer the question by reading only the sentence but failed, went back to read carefully the whole para. 5, but couldn't understand anything.
49 (X)	Cannot understand the sentence, so analysed the structure (subject clause introduced by 'that').
50 (X)	Cannot understand the long sentence, so analysed the structure but still failed (cannot find the subject of the sentence).

Appendices - Chapter 6

Student No. H9   Total: 5 (AH test)   Subject: Teaching Chinese to Foreign Learners

Section	text-processing performance
1 careful global passage 1	- Read the text carefully, word by word. - No translation, no re-reading, at a slow speed. - Finished first reading in c. 6 minutes. - Simply matched the words in the questions with those in the text and didn't read carefully. This led to the wrong answer of Q2. - Found it difficult to locate relevant information for answering the questions if there are no words that can be exactly matched. e.g., Q3: first matched the word 'biggest' and happened to find it in para.2 but could not answer the question then went on to match 'biggest problem'. - Didn't seem to have comprehended the text.
2 skim passage 4	- Read paras. 1 to 4 quite carefully, almost word by word, at a slow speed. - No re-reading, no translation. - Realising the time pressure, started to read paras. 5 to 9 selectively, jumping here and there, but without a clear pattern.
3 search reading passage 4	- Started passage 9 (the scanning section). Didn't read the instruction carefully. - Didn't realise his mistake until he finished the whole section (he was answering the questions of Section 4).
4 scan passage 9	- Word by word careful reading. - No selectivity at all since the 7 minutes in the previous section was used for this section as well. - No idea of scanning whatsoever.
5 careful local passage 10	- Read the text carefully word by word, with no translation, no pause, at a very slow speed. - Showed no comprehension of the text at all. - In answering the questions, all are pure guesses. - The only means used is the part of speech.

Item	task-completion performance
1 (✔)	Located the answer using the clue: 2000 in para. 2. Read carefully and got the answer. Took him quite long to put the answer in 8 words. c. 3 minutes.
2 (X)	Looked for 'middle class Asia' in the text. And found it in para.1, without understanding the question and para.1, answered it wrongly.
3 (X)	More than 5 minutes. Matched the word 'biggest' in para. 2 but failed to answer it. Matched 'biggest problem' in para. 4. But the key is in para. 3.
4 (X)	Failed to locate the answer anywhere, so started from para.1. Finally arrived at the right place (last paragraph) but failed to make inference.
5 (✔)	Read the last paragraph carefully and arrived at the correct inference.
16 (X)	Didn't catch the main idea of the text, instead copied two sentences from the first paragraph.
19 (X)	All questions were left unanswered because he didn't read the instruction carefully. Instead of working on the same passage for search reading, he went on to the next passage after he had read passage 4 for the skimming section. So he missed this section totally.
20 (X)	
21 (X)	
22 (X)	
41 (✔)	Got the answer through careful reading.
42 (X)	Missed the answer even though he had come across the relevant part of the text in careful reading.
43 (✔)	Got the answer through careful reading.
44 (✔)	
45 (X)	Missed the answer even though he had come across the relevant part of the text in careful reading.
46 (X)	Finished the item after he read para. 1 to 3. But just a guess.
47 (X)	Guessed between several verbs: reinforced, concealed, revealed, approved and compelled.
48 (X)	Pure guess.
49 (X)	Guessed between several nouns: sensitivity, source, evidence.
50 (X)	Pure guess.

Appendices - Chapter 6

Appendix 6.3 3
Use of skill/strategies and performance on the test

AH subtest

Subject Score Item No	Subjects' Performance								
	H12 17	J10 16	J15 14	H8 12	M15 12	J16 11	M8 8	M14 6	H9 5
1	W ES	C ES	C ES	C ES	C ES	C ES	C ES	W ES	C ES
2	C ES	C ES	C ES	C ES	C ES	C ES	W ES	C ES	W ES
3	W ES	C ES	WUES	WUES	WUES	C ES	C ES	WUES	WUES
4	C ES	C ES	C ES	WUES	WUES	W ES	W ES	WUES	WUES
5	C ES	C ES	C ES	WUES	WUES	WUES	W ES	WUES	C ES
16	C ES	CUES	C ES	WUES	CUES	C ES	W ES	W ES	WUES
19	C ES	CUES	CUES	C ES	CUES	C ES	C ES	CUES	WUES
20	W ES	CUES	W ES	C ES	WUES	W ES	W ES	WUES	WUES
21	C ES	CUES	C ES	W ES	WUES	W ES	W ES	WUES	WUES
22	C ES	CUES	WUES	W ES	C ES	C ES	W ES	WUES	WUES
41	C ES	CUES	C ES	C ES	C ES	C ES	C ES	CUES	CUES
42	C ES	CUES	C ES	C ES	C ES	C ES	W ES	CUES	WUES
43	C ES	WUES	W ES	C ES	C ES	W ES	W ES	WUES	CUES
44	C ES	CUES	C ES	C ES	C ES	C ES	C ES	WUES	CUES
45	C ES	CUES	C ES	C ES	C ES	W ES	W ES	WUES	WUES
46	C ES	C ES	C ES	C ES	W ES	C ES	W ES	C ES	WUES
47	C ES	C ES	C ES	C ES	W ES	C ES	C ES	C ES	WUES
48	C ES	WUES	CUES	W ES	C ES	WUES	C ES	WUES	WUES
49	C ES	WUES	W NC	W ES	WUES	WUES	W ES	WUES	WUES
50	C ES	WUES	WUES	C ES	C ES	W NC	C ES	WUES	WUES

CES	- correct answer using expected skill/strategy
CUES	- correct answer using unexpected skill/strategy
CNC	- correct answer arrived at through unclear means
WES	- incorrect/wrong answer using expected skill/strategy
WUES	- incorrect/wrong answer using unexpected skill/strategy
WNC	- incorrect/wrong answer arrived at through unclear means

Appendices - Chapter 6

ST subtest

Subject Score Item No	H18 18	J20 17	H17 15	M2 12	J25 11	M5 11	M6 6	J24 5	H15 2
11	C ES	W ES	C ES	C ES	C ES	C ES	C ES	W ES	WUES
12	C ES	C ES	C ES	W ES	C ES	C ES	C ES	C ES	WUES
13	C ES	C ES	W ES	WUES	WUES	C ES	WUES	WUES	WUES
14	W ES	C ES	C ES	WUES	WUES	C ES	WUES	WUES	WUES
15	C ES	WUES	C ES	WUES	C ES	C ES	WUES	WUES	WUES
18	CUES	CUES	C ES	C ES	WUES	CUES	WUES	C ES	WUES
27	C ES	CUES	C ES	C ES	CUES	WUES	WUES	WUES	WUES
28	C ES	CUES	W ES	C ES	CUES	WUES	WUES	WUES	WUES
29	C ES	CUES	C ES	W ES	WUES	WUES	CUES	WUES	WUES
30	C ES	CUES	C ES	W ES	WUES	CUES	CUES	WUES	WUES
31	C ES	CUES	C ES	C ES	C ES	C ES	WUES	WUES	WUES
32	C ES	CUES	C ES	C ES	C ES	W ES	WUES	CUES	CUES
33	C ES	CUES	W ES	C ES	C ES	W ES	WUES	WUES	WUES
34	C ES	C ES	C ES	C ES	W NC	C ES	C ES	WUES	WUES
35	C ES	C ES	C ES	C ES	W NC	C ES	WUES	WUES	WUES
51	C ES	C ES	W ES	W ES	C ES	WUES	W ES	WUES	WUES
52	C ES	W ES	W ES	W ES	C ES	WUES	W ES	WUES	WUES
53	C ES	C ES	C ES	C ES	C ES	C ES	W ES	CUES	WUES
54	W ES	C ES	C ES	C ES	W ES	WUES	C ES	WUES	CUES
55	C ES	C ES	C ES	C ES	WUES	WUES	W ES	CUES	WUES

CES	- correct answer using expected skill/strategy
CUES	- correct answer using unexpected skill/strategy
CNC	- correct answer arrived at through unclear means
WES	- incorrect/wrong answer using expected skill/strategy
WUES	- incorrect/wrong answer using unexpected skill/strategy
WNC	- incorrect/wrong answer arrived at through unclear means

Appendices - Chapter 6

ML subtest

Subject Score Item No	J9 17	M22 17	H6 15	M20 12	H2 12	J1 10	M16 7	J3 6	H4 4
6	C ES	C ES	C ES	C ES	C ES	C ES	W ES	W ES	C ES
7	W ES	C ES	C ES	C ES	W ES	C ES	W ES	W ES	C ES
8	C ES	C ES	C ES	C ES	C ES	W ES	WUES	WUES	WUES
9	C ES	C ES	C ES	W ES	W ES	W ES	WUES	WUES	WUES
10	C ES	C ES	W ES	C ES	W ES	C ES	WUES	WUES	WUES
17	CUES	CUES	CUES	W ES	C ES	WUES	WUES	W ES	WUES
23	C ES	C ES	CUES	C ES	C ES	CUES	WUES	C ES	CUES
24	CUES	C ES	CUES	C ES	C ES	WUES	WUES	W ES	CUES
25	C ES	CUES	CUES	C ES	W ES	WUES	WUES	C ES	WUES
26	C ES	CUES	CUES	C ES	C ES	WUES	CUES	C ES	WUES
36	C ES	CUES	C ES	C ES	W ES	WUES	W ES	CUES	WUES
37	C ES	CUES	C ES	C ES	C ES	WUES	C ES	WUES	WUES
38	W ES	CUES	C ES	W ES	C ES	CUES	C ES	CUES	WUES
39	C ES	WUES	C ES	W ES	C ES	CUES	C ES	CUES	WUES
40	C ES	WUES	C ES	W ES	C ES	CUES	C ES	WUES	WUES
56	W ES	C ES	W ES	C ES	C ES	W ES	W ES	WUES	WUES
57	C ES	C ES	C ES	C ES	W ES	C ES	W ES	WUES	WUES
58	C ES	W ES	W ES	WUES	WUES	W ES	W ES	WUES	WUES
59	C ES	C ES	W ES	WUES	WUES	C ES	C ES	WUES	WUES
60	C ES	C ES	W ES	WUES	C ES	C ES	C ES	WUES	WUES

CES	- correct answer using expected skill/strategy
CUES	- correct answer using unexpected skill/strategy
CNC	- correct answer arrived at through unclear means
WES	- incorrect/wrong answer using expected skill/strategy
WUES	- incorrect/wrong answer using unexpected skill/strategy
WNC	- incorrect/wrong answer arrived at through unclear means

Subject Index

A

AERT prototype   71-74

B

background knowledge   14, 17-19, 24-27, 40, 43, 61, 64, 69, 72, 91, 102, 104, 105, 117, 119, 120

C

careful reading   1, 4, 6, 7, 15-20, 23-25, 33, 35-38, 40-41,43, 46, 49, 50, 59, 60, 64, 67, 70-73, 75,78, 79, 82-84, 86, 94-96, 98-103, 106, 107, 109-111, 113, 115-116, 118-119

comprehension   1, 4, 6, 7, 14, 15, 17-23, 25-28, 41, 42, 44, 59, 67, 75, 76, 82, 84, 87, 96, 109, 111-113, 115, 119

D

data analysis
    analysis of variance (ANOVA)   9, 19, 69, 82, 84, 85, 91, 119, 120, 243-254
    correlations   5, 22, 90, 91, 195, 226-227
    cross-tabulation   3, 9, 74-76, 81, 82, 116, 118, 187-189, 217-223
    descriptive statistics   3, 5, 12, 74, 80, 84, 178-180, 185-188, 206, 213-216
    factor analysis   20-22, 78, 79, 83, 108, 193-198, 228-242
    profiling   84, 119
    reliability   5, 12, 21, 75, 81, 82, 102, 117, 183-186, 211-213
    t-test   5

E

English for Academic Purposes reading
    teaching tasks   12, 41, 44, 46, 49
    teaching task operations   139-141
    teaching task conditions   148-154
    testing tasks   12, 37, 44, 49, 69
    testing task operations   53, 142-146
    testing task conditions   55, 60, 155-165, 265-277

expeditious reading   7, 15-19, 23-25, 35-37, 46, 49, 50, 59, 60, 67, 70-73, 79, 81, 82, 84, 86, 87, 89, 95, 96, 98-101, 116

G
goal setting 6, 18
grammar *see syntax*

I
inferences 22, 39, 40, 50, 72, 107, 109, 115

L
lexis 15, 17, 18, 23, 34, 48, 49, 50, 67, 83, 91, 98, 113
literacy 2, 18, 19

M
main ideas 7, 8, 15, 18, 23, 24, 34-36, 38-40, 42, 43, 48-50, 59, 66, 67, 72, 94-100, 107, 108, 116
models of reading
    bottom-up 15, 24, 26
    compensatory 26
    compontential (also componentiality) 4-6, 11, 14, 15, 17, 19, 29, 22, 28, 61, 72, 83, 118, 119
    interactive 15, 24, 44
    process(es) 5, 7, 9-11, 14-20, 22-25, 38-42, 45, 64, 66, 67, 74, 80, 82, 92, 96, 101, 104-107, 110, 112, 114, 116-118, 121
    sequential 17, 24, 39, 106
    top-down 15, 24, 26, 42
monitor (also monitoring) 2, 3, 13, 18, 19, 105, 107

N
needs analysis 6, 16, 28-36, 59. 128. 129-131

P
performance conditions 6-7, 11, 13, 35, 44, 46, 66, 78, 89, 121
propositions
    macroproportions 8, 23-25, 36, 39, 42, 62
    microproportions 8, 23

Q
questionnaires
    expert judgement 5, 9-12, 93-199, 108, 276, 287
    students 60, 93-97, 199-206, 255-262, 276-280
    subject matter teachers 29, 94, 98-107

R

reading
  global   16, 18, 24, 37, 49, 60, 67, 70,-73, 76, 85, 98, 99, 102
  Chinese universities   1-3, 28-36
  local   4, 7, 24, 26, 37, 59, 67, 72, 75, 85, 98, 99, 102

S

schemata   27, 40, 42, 44
skills   1, 2, 4-7, 9-11, 14, 15, 19-24, 27-29, 34-39, 41, 50, 57, 59, 61, 64-66, 68, 71-72, 82, 86, 87, 93-105, 107, 114-119, 121
strategies   1, 2, 4-7, 9, 10, 14, 16-24, 26-29, 34-50, 57, 59-61, 64-66, 68, 71-73, 75, 82, 86-87, 93-105, 107, 114-119, 121
  scanning (also scan)   4, 7, 16, 17, 24, 25, 34, 37-39, 41-44, 47-50, 60, 62, 64-67, 70, 72, 75-76, 78-79, 81, 82, 89, 91, 93, 94, 96-103, 110-112, 115, 116, 119
  search reading   4, 10, 16, 17, 24, 25, 36-39, 41-43, 48-49, 59-60, 64, 66-67, 70, 72, 75-76, 78-79, 81, 82, 89, 91, 93, 94, 96-103, 110-112, 115, 116, 119
syntax   17, 18, 38, 42, 49

T

task
  format(s)   5, 8, 16, 23, 47-50, 73, 77, 78, 86, 166, 170
  gap-filling   48, 50
  information transfer   48-50
  MCQ   48, 50, 69, 70, 88
  SAQ   48, 50, 70, 73, 72, 82
text
  diagramming/mapping   66-69, 173-178
  selection   45, 57-65, 66, 69, 121
  structural/rhetorical organisation   41, 57, 58, 60, 147, 164, 165
  suitability   31, 57, 58, 60, 62, 86, 87, 171, 173

V

verbal report(s)   10, 21, 102, 104-106, 114
  recall   15
  introspection   5, 9, 10-12, 21, 93, 97, 101-105, 109, 116-118, 281-297
  retrospection   5, 9-12, 57, 58, 93, 96, 97, 101, 103, 118, 276-280